T0315732

High Flying Around

Memories of the 1960s
Leicester Music Scene

High Flying Around

Memories of the 1960s Leicester Music Scene

Shaun Knapp

This book is dedicated to Rod Read, Legay Rogers, Alan Hornsby, Jimmy Rose, Paul Wolloff, Clive Jones, Clive Box, Ric Grech, Jim Smith, Pete Illiffe and every other musician who was involved in the 1960s Leicester music scene who are no longer with us.

And to my father-in-law, Tony D'Arcy, a lovely man who sadly passed away before it was published. He will always be greatly missed.

First Published in Great Britain in 2017 by DB Publishing,
an imprint of JMD Media Ltd

© Shaun Knapp, 2017

All Rights Reserved. No part of this publication may be reproduced, stored in a retrieval system, or transmitted in any form, or by any means, electronic, mechanical, photocopying, recording or otherwise without the prior permission in writing of the copyright holders, nor be otherwise circulated in any form or binding or cover other than in which it is published and without a similar condition being imposed on the subsequent publisher.

ISBN 978-1-78091-550-0

Printed and bound in the UK

Contents

Acknowledgements

Many thanks to all of those who have contributed or offered help and advice, it couldn't have been done without you: Austin J. Ruddy, Brian Plews, Callum Wright, Chris Busby, Chris Dredge, Clive Jones, Chris Lewitt, Colin Hyde, Dave 'Moth' Smith, Dave Dean, Dindy Outen, Ed Stagg, Gary Knapp, George Parker, Georgie Wright, Gus Turner, Harry Ovenall, Helen Garner, Jim Gregan, Joel LaRosa, John Aston, John Butler, John Knapp, Julia Read, Kassy Parker, Kate Kissane-Rogers, Kathy Chamberlin, Kenny Wilson, Kevin Knapp, Linda Knapp, Louise Knapp, Mark D'Arcy, Matt Rogers, Maria Veall, Marilyn Lawrence, Michael Smith, Mick Pini, Mick Reynolds, Natalie Kent, Nick Hairs, Paul Coles, Peter Feely, Peter Burnham, Peter Wild, Ray Percival, Ray Read, Richard Read, Robin Hollick, Rob Townsend, Robin Pizer, Rod Brown, Sally Coleman, Sarinda Bains, Steven Parker, Su Barton, Terry Gannon, Yvonne Kennett.

All *Leicester Chronicle* articles used courtesy of the *Leicester Mercury*.

Cover design by Brian Plews: www.bcreatif.com

Many thanks to Yvonne Kennett, Julia Read, John Imbush, Kate Kissane-Rogers, John Knapp, Mick Reynolds, Chris Busby, Kenny Wilson, Rod Brown, Gus Turner, Robin Hollick, Brian Plews and Chris Dredge for supplying the photographs used in the book. Every effort has been made to trace copyright holders and to obtain their permission for the use of copyright material. The publisher and the author apologises for any errors or omissions in the above list and would be grateful if notified of any corrections that should be incorporated in future reprints or editions of this book.

This book was edited by Louise Knapp BA (Hons).

Special thanks to Chris Lewitt for kindly allowing the use of his interview notes with Robin Hollick and John Butler and to Kenny Wilson for the use of his blog as a reference (kennywilson.org/my-life-in-music/).

Finally, a massive thank you to my wife, Lisa, and daughter Louise, who between them have had to put up with my moaning, whingeing and rambling on about mods, rockers, hippies and publishers for the last five years.

Preface

We all know how fantastic Manchester, Liverpool and London were during the 1960s, but the music scene in Leicester during this period was just as electric, even if it was scaled down due to the comparative size of the city. There were venues galore for bands to play in – the Il Rondo, Nite Owl, The Casino and The Green Bowler to name just a few. Some of the bands that came from Leicester – Legay, Family, The Broodly Hoo, Pesky Gee!, The Farinas, Deuce Coupe, Vfranie – were producing different styles of music and packing in the fans wherever they played.

Although I was only two years old when Legay formed, I feel that I grew up with them – my brother John Knapp was in the band. I can remember (vaguely) seeing them play at Birstall Village Hall (I must have been four at the time) and 'No-One' was, and still remains, one of my favourite songs. It sounds just as exciting today as it did then and is crying out to be covered and re-interpreted by a new band. The B-side, 'The Fantastic Story of the Steam Driven Banana', was a nursery rhyme put to music, an incredible story that fired my imagination as a child – just think about it, a steam driven banana …

For me to even remotely attempt to get into the zone of what it must have felt like to follow a band such as Legay, with all of the excitement of the live gigs and the anticipated success, I can only compare it to when I used to follow a Leicester band called The Filberts. They were a fantastic band with a unique sound and a fast-growing fan base who used to play regularly at the Princess Charlotte. They changed their name to Diesel Park West and went on to release what I believe to be one of the best albums of the 1980s, *Shakespeare Alabama*. The anticipated excitement of wanting to see them live, waiting for the records to be released and following them around is something that I will never forget and is a feeling that strongly resonates from those that followed Legay back in the 1960s.

The inspiration for writing this book was to record the story of Legay and other memories of the 1960s music scene in Leicester before it was too late as, sadly, a lot of the characters from that period are no longer with us. This was recently demonstrated by the sad loss of two members of Pesky Gee!, Clive Jones and Clive Box, who passed away while this book was in its infancy. I interviewed Clive Jones via a series of email exchanges not long before he passed away, so thankfully part of his story has been recorded and saved. Ultimately, I've tried to let the people who were there tell the story as much as possible – it is, after all, their story. The book is about an era in history that, without a shadow of a doubt, was by far one of the most exciting and original that we have ever seen. In the years that the book covers, I've tried to tap into the various elements that made up the 'scene' in Leicester; the bands, the agents, the venues, the designers, the musicians, the fans and the fashion. My role within this project was to listen to the memories, establish the facts and to stitch it all together with the minimum of waffle from myself. Those memories, however, may be a bit jaded, so please be kind in your thoughts if some of the detail is a tad out of sync with how you remember it. At times, it really has been like completing a 1000-piece jigsaw puzzle without having a picture to go by.

Today, this era can only truly be revisited by the memories of those who were there. Most of the bands have gone and those iconic venues – which once pulsated to the sound of raw, live music – are no more, they've either disappeared or have been converted into something completely different. The Nite Owl burnt down, The Green Bowler is now a shop, The Casino has been converted into student accommodation and the Il Rondo, which played host to Rod Stewart, The Who, Cream, King Crimson, Howlin' Wolf and The Action to name but a few, is now a restaurant. Today, people walk past these innocuous-looking buildings on a daily basis, completely oblivious to their history and the exciting, positive impact they had on young people's lives during the 1960s.

For the vast majority of the people interviewed, this really was their 'golden age', a unique era which, regardless of how they try to recapture the moment today, will simply never be the same.

Foreword

Leicester in the 1960s by Dr Su Barton

The 1960s was a time of rapid change, materially and also in social attitude, particularly amongst young people. Young adults in the 1960s were the first generation of the twentieth century not to have had their youth blighted by world war. After 1962, young men were free from compulsory National Service in the armed forces, a fact some older people never let them forget. A generation was reaching adulthood after having been raised in households where they were well fed on nutritious home cooking and nurtured in infancy with National Dried Milk, orange juice and vitamins from the Welfare Clinics. They were cared for by the National Health Service in times of illness. They were brought up by parents who hardly ever considered separating and whose fathers were authoritarian figures, the head of the house. If they were naughty, they expected to be smacked. Homes, which were made comfortable with increasingly available and affordable mass-produced consumer goods, were kept clean by the hard work of a mother who, as well as doing the housework and cooking, most likely contributed financially through her work, probably in the hosiery or boot and shoe industries. This coincided with the zenith of the post-war economic boom which had seen a continuous rise in living standards since the end of post-war austerity. Even so, many homes in the inner city terraced streets still had no bathroom or inside toilet. Since the city became a smokeless zone in the mid-1960s, most Leicester houses were heated by gas fires in the living room and front room. Upstairs was often cold so the whole family would gather in the one room around the television unless they went out. Children had a lot of freedom, playing in the streets and wandering around their neighbourhoods alone.

Most young people left school at the age of fifteen with no qualifications and went to work in industries characteristic of Leicester until the 1980s. Hosiery, boot and shoe, engineering and printing industries, as well as shop and office work, were popular choices. Of course, not everyone left school so young. There was a bi-partite education system in the city at the time, some children passed their eleven-plus exam and gained a place at one of the grammar schools. These were sexually segregated and all pupils were expected to 'stay on' until sixteen and take O level exams. A smaller minority continued their education in the sixth form and took A levels, and an even smaller group went to university or polytechnic. The majority, about eighty per cent, went to secondary modern schools and left as soon as they were old enough to start work, for many of them the Easter after they turned fifteen. Not all secondary modern pupils left at fifteen, some of them 'stayed on' and took CSE exams and went on to take up five-year apprenticeships to become skilled workers in one of Leicester's booming industries or office jobs. There was well-paid employment for everyone who wanted it.

People married young and expected to stay together for life as the Divorce Reform Act had not yet simplified the process of ending an unhappy marriage. For the majority of young people, life was safe and secure. But not everyone wanted this security. Having a life mapped out, determined by class and gender, felt cloying to some who rebelled against their parents and social conventions. Rebellion took the form of dressing in a way that distinguished them from their parents' generation. Subcultures gave a lot of young people a sense of identity separate from mainstream adult society. The decade opened with teds and beatniks and was soon superseded by mods and rockers in the early sixties. The middle and end of the decade saw a burgeoning of different youth cultures – skinheads, Hell's Angels, greebos and hippies as well as the archetypical image of the era, the mini-skirted, so-called 'dolly bird' and young men in flared trousers.

Working from the age of fifteen onwards gave youth economic independence, the freedom to spend the wages they earned on whatever they chose, after giving a proportion of their income to their mum for their 'board.' Strangely, despite this array of subcultures, in Leicester there were few specialist shops selling fashion clothes aimed at young people. By the late 1960s there was Chelsea Girl on Eastgates and Miss Selfridge inside Lewis's. Fortunately, the nature of Leicester's industrial base meant that there were plenty of factory shops selling the latest fashions and, of course, there were the stalls on Leicester Market. Almost everyone knew someone who could get cheap clothes and footwear, sometimes big name brands like Fred Perry and Dunlop, through their staff discount at the factories or shops where they worked.

Another source of affordable fashion was making it yourself. At its most simple, this could be turning up the hem of a dress or skirt or, if a conservative parent disapproved of too much leg on show, rolling up the waistband when out of the house to create a short mini. All girls and their mums had learnt how to sew in childhood, it was a compulsory subject for females at school. Many homes had a sewing machine or even an over-locker if one of the women in the family was an outworker for one of the local clothing factories. The latest fashions were available in paper patterns that could be customised to suit the individual and made up at home in a few evenings with reasonably priced material from the market. Some garments were even run up at work on the factory's machine in the lunch hour or breaks, 'doing a foreigner' as the practice was known.

Hairstyles for young people became more natural and easy to manage than those of their parents, especially for girls who could choose a short, easy-to-manage crop or a long loose style that could be washed at home. This was a massive change to the coiffure of their mothers whose shampoo and sets involved weekly or fortnightly visits to the hairdresser. Many adult women did not wash their hair at home between sets and slept in curlers or rollers to keep their stiff, lacquered hair in place. For some reason, when a woman had grey hair, it was often a mark of status to tint it blue with setting lotion or dye, a blue rinse. Boys began to wear their hair longer by the end of the decade, in contrast to the short haircuts held in place by Brylcreem which had been popular in the fifties and were still sported by their fathers. 'You can't tell if they're boys or girls,' was a common derisory comment of the older generation.

Of course, adults and young people had different tastes in music. For young people, music was an important aspect of self-identity. Many houses had a gramophone, the more affluent a radiogram, on which to play their 45 rpm singles and 33 rpm long players or LPs, in mono of course for most of the decade. Most records were purchased at small independent shops, many of which offered records as a sideline to the electrical goods they sold as the main part of their businesses.

Entertainment often consisted of listening to live music. In Leicester, the working-men's club movement was particularly strong and every neighbourhood as well as the city centre had a club with a concert room where bands and singers performed cover versions of hits. Many young people accompanied their parents to the club on Saturday nights. When these young people began to venture out themselves, their first experience of independent nights out was to the Palais, a dance hall on Humberstone Gate, where most of the music was covers of the latest pop songs played by a house band. Technological developments and changes in the law allowed recordings to be played in public and discotheques – nightclubs playing records – began to appear around town. Disc jockeys played original versions of the hits and introduced new styles of music, such as soul and ska, often imported from America or the Caribbean. Catering for the different sub-cultures meant that the clubs would have sessions targeted at particular groups with their own tastes in music on different nights of the week.

For most young people, this new found freedom of youth culture was a brief interlude before the responsibility of relatively early marriage and parenthood. As well as pubs, dance halls and discos, there was a cinema in nearly every neighbourhood as well as more luxurious ones downtown. New films were first shown at one of the national chains, such as the Odeon or ABC, in the city centre before appearing in local cinemas where admission prices were cheaper. Going to the pictures locally was still popular in the sixties before some of the cinemas started to be converted into bingo halls from the end of the decade. At the end of every performance the national anthem was played. The audience was obliged to stand up and not move or talk while 'God Save the Queen' was played. There was a rush to escape the auditorium before the anthem came over the speakers. The more overtly rebellious had the audacity to walk out while the music was playing, to the indignation of the more conservatively minded, usually older, members of the audience.

In Leicester pubs, 'last orders' was at half past ten and everyone had to leave by 10.50 p.m. after 'drinking-up time', just in time to catch the last bus home at about 11 p.m. On Sundays, 'last orders' was even earlier at 10.00. Just over the city boundary in the county and suburbs like Oadby, Wigston and Braunstone Town, the pubs served until 11 p.m. or 10.30 p.m. on Sundays. The motorway services, Ross's at Leicester Forest East, was popular among young people who wanted somewhere to go after the pubs closed other than a nightclub. Ross's café was open twenty-four hours a day, although it didn't serve alcohol, and transport was needed to get there. Rising living standards in the 1960s meant that many, even teenagers over sixteen, had the archetypical youth transportation of a motorbike or scooter or even a second-hand car.

A takeaway on the way home was unlikely to be anything other than what was available in the fish and chip shop. In the 1960s, few people would have known what pizza was or ever have tasted curry unless they were of Asian heritage, although a few Chinese restaurants and takeaways had begun to appear around the city. Only a few hippies and eccentrics were vegetarian. Dinner, cooked by mum at home, was invariably meat or a dish containing meat like a pie or sausages, potatoes in one form or another but often mashed, accompanied by vegetables such as peas, carrots or cabbage. Pasta and rice were not commonly eaten at home until a potato shortage in the mid-1970s led people to search for an alternative filling food. White sliced bread and butter was eaten with almost everything, even with tinned peaches or fruit salad with condensed milk for Sunday tea.

There was an air of confidence in Leicester and, indeed, in England generally in the 1960s. Demand for labour outstripped supply for both males and females. It was a truism that if you were sacked or didn't like your job you could walk out and find another one later the same day or at least the day after. In football, England's World Cup victory in 1966 with goalkeeper Gordon Banks of Leicester City, the team then in the First Division of the Football League, contributed to this confidence. So too did the cultural meme of Swinging London, with Carnaby Street the centre of youth fashion. Increased prosperity, the space race, Concorde and growing ownership of motorbikes and cars made people believe that this was the dawn of an age of plenty in which things would continue to progress and people prosper. The recession of the 1930s, the deprivations of the war and the austerity of the post-war years were confined to an increasingly remote past.

So far it appears that life in the sixties was fun, safe and secure. However, social attitudes among the older generation did not seem to be changing at the same pace as material progress. There was a division of gender roles in employment, where women had no or little access to professions and were almost always paid less than men whatever job they had, irrespective of skills, qualifications and experience. The many pubs of Leicester were almost entirely a male preserve, or at least the bar was. Women might go to the pub, to sit in the lounge, if taken by their husbands or boyfriends. Few women would go to the pub alone or in female-only groups. Many pubs would not allow women to drink pints, a half was acceptable but more feminine drinks such as Babycham, Cherry B and Snowball were popular. In the Working Men's Clubs, women could not be served at all as the rules would not allow them to go to the bar. Children were allowed in clubs with their families on Saturday nights but at the pub they had to sit on the doorstep, if they were lucky with a bag of crisps and some pop.

The image of the so-called Swinging Sixties is in many ways a misnomer. Sexism and discrimination against women and girls was rife and accepted as the norm. Although the sixties is seen as the time when the Pill began to give women control of reproduction and their sexuality, women who wanted to go on it could only obtain prescriptions by paying their GP as private patients. Contraception wasn't available on the National Health until April 1974, although condoms could be purchased by men in the barbers. These could also be bought in chemists by those confident enough to go to the counter and ask for them. In 1970, the National Council of the Family Planning Association mandated that its clinics should give family planning advice to anyone, irrespective of marital status. In Leicester, though, there was only one FPA clinic, in St Peters in Highfields, and not everyone would be aware of its services or how to access them. Abortion was illegal until 1967 although a few desperate women resorted to illegal termination of an unwanted pregnancy, often at risk to their health or even their life, as well as being involved in a crime. Unplanned pregnancies were usually followed by a hasty wedding, 'having to get married' as they said. Few women would want the stigma of a child born outside marriage.

Another aspect of gender discrimination and clearly defined roles was that if a man wanted to go out with a woman he would be expected to pay for everything, at least in the early days of a relationship. In some ways this could be seen as fair as a young man who earned more would probably have more money available to spend, in pre-decimal pounds, shillings and pence of course. Young women and girls always claimed they had to spend a lot on clothes and make-up to look nice for their date when they went out so they could have spent as much as, if not more than the men.

Gender oppression was restricting enough for straight people but if you were gay it was even worse. It wasn't until the Sexual Offences Act of 1967 that consensual relationships between men were decriminalised in England and Wales for those over the age of 21. The Act did not apply in Scotland until 1981 and Northern Ireland until 1982. Although women in same sex relationships did not face legal penalties and criminalisation, social pressure and discrimination could be just as oppressive. For those who were transgender, no one had the legal right to change gender until 2005.

Racism blighted relationships between some individuals and groups. The newly arrived immigrants from the West Indies were soon followed by Asian people who were to add so much richness to cultural life in the city. Casual racism was endemic as was discrimination and abuse both in the social sphere, employment and institutional life. A Leicester child starting school in the early 1960s may never have seen a person who wasn't white. By the time they were in secondary school at the end of the decade, that child would probably have a number of playmates of other ethnicities. These early friendships were a challenge to some of the racism in adult society and were the first stage in the development of Leicester's multicultural society.

A paradox of being young in the 1960s was that while many working-class young people left school at fifteen, worked full-time, had a lot of financial independence and saw themselves as grown-up, they were not legally adults until they were twenty-one years old and could not vote in elections. At the same time, television brought an awareness of the wider world and international politics, including the Vietnam War, leading to a growing radicalisation and demonstrations by young people for civil rights, peace and social and economic change, especially in the USA and Paris in 1968 and beyond. Young people in Britain, including some in Leicester, were also influenced and joined protest movements, went on demonstrations or joined political organisations and pressure groups like CND early in the 1960s and the Anti-Apartheid Movement at the end.

A small minority of young people began to look for something more than what they saw as the predictable lives of their parents and most of their peers. The tedium of a lot of jobs, many of which involved doing repetitive tasks in factories, was boring for bright teenagers whose background often denied them the opportunity to aspire to anything more. A few young people, from among those who had stayed on at school into the sixth form, became the first in their families to experience student life along with the new ideas and independence that went with it. This was thanks to grants that removed financial barriers to higher education for ordinary people. For some of them as well, this alternative life led them to experiment with different and distinctive styles of dress, including long hair for both boys and girls, to the horror of the older generation. Sex outside marriage began to lose its stigma and a few daring couples even lived together openly before or even instead of marriage. Some of them experimented with recreational drugs such as the illegal cannabis and the hallucinogenic LSD, legal in the UK until 1966. Those with a talent for music formed bands, typically electric guitars and drums with vocals. Developments in musical technology, as well as influences from around the world, led some to experiment with synthesisers, creating new sounds and musical forms made louder by modern amplification and enhanced by new electronic technologies in the recording studio. A distinct counterculture emerged originating in these alternative lifestyles and values.

Physically, Leicester was undergoing massive spatial and architectural change as whole areas of the city underwent redevelopment. Entire communities of older terraced houses were demolished and residents moved out to expanding outer estates. In the city centre familiar and sometimes loved landmarks and streets, some of which had stood for centuries, were swept away. Tower blocks began to appear and modern, almost brutalist, steel and concrete office and residential developments were added to the architectural mix alongside the familiar red brick. Flyovers, the underpass and subways transformed the road layout, creating a new and dynamic urban landscape which could be both exciting and threatening. Rapid change of the built environment reinforced the idea that the world was changing and nothing was permanent. A proposed monorail for Leicester as well as the space race showed that technology-wise almost anything was possible.

It was against this background of a country and city going through rapid, profound and dramatic social and cultural change with its conflicts and contradictions that the scene was set for the story of Legay and the other Leicester people featured in this book.

Part One:

Something Quite Indescribable

The Story of Legay

Introduction

'History tends to be written about the rich and famous but there is a much broader story to tell about the mass of people who live rich and varied lives and make a real impact on their local culture. This is the case with the local music scene. Although few achieved national or international success, there is a legacy of real talent, happenings and events that changed people's lives and made the world a better place to live in. Legay were one of these. Even now I think they were the best band I've ever seen live and I've seen a few! They were as big as The Beatles to awestruck teenagers like me ...'
Kenny Wilson

Influenced by Tamla Motown, The Who, The Action and The Rolling Stones, Legay launched themselves onto the Leicester public in 1966 at The Casino Ballroom on London Road. Within months, they were packing out venues across the city and county. By 1967, the band's reputation as a live act had accelerated, playing sell-out gigs across the Midlands, the north-east and London. Playing a mixture of their own material plus heavy versions of Tamla classics, all with their Marshall amps switched up to the famous number 11, a Legay gig would have been loud and, much to the angst of some of the other bands, full of the best looking women in town. The guys in the audience wanted to be them and the girls wanted to be with them. In 1968, Legay released 'No-One' on the Fontana label, the single that should have launched them into UK-wide psychedelic stardom. It didn't. A lack of national radio airplay and poor promotion by Fontana put paid to that. Just over a year after the release of 'No-One', Legay were no more, swapping psychedelia for the imported sound of the American West Coast. With a focus on the likes of Moby Grape, Buffalo Springfield and HP Lovecraft, Legay slowly morphed into a new band with a new sound, look and name: Gypsy.

Legay had the potential to have been huge. The fact that they weren't is a question that even today baffles fellow musicians and fans alike, including Diesel Park West singer, John Butler: 'You've got to ask yourself the question: what made it so special? And it can only be an alignment of personalities. If you break down the band to the individuals in it, there was nothing outstandingly special about them. But put them all together and you had something quite spectacular.' Within three short years, Legay had developed a unique look, sound and image that was a major influence on other bands. In Rob Townsend, they had a powerhouse drummer who played in what many believe to be the four best regional bands of the period: The Beatnicks, The Broodly Hoo, Legay and Family. Legay had developed a regional fan base that would travel to see them wherever they played. Their reputation as a live band was non-comparable, they were quite unique in the way they approached performing live. They didn't simply cover other bands songs, they reworked and reinterpreted them. Some would say that they were pioneering the remix before it had ever been heard of.

If Legay had remained as Legay, would they have gone on to greater things? The Who, The Beatles, The Rolling Stones all changed/adapted to a new scene while retaining the essence of the band. Legay didn't – they literally changed into a new group, opting for a change of name, a different look, a new sound and a radical rethink of how they played/performed live. While Gypsy went on to achieve modest success, a reputation for being an exciting live band and a passionate fan base (which is still the case, some forty years after they split up), for many there is still the doubt that they got it wrong by dropping the originality that defined them. The latter is probably summed up best by band member, John Knapp: 'My biggest regret is that we turned into Gypsy. Legay were very English, a totally original band, the look, the sound, everything. We didn't owe anything to anybody. We threw all of that away and turned ourselves into a completely different band, a copy of Buffalo Springfield and Moby Grape.'

The story of Legay is one that I'm sure can be told in every city and town across the country. It's the story of five school friends who wanted to be in a band and make it. Although they weren't successful in a commercial sense, Legay were hugely successful in another; they succeeded in bringing an incredible feeling of joy, happiness and excitement into the lives of thousands of young people across the region and beyond. And that excitement is still evident today, it was there to be seen in the eyes of everyone I interviewed. People looked totally energised when they chatted about Legay and the era of flower power, the Il Rondo, Youth Dew and the delights of buying material, zips and buttons from Geoff's Fabrics in Leicester Market.

While making some cash from it along the way would have been good, I can't help thinking that if that was the case, some members of Legay probably wouldn't be around today as a result. Perhaps the legacy of making a lot of people very happy and to have survived is a far better reward than becoming yet another member of the 27 Club.

'We Were Very Loud ...'

'They were electric live, you couldn't wait for them to come on. It was like listening to blitzkrieg Motown ...' **Paul Coles**

Formed in 1966, Legay consisted of two sets of friends from Longslade and Stonehill schools in Birstall. 'Rod and I used to go to the Palais together and we often used to see the others hanging around,' recalls keyboard player, John Knapp. 'Robin, Mac and Legay came over to us one night and asked Rod to be the singer and myself to play the pianotron. We'd never done it before but we said yes, straight away.' Legay were Rod Read (vocals), Robin Pizer (lead guitar), Dave 'Mac' McCarthy (bass guitar), John Knapp (pianotron) and Legay Rogers (drums). Legay Rogers lived in Birstall and worked at Chapman and Fraser, a warehouse in Thurcaston. Working in the same warehouse was Robin, who lived in Syston, and Mac, who was from Thurmaston. John and Rod were best friends who grew up together in Birstall. John was a reproduction artist at Wintertons Printers and Rod was a junior shoe designer at Clarkes Shoes. 'I worked at AEI as an apprentice car mechanic but didn't like it so I joined Legay and Mac at Chapman and Fraser,' said Robin. 'Legay was the instigator of the band, he thought he was Brian Jones. He was the one who was chatting to Mac about getting something together. I remember the three of us auditioned somebody as a singer, a guy with a crew cut, but it wasn't right. Legay suggested we ask John and Rod, they knew each other because they all lived in Birstall.'

By the time Robin was nine years old, he had learned to play the trumpet. At thirteen, he'd joined a brass band in Sileby playing the baritone horn. 'I used to cycle from Sileby to Birstall to visit one of my uncles, who was a multi-instrumentalist,' said Robin. 'It was there that I learned to play the guitar. I bought a Watkins Rapier and added a seventh string.' Robin's uncle also taught the rudiments of the guitar to Mick Reynolds, one of the band's earlier roadies, and Dave McCarthy. 'Robin was definitely the most important musically,' said Mick. 'He would be responsible for teaching the others their parts and was at the time not only the best musician but probably the most accomplished singer.'

While John Knapp was from Leicester, Rod Read was born further afield in Egypt, on British Army territory. His dad, Les, was in the army during the Second World War and it was while he was in Italy he met his future wife, Nina. After the war, Les and Nina lived in Egypt, Austria, Scotland and various places in England before they came back to Leicester. Rod was nine years old when the family moved to Birstall. 'He had an amazing presence, even as a nine-year-old kid,' said John. 'The first day he walked into school, all the girls fell in love with him.' The two became best friends, later becoming mods who would regularly hitch lifts to London's renowned Carnaby Street to buy clothes. 'We used to save up as much cash as possible and go down there at least three times a year,' said John. 'We'd wait for hours on the slip road near the M1 junction for someone to pick us up. We didn't want to waste money on transport, we wanted to spend it all on clothes. We'd be speeding as well, which meant we didn't have to spend much cash on food either. We'd go to Lord John's – I can remember buying a mohair burgundy jacket and trousers from there, Rod bought a candy striped jacket. We'd also buy patterns, adapt them and get Burton's to make them up for us in Leicester. Even then, we didn't want to look like typical mods, we wanted to look different.'

Robin Pizer and Mick Reynolds were classmates at Roundhill School and from the age of thirteen hung out together in their home town of Syston. In the summer of 1963, they both left Roundhill and started at Longslade School in Birstall where they met Rod and John. Musical influences and allegiances were already forming. 'One day in 1964, Robin and I were walking down a corridor at Longslade,' said Mick. 'He said to me that The Beatles weren't his favourite group any more, it was the Stones. It sounds a bit stupid now but I was really taken aback by this but at the time, it was a big thing to say. But it showed how forward thinking he was because the Stones were doing a lot of Chuck Berry stuff which would be a huge influence later on.' During the same year, Robin, Mac and Mick formed a band with two other friends, calling themselves Route 5, an adaptation of the Chuck Berry song, 'Route 66'. They were influenced by British R&B, The Rolling Stones and the first Kinks LP. 'At the time, I had an old Spanish guitar which was detuned to sound like a bass,' said Mick. 'Dave (Mac) was taught rhythm guitar. Bass guitar did not come naturally to me and I had to rely on Robin to show me what to play and then learn the parts parrot fashion. We played a few local gigs, schools, village halls, et cetera, then eventually went our separate ways.'

During the same period, Legay Rogers was spending as much time as possible learning to play the drums whilst listening to Elvis's 'Heartbreak Hotel' or 'Hound Dog'. Affectionately known around Birstall as 'Lurgy', Legay took advantage of his dad's position as caretaker at Stonehill School by practising in the music room. Ray

Read, brother of Rod and one of the band's roadies, remembers the aspiring young drummer. 'I knew Legay Rogers before the band started. He was a delivery boy for the Co-op, he used to ride around Birstall on his pushbike, it had a basket on the front. There were a few of us at the time who were all into drumming. He was a real character, full of charisma. He was worth three blokes in a band.'

Robin and Mick briefly lost contact when they left school in 1965. When they next met, on a bus the following year, they immediately got back to discussing their musical influences. 'Robin told me that he was in another band with Legay, Dave, Rod and John and that they were practising in a barn on Threeways Farm in Queniborough,' said Mick. 'He asked if I'd like to come and listen.' Threeways Farm was the home of Syston Boys FC, an old farm building which was at the time used as the football club changing rooms. 'I went along the next night and liked what I heard. They knew the basics of about two songs and things progressed from there. What struck me the most was the sound – the only other band that were doing something different at the time were The Who.' John Knapp: 'Queniborough was before we had the van so we used to have to get there by bus, taking the guitars, keyboards and drums with us. It wasn't ideal but that's what we had to do. To accentuate practice time, we also used the garage at the rear of Mick's parent's house in Syston, we used it to store the kit. It was standing room only, with no space for the drums. It was a great atmosphere though, there was an instant reaction between each other right from the start.'

Family guitarist Charlie Whitney, who during the early days at Klock Agency managed the Broodly Hoo, came down to Threeways Farm to watch Legay rehearse. 'I think the idea was that he was going to manage us,' explains John. 'But we didn't want him to do it, don't ask me why. The history of the band is immersed in turning down people we should have been involved with and going with those that we shouldn't!' The rehearsals at Threeways Farm led to Legay's first live performance at Birstall Village Hall. It was organised by Klinch Promotions, an agency run by Rod's other brother, Richard. John's parents ran the door and the refreshments table, selling pop, crisps and sweets. 'The Birstall Village Hall gigs were important to us,' said John. 'It gave us our first taste of performing live, an opportunity to bring what we had learned at Threeways Farm to an audience and to see if it worked.'

So, what's in a name? 'Legay Rogers was very proud of his unusual Christian name,' said Mick Reynolds. 'So proud that in the early days before gigs he had his name placed on the front of his bass drum in large letters. Whilst pondering over different names for the band, someone suggested Legay as it was already on the drum kit. It stuck from thereon in.'

....

Legay's first official gig was at The Casino on London Road, Leicester, in July 1966. Also on the bill were The Matadors and Mike and the Planets. 'I was playing an Echo 12-string at the time,' said Robin. 'I wore my nail away, which caused a bit of blood, and broke a couple of strings.' Chris Busby, guitarist with Vfranie, recalls that first gig: 'It was packed. There was a huge buzz of expectation and a really good vibe. When they came on it was great, really exciting. We all loved them – the image, the sound, everything, we were all big fans of them.' Due to illness, John Knapp didn't play the Casino gig, instead he watched it with the rest of the audience. 'I came down with jaundice, conjunctivitis and chickenpox all in one go. I had to take six weeks off work and missed rehearsals. It was all down to lifestyle – too many pills and not enough food or sleep. It always catches up with you in the end, regardless of how much you think you'll get away with it.'

The Casino, along with the Frollocking Kneecap in Market Harborough, would virtually become Legay's second home with the band playing there on numerous occasions over the next couple of years. 'The Casino gigs were the best,' said John. 'It wasn't that big a place but it felt huge because it was always packed. We called the guy that owned it "The Penguin" because he was always wearing a tuxedo and dickie bow. There was a bar at one end and I think there was another one upstairs.'

Shortly after their first gig at The Casino, Legay played The Latin Quarter, a tiny cellar club on Belgrave Road. 'The gig at the Latin Quarter was held downstairs, whilst the nightclub was upstairs,' said Mick Reynolds. 'The cellar was quite a cool place, you just couldn't get enough people down there. A guy turned up who wanted to manage us, Legay Rogers had been talking to him. We all stayed at his house … well, he made out it was his house, turns out his landlady was away for the weekend. He was all talk, he thought he was Brian Epstein.'

The mods were an early influence on Legay both in look and sound, the songs they played being a derivative of American R&B, particularly Tamla Motown. 'We would go and watch bands such as The Who, The Action, The Creation and The Kinks,' said Mick. 'At the time, the Il Rondo was probably the main source of regular, good live music in Leicester. We'd occasionally go to The Dungeon in Nottingham, it was more of a disco though, very similar to the Nite Owl on Newarke Street. They played a lot of mod-related American music, mainly Tamla derivatives. You've got to remember that there was very little radio airplay for this style of music at the time, you really only heard it in clubs.' John Knapp: 'When we used to go up town, we'd call into a coffee bar on Duns Lane called The White Cat. It was great, had a fantastic aroma. It was how a lot of us got into music, you'd hear songs being played there on the jukebox that you'd never heard before, a bit of Tamla, a bit of blues, Howlin' Wolf. Great stuff.'

A gang of Leicester mods – including John, Rod and Ray Read – would often go to Nottingham to sample the bars, clubs and coffee shops. Most of the time, the visit would end in a skirmish, something that Ray Read remembers all too well. 'Just by the marketplace was a hill. On this one occasion it was black, full of leather jackets, loads of rockers marching down towards us. There we were, four or five Leicester mods, surrounded by these black leather jackets. Rod told us to stay put and started to move through them, pushing them to the side, one by one. It was like the parting of the waves. I was nervous but Rod started to lead us out. We managed to get ourselves into a café and they followed us in, making knuckledusters out of the tin ashtrays that were on the tables. We made another run for it and managed to hide in a graveyard. To this day, I don't know how we got away with it.'

On a visit to the Il Rondo in early 1966, the three friends didn't even manage to get to the end of their street in Birstall when they ran into trouble. 'We were walking from my house to go into town,' said Ray. 'I was copying a call I'd just heard from Tarzan, it was on the telly before we came out. This guy thought we were taking the mickey out of him, an argument started and he set his Alsatian dog onto us. It bit a lump out of Rod's arm. I had to punch this guy to get him off of me and kick the dog so that it would let go of Rod. We thought "let's get out of here" so we ran for the bus with this guy chasing behind us. We'd just jumped onto the bus and he stuck a screwdriver into John, there was blood everywhere. When we got to St Margaret's Bus Station, the police were waiting for us. It went to court and we were charged with attacking him. We got off with it though, it wasn't the first time this guy had done something like that and he also lost his temper in court. Case dismissed.' John Knapp: 'I've still got the scar from that. Looking back, that's all we seemed to do during the mod years, get into scraps. We'd either go looking for it, especially if Rod was with us, or it would find us.'

During these early days, every available hour was spent on developing the band's sound and visual identity, especially with regards to sourcing new material to play.

'Rod, John and I used to meet during our lunch breaks from work,' said Mick Reynolds. 'When not sourcing material for new shirts, we used to go to Advance Records on High Street which sold obscure and often imported American/Tamla style records. Rod would rummage through these to find new songs, Barbara McNair is one that springs to mind. We'd listen to it in the shop and if we liked it, we'd buy it.' Legay would take these harmonious and melodic Tamla songs and play and interpret them in a totally different way, turning up the volume but retaining the harmony and melody. 'They adapted each song to the Legay style,' said Mick. 'That was the difference between them and the other bands that were around Leicester at the time, most of them were playing soul music. We hated it because everyone was doing the same thing, exact copies of the originals.' Robin Pizer: 'We didn't really do covers as such because they sounded nothing like the originals, they were all completely different. We were also very loud. The first thing we did was turn our amps straight up to maximum.' Paul Coles, drummer with Leicester band Vfranie, also recalls Legay's unique take on the Tamla classics. 'They were electric live, you couldn't wait for them to come on. It was like listening to blitzkrieg Motown, it wasn't light and airy like the original stuff, it was totally in your face and loud. They did a version of "You're Ready Now" by Frankie Valli. You wouldn't have recognised the original, it came at you like a steam train.'

The source of the newly discovered volume came after a visit to Moore & Stanworths on Belgrave Road. 'Early on, Legay weren't that loud because the equipment was pretty mediocre,' explains Mick. 'Then we went to Moore & Stanworths and bought all the kit on hire purchase, the income from the gigs was used to pay for it all. I used to go there on Saturdays and pay the weekly instalments on perhaps five or six different purchase agreements. They were all guaranteed by various parents as we were all too young at the time to have a hire purchase agreement in our own names. It was here that we picked up the first Marshall stacks. At the time, no other band in Leicester had anything like that, only those such as The Who had that sort of system. From then on, Legay became really loud. Inevitably, club owners would tell me to turn the volume down so I'd lower it by one unit then turn it back up again for the next song.'

For young musicians, Moore & Stanworths was *the* place to go in Leicester for advice and information on instruments and amplifiers. With the help of Phil and Dave, in their gleaming white overalls, many purchases were made by guitarists in their quest for the best equipment. 'It was the place to meet colleagues, friends and the celebrated musicians of the Leicester music scene,' said Leicester musician, Terry Gannon. 'I bought my Rosetti Lucky 7 from there but, much more importantly, my Hofner Verithin Custom Committee. It was a rare and gorgeous instrument, blonde with the most beautiful wood grain and mother of pearl binding and flowery motif headstock. I didn't know whether I should polish it, play it or just look at it.'

....

Legay dressed in what they liked to wear, usually very trendy clothes inspired in particular by Rod's shirts which, after buying material and buttons from either a stall on Leicester Market or from Lewis's department store, he had designed and made up by his grandmother. 'She used to make a lot of his shirts,' recalls Julia Read, Rod's girlfriend and future wife. 'She was a seamstress. She had to stop making them though as she had arthritis. As I used to make a lot of my own clothes, I made a few for him afterwards. Rod would see shirts that he liked and I'd add embroidery to them.' Eventually, Rod's grandmother would make shirts for each member of the band with the exception of John. 'They didn't last five minutes,' said Robin. 'They would fall apart after a couple of gigs, we'd wear them out. We'd never make the same design again though, we'd move on to something else.'

Rod and John were the first ones to wear custom-made shirts, even during the early mod days. 'I remember seeing them at The Palais on Sunday nights,' said Mick Reynolds. 'They'd come in wearing these shirts and jackets that were completely different to what everyone else was wearing. The ethos of that evolved into Legay, especially with the shirts. I wouldn't class it as outrageous, more outlandish, and completely different to anything else that was around, including the bigger bands that were on the circuit. They weren't wearing anything like what Legay were wearing.' All of the ideas on presentation were down to John, who designed and made his own clothes, and Rod. 'It was a great image, nobody looked like we did,' said Robin. 'Our clothes had nothing to do with fashion, there was no trend. We weren't afraid to try out anything new.' John Knapp: 'We just loved dressing up, it seemed right at the time. We used to attract a lot of girls because of what we wore and the fact we were wearing make-up. A lot of the clothes were from a theatre hire shop on Silver Street. Two of the girls that worked there, Sue and Jane, were fans of the band so we used to get outfits from them for free.' However, not all of the clothes were designed by Rod and John, nor were they handmade. 'I can remember Legay playing a couple of gigs in a village hall and the next day there was a rummage sale,' said Mick. 'We all went through the clothes and I think each one of us came back with a shirt or jacket. I think there's even a photo which shows Rod wearing a woman's pinstriped jacket, he might have got that from a rummage sale.'

Legay's look, stage presence and ability to attract the ladies hadn't gone unnoticed by other bands. 'I'm sure there was some jealousy from others because Legay always had their own fan base, usually girls that fancied them,' said Clive Jones, saxophonist and flute player with Leicester soul band, Pesky Gee! 'We may have been jealous of their following but not of the band as we played a different type of music in the early days.' Chris Dredge, guitarist with Pesky Gee! adds: 'It was just friendly rivalry, we were at opposite ends of the scale to be honest. We used to take the mickey out of them by saying that their voices hadn't broken because they could reach all of the high notes and that we had a bigger van – ours was like a bus compared to theirs. We thought Legay were similar to the Small Faces but a bit more hard and heavy. And like the Small Faces, they didn't make any money either.' John Butler, singer with Diesel Park West, continues: 'Some of the other bands that were around were quite conservative and had been trying for ages. They were jealous of Legay because they just seemed to have appeared from nowhere.' Paul Coles remembers the vast repertoire of the band. 'You kept thinking, where are they digging these songs up from? So we kept an eye on them, see what they were doing, go and watch them as much as we could. Then when we got to know them it was great, it was like hanging around with royalty. I remember when Vfranie had just done a gig at Roundhill School, John was in the audience and we gave him a lift back home to Birstall. I kept thinking, bloody hell, Knappo's in the back of the van!'

....

Those initial, early days of balancing a full-time job and being in a band proved to be difficult for Legay. 'When we used to gig, we didn't get back until late, which meant we'd be completely exhausted the next day,' said John Knapp. 'I used to sneak off to the toilet at work and grab some sleep while the rest of the guys would cover for me.' Although the band members would eventually leave their jobs and go professional, Mick Reynolds still continued with the day job. 'I always worked. After a London gig, by the time we'd driven back to Leicester, dropped everybody off and parked the van up, it would have been about 6 a.m. I'd grab an hour's sleep and then get to work for 8 a.m., feeling dreadful.'

The first van that Legay used has developed something of an iconic status in its own right and to this day it is remembered with great fondness by both fans and band members alike. 'We ended up with a blue Commer van that didn't have proper windscreen glass, it had been fitted with normal house glass,' said Robin Pizer. 'The glass was already in when we bought it, it would have cut people to shreds if it had smashed. We used to park it either at Mick's place in Syston or at the bottom of Kingsgate in Birstall.' The van, which was constantly breaking down, was driven by Richard Read, who was a roadie for the band in the early days along with his brother, Ray. On top of the dodgy windscreen, its general unreliability and cleanliness, Richard also had to contend with another major problem. 'We played a gig at the Rugby Corporation Hall and I drove the Commer without any foot brakes, I had to keep using the hand brake. I've never been so bloody nervous in my life, I was a quivering wreck by the time I got out.' Richard continued to drive the van until Mick Reynolds passed his driving test in 1967. 'We used to have a policy of never cleaning it,' said Mick. 'It looked filthy with names and messages written in the dirt. I was stopped by the police once on the dual carriageway in Thurmaston. I asked why I had been stopped and was told that the van needed cleaning – I didn't realise that it was an offence! In the end, the officious officer of the law gave me a ticket for too much smoke coming from the exhaust. I was given a £5 fine and had my licence endorsed. On another occasion, I remember we were driving out to Uppingham in the van, it was a winter's night and in those days the roads didn't get gritted. We had a portable radio and record player, every time we went around a corner it used to slide all over the place. There was ice all over the road and we came to a bend, skidded off through a hedge and down a field on the other side. All the equipment came off the roof rack and we had to look around in the dark for all of this stuff, including John's pianotron. Somehow, we managed to get everything back up to the van and carry on.'

In January 1967, David Sandison (who would later become a major influence on the development of the band), filed his first report on Legay in the *Leicester Chronicle*. With nine months of performing under their belts, and now being managed by John Aston of Klock Agency, the article provides an interesting and accurate glimpse into where the band were and where they wanted to be.

Can Legay Exploit Their Thunder?

By David Sandison

Legay are a group most Leicester club fans will have seen by now at one time or another. Few – except close friends and families – would credit them with outstanding musical ability, yet there is something about that which commands attention and respect.

The first time they appear anywhere, the atmosphere becomes tense as people react to their screaming guitars and thundering attacks on songs. The next time they appear, the place is full, as word has spread.

This is the sort of thing agents and club owners like, and so it is no surprise to learn that in the nine months that Legay have been playing together, they have built a solid reputation with managers (who count) and fans (who pay). This, too, is the stuff that makes stars.

Which way are Legay looking? Which way do they hope to go next year? I spoke to the group over a cup of coffee, and found out what makes Legay tick.

Which Way To Go?

Do they want to be 'stars'? How important is the group to each member? Which way do they want to go with their music? How important do they think gimmicks are?

'We want success more than anything,' they all admitted, Robin Pizer was most vehement. 'I think we'll get it,' he said. 'We cater for ourselves, and there's a lot of people like us around, so we cater for them as well. We aim for the best visual effect possible.'

'I think we're the only really vocal group in Leicester,' added John Knapp. 'The music we do is exciting, and this is fine, because we just set out to excite people.'

Robin came back. 'I don't agree that concentrating on excitement means you lose musical quality, but even if we are not exceptional musically it doesn't matter. I think people buy records for music and go to dances for excitement.'

How much are Legay prepared to do to become a success? 'We'll do almost anything to make it,' said David McCarthy, while the others nodded in agreement. 'We'll wear anything, play anything, do anything that we think will help us get on. We want to succeed in this field.'

Optimistic words. But there are hundreds of groups currently knocking on doors all over the country, trying to get the 'in' to the big money clubs and halls.

What do Legay think about this?

Back came Robin. 'If we thought that we were a run-of-the-mill group, we would pack it all in now. If we thought we could do nothing else and give nothing else to audiences, then we would finish, because there are hundreds of groups who could do with the work we were taking.'

Legay are a wild looking bunch, with their specially designed clothes and their uninhibited act. But appearances can be deceptive. They are planning all of the time, calculating away like five computers.

....

In early March 1967, the band endured their first major setback when founder member Legay Rogers had to leave due to ill health. Having just finished a gig at the Boat Club in Burton upon Trent, Legay complained of feeling unwell and collapsed outside. 'We'd just played a really good gig,' said Robin Pizer. 'He was walking down the path, carrying his drum kit back to the van and he just collapsed, writhing around on the floor. It was an incredible shock to all of us.' Mick Reynolds: 'We took him from the path and into the van, he was shaking for a long time. It was very scary because none of us knew what to do, we didn't really know what was happening. We kept saying to him, "what's wrong, what's wrong". He was taken away in an ambulance and that was it.'

Shortly afterwards, Legay Rogers was diagnosed with having a stomach ulcer. 'Lurgy', the founding member who gave his name to the band, never played with them again. 'We were devastated when he left,' said Mick. 'Looking back though, it might have been the best thing for him that he went when he did. He had become increasingly unhappy about gigging at the weekends, he wanted to spend the time with Kate, his girlfriend and future wife. In an odd way, I think he was relieved that he could leave this way as opposed to resigning, his hand was forced in the end.' Kate Kissane-Rogers, Legay's girlfriend, remembers his departure: 'Gay was ill for quite a while, we discovered he had a stomach ulcer after the gig in Burton. He said he thought it could have been caused by eating bacon sandwiches and fry ups at three in the morning after gigs! The doctor told him he had to leave the group and live a normal life so he sold his drums and bought me an engagement ring. His ulcer played him up for years, he eventually had to have surgery on it but he made a good recovery and played with many bands afterwards.'

With Legay Rogers gone, the remaining band members spent time considering their options. 'While we would have known what was going on regarding Legay Rogers at the time, there was no way we would have got involved with it,' explains band manager, John Aston. 'It would have been tough for them though as they were all good friends.' Friendship aside, Legay's departure left a massive hole within the structure and make-up of the band. Not only had they lost a drummer, they had also lost a great character and showman, something which the remaining band members even today acknowledge was never recaptured. His replacement, however, would turn out to be someone who many consider to be one of the most powerful and creative drummers that emerged from the 1960s …

Charles Keene College, 1966.

Early publicity shot. John, Dave, Robin, Legay and Rod, 1966.

Unknown venue, 1966.

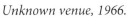

Unknown venue, 1966.

Backstage, 1966.

*Legay Rogers, founder member
and instigator of the band.*

Klock publicity shot with Rob Townsend, 1967.

Publicity shot, 1967.

Publicity shot, 1967.

Upstairs in a bedroom, 1967.

Backstage, 1967.
With Mick Reynolds
(centre).

The gleaming, white van,
before the policy of never
cleaning it.

Robin, Dave and Rod,
1967.

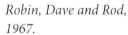

Julia Read, 1967.

The Stuff Stardom's Made Of ...

'He started to play the drums and the whole room shook, he was incredibly loud, it was an unbelievable sound. We had to change how we played to accommodate his style – we had to become louder ...' **John Knapp**

The search for a new drummer led to Rob Townsend, who was a friend of John Knapp. 'We just didn't know what to do when Legay left,' said Robin Pizer. 'John worked with Rob and he sounded him out about joining.' Rob, who lived on Bassett Street in Leicester, was a former member of The Beatniks and was now playing with The Broodly Hoo, a local band who mainly performed soul covers. 'I was working with John at Wintertons, he was getting into playing the piano,' recalls Rob. 'I was playing in the Broodly Hoo, who were a quite successful band managed by Charlie Whitney and Klock Agency. I was the oldest, probably about seventeen, the rest were all sixth formers. We used to play stuff by the likes of Geno Washington, The Ram Jam Band and Jimmy James and the Vagabonds.'

Rob's main musical influence was traditional jazz, following the likes of Acker Bilk and Chris Barber. 'I didn't have a record player so I would go round to my cousin's house, he was a big traditional jazz fan,' said Rob. 'He took me to De Montfort Hall to see Acker Bilk and in those days he was playing very good traditional jazz, especially the marches, they were really good. I also used to go with a kid from school and we saw everybody from Duke Ellington to Count Basie, Louis Armstrong and Dave Brubeck. I took drumming very seriously, I studied it, I listened a lot. Anything that was on at De Montfort Hall I went to because I really wanted to play the drums. And the jazz boys really had the best drummers.'

On one occasion, Rob was on the bus home from school when he heard 'Apache' by The Shadows. 'They had a great drummer called Tony Meehan and he became my hero. In those early days, I was still at school and I was playing with guys that were a lot older than me, they'd come out of the rock and roll era. I was in two bands, the first was called Buzzford and the Classics and then I went on to The Beatniks. Both bands were led by piano players who taught me how to play Chuck Berry and Jerry Lee Lewis songs so I became quite proficient at playing those.'

Rob joined The Broodly Hoo after their drummer took ill and Klock Agency recommended him to the rest of the band. He played a gig with them at Wyggeston

Girls School and then, about a month later, another one was scheduled at The Casino on London Road. 'They came round my house on the Sunday afternoon and said that the drummer had taken ill again and was there any chance I could do it. I did and they asked me to join. I think it was because I'd been doing it a bit longer than them, I had more experience.' At the time, The Broodly Hoo were a blues outfit, playing numbers by musicians such as 'the father of British Blues harmonica', Cyril Davies. 'When the brass came in, one of the singers turned to the sax and we brought another singer in,' said Rob. 'It was starting to go the way I wanted it to. It was jazz and I loved the big bands.'

....

Rob was about eighteen when The Broodly Hoo started to break up. It was at this time that he joined Legay, at first temporarily covering for Legay Rogers, who was ill. 'I saw Legay Rogers a few times with the band, once I think was at Leicester University or somewhere similar, he was sick on stage. On this particular occasion he was ill again and I think I said to Charlie Whitney that I'd join them if they wanted a drummer, it was quite casual. My first gig in Leicester with them was near St Margaret's Bus Station. We were in a cellar with a little stage in the corner, I just about got the drum kit on it.'

The news that Rob Townsend had left The Broodly Hoo to join Legay was covered via the *Leicester Chronicle* on 24 March 1967. It's interesting to note that while the journalist believed that 'Rob's presence has not meant a great deal musically', the band on the other hand thought completely the opposite, so much so that they had to adapt to Rob's sound and technique.

Broodly's Break Up – Future Uncertain

Drummer Townsend finds freedom after discipline

Rob Townsend, former drummer with Broodly Hoo, has joined Legay. Old news maybe but worthy of recording on this page for future generations.

His decision was not a hasty one – Rob had been discontented with his role in Broodly Hoo for about two months. He had been offered a job by Legay but decided to see how things went with the Broods before committing himself.

When Phil Wright left the Broods a month ago, Rob had a re-think and went to see Legay. The clinch to the deal came when drummer Legay (Rogers) felt ill after a booking. Rob sat in for him, liked the freedom of Legay after Broodly Hoo's disciplined music and asked to join.

Working out songs

Before he did however, drummer Legay had resigned – 'so that I can work out a lot of songs I've been thinking of for some time' he told me over the weekend. Rob was in and has already played with the group at Nuneaton, the Rag Rave and The Casino.

So far – and no-one would really expect such a thing – Rob's presence has not meant a great deal musically. But I think he can help Legay a lot, and his knowledge of the pop scene and its music should provide the group with plenty of ammunition in their fight to the top.

The difference to Rob is quite great though. For the first time for ages he has been told to drum exactly how he wants. And he is revelling in this.

Another early Legay gig with Rob was in a village hall in Leicestershire. 'There was nobody there really,' admits John Knapp. 'He started to play the drums and the whole room shook, he was incredibly loud, an unbelievable sound. We had to change how we played to accommodate his style, we had to become louder because he was the dominant sound. Legay Rogers' style of playing was mainly cymbal led, Rob's was about power and inventiveness, his technique was awesome. During this time, Robin had also started to write his own songs and Rob put the backbone to them, that's how "No-One" developed.'

Today, Rob remembers how everyone had their own roles within the band: 'The musical director as it were was Robin, who had started writing his own material. John and Rod were the fashion boys. They were all great looking guys, they had this mod type image. I had clothes made by Rod's grandma in Braunstone, we used to go to Lewis's to buy cloth and she used to make them. I remember I had a blue flowery shirt. I can also remember buying a white fur coat from Leicester Market and cutting the sleeves and collar off so that it became almost a waistcoat.' Rob quickly realised that Legay weren't a run-of-the-mill band with regards to how they looked. 'We had a really big female following, it was quite exciting. You concentrated more on what you were trying to play and how you looked. It wasn't musical perfection but we had a lot of presence on stage – and we had Rod Read. He wasn't the greatest of singers but the women flocked to see him.' Rod's presence on stage was something that was picked up by Leicester singer/songwriter, Kenny Wilson: 'Rod Read was incredibly charismatic and they had a huge fan base of mainly attractive girls. As you can understand, this served as an inspiration to me to follow a musical career …'

Unbeknown to the band's legion of female fans, most of Legay were in steady relationships. 'I started to go out with Rod a couple of months before they went on the road,' said Julia Read. 'They were practising at the time, getting ready for the big launch at The Casino. It came to light that we both liked each other but we didn't know so somebody set it up. Our first date was on Friday, 13 May 1966, it had all been arranged the week before in the Il Rondo. Everything went wrong – I ripped my dress, the bus broke down on the way and I was late.' Mick Reynolds: 'Rod didn't have a lot of confidence with girls at the time, I remember that I had to ask Julia if she would go out with him. All the girls used to fancy Rod but he wasn't interested, he was going steady with Julia.'

Rod wasn't the only member of the band in the early stages of a relationship. 'I first met John at a Legay gig in 1966,' said Linda Knapp. 'They were playing the Raven Youth Club in Thurnby Lodge – he tripped me over as I walked across the room. I'd only just left school when I met him, I was as green as they come, and so naïve it was untrue.' As money was tight during the early days of the band, it was down to Linda to make the effort to see John. 'I had to catch two buses to get to Birstall, I remember the walk up Greengate Lane was a killer. It was all a bit hit and miss to begin with because they were always playing, sometimes six nights a week. It was difficult, he'd say I'm playing at so-and-so, if you want to see me, that's where I'll be.'

As with most other bands at the time, partners were kept out of the limelight. The consequences of fans discovering that band members were in relationships and unavailable could have been disastrous to their overall commercial success and marketability. 'We used to hitch all over the place to see them,' said Linda. 'We wouldn't get a lift with them because they didn't want the fans to see girls getting out of the van. On one occasion, we hitched down to London to see them and I don't think they were best pleased to see us.' Band manager, John Aston: 'They didn't have girlfriends as far as the fans were concerned. Taking girlfriends with a band could cause trouble, one would want to take theirs and then the other five guys would want to take theirs, you simply couldn't accommodate them. I'm sure they all had someone in the wings whose company they enjoyed but they were a good looking bunch of lads who appeared to be as carefree as they could possibly be, that was the attraction.'

The friendship shared by the band's girlfriends was based almost exclusively around the ability to be able to understand the complexities of band life. 'I can't say that I really knew the other guys in Legay,' Linda reveals. 'When you are going out with somebody in a band, you don't get into too many deep conversations with the others, people don't like it. And because you never knew what anyone was doing, you had to have a friend within the band. Things could change at the last minute, a gig could be arranged or cancelled and because of that, you couldn't really have a proper friendship with someone outside of the band. Friendships formed within the band and in our case, it was Julia and Kathy (Robin's girlfriend) and me and Lorraine (Mac's girlfriend). It's odd but I probably know more about Kathy and Julia now than I did then.' Julia Read: 'I was probably friendlier with Kathy than any of the others. We were quite different in the fact that while she probably wouldn't be wearing make-up, I'd always have my false eyelashes on. She'd be wearing a duffle coat and I'd have a velvet coat on. She wasn't interested in fashion but we still got on. When Kathy's mum and dad went away, Rod and I used to stay round there with her and Robin and when my parents went away, we used to stay round my house. Robin used to cook us breakfast!'

Julia and Kathy would often link up to go and watch Legay when they were performing outside of Leicester. As with today, train timetables back in the 1960s weren't designed to accommodate gig times. 'Kathy and I went to Birmingham one Sunday night to see them at The Swan at Yardley,' said Julia. 'They asked us if we wanted a lift back and we said no, we're going back on our own. We got to New Street Station and were told that the next train to Leicester was the following morning. I rang my mum and she told me to tell a policeman but he couldn't help, he told us we'd have to sleep in the ladies waiting room, which we did. We didn't get back to Leicester until gone 8 a.m. and I had to be at work for nine. So I went straight to work, still with my going out gear on. I was alright until about two and then it hit me.'

....

In 1967, Legay embraced the psychedelic scene, absorbing new influences such as the Electric Prunes, Jefferson Airplane, The Move, The Beatles (in particular *Sgt Pepper* and *The Magical Mystery Tour*) and Pink Floyd. Jumping head first into the visual ethos of 'Flower Power', Legay were seen in Leicester, and by the media in particular, to be at the forefront of the American-led ideology. This article from the front page of the *Leicester Chronicle*, August 11:

Flower Power comes to Leicester

Flower Power has come to Leicester. To join the movement, just think happy thoughts, love your neighbour and accept that pretty flower when it's offered ...

Non-violence is the theme of the Flower Power cult. Their symbol – the flower – stands for gentleness.

Leicester's Legay are the city's first beat group to pioneer flower clothes, which they make themselves, adding beads, pendants and bells. On stage, painted faces are used to add atmosphere.

Weird? Certainly. Effeminate? Legay say no, despite the jibes they have to face.

In amongst the flowers, you (will) see Legay leader, Robert Pizer (sic). Robert now lives almost permanently without shoes. The face paint is reserved chiefly for the stage act, but he has worn it off stage.

Caught in mid-leap by our photographer is Howlin' Robin, resident master of ceremonies at a Leicester club. Disciples of the new cult maintain that the essence of life is to 'be happy'. Leap about, sing, wear strange clothes but, above all, be happy.

The *Leicester Illustrated Chronicle* took great pleasure in reporting/mocking the fact that Legay had a 'typical flower power cult retort' to those that abused them – they would hand their detractors a gift of either a flower or an apple. 'Someone who had too much to drink at a venue last week tried to pick a fight,' reported the *Chronicle* in 1967. 'Legay gave him an orange.' (John Knapp: 'We were playing at a barbeque in Whetstone with Unit Four Plus Two when we gave the oranges out.') 'The whole idea was great,' said Pesky Gee's Clive Jones. 'Legay took it up and so did we to a point even though we still played some soul songs in the set. I remember we all had flower power style shirts in the brightest colours – what a pity it only lasted that one year.'

With Rob Townsend in the drum seat, Legay went to Derek Tompkin's studio in Kettering to record a series of tracks including 'Out Of My Mind', 'Barmy the Policeman', 'Take Me In Your Arms', 'Why Do You Wanna Make Me Blue' and

'You're Gonna Love Me Baby'. 'David Sandison introduced us to Derek Tompkins and Klock booked us in,' said Robin Pizer. 'The change over to the psychedelic sound was happening way before "No-One". We recorded songs such as "Television", which was a bit strange, and "High Flying Around" although with the latter, I have no recollection about writing it, singing it, recording it or even playing on it. *Sgt Pepper* changed a lot of things, we were talking about it a lot at that point.' Mick Reynolds: 'The studio was a bit of a homemade job but at the time we really didn't know what a proper one should have looked like.' Although the sessions went well, the band refused to bring in a producer to oversee the recordings. 'It would have been pointless, they couldn't have directed us to do anything,' admits Robin. 'We were pretty arrogant in the way we thought, we couldn't handle anyone telling us what to do. To be honest, I don't think anybody would have put up with us.' 'Out Of My Mind' was a cover of the Buffalo Springfield track. After the recording session, Legay played a gig at the Frollocking Kneecap in Market Harborough and they took a copy of the demo with them. By the end of the night, however, they discovered it had been stolen. 'They played it and we never saw it again,' said Robin. '"Out Of My Mind" was a good song, I took out the pianotron's tremolo unit and ran the guitar through it. It totally altered the sound. You could play one chord and it went on and on forever.'

David Sandison wrote about Legay in the *Leicester Chronicle* in June 1967. This extremely positive review, made on the back of the band recording the four demos in Kettering, if nothing else, promised great things ahead:

Legay: The Stuff Stardom's Made Of

When they hear the demonstration record Legay have just made, a lot of people in the business are going to wonder where the group has been all this time. Answer coming up: Legay have been gradually building up an act that pales into insignificance the efforts of similar-styled outfits and out-dates the tepid and insipid dirges ground out by so called 'soul' bands. They have also written a song that should set them well on their way to stardom – and the hit parade. It's called 'Barmy the Policeman' and it was written by Robin Pizer. Its story line is funny and the song construction is excellent for a first production.

Legay have also recorded three other tracks – all of which would make a very commercial record for general release. Titles cut by them at Derek Tompkin's studio in Kettering were 'Take Me In Your Arms', 'Why Do You Wanna Make Me Blue' and 'You're Gonna Love Me Baby.'

Legay come into quite a bit of criticism for the volume of their music during personal appearances. With their personal sound cut down and split into tapes, they sound very good to me. The loudness is incidental. They were recording from 10.00 a.m. until 4.30 p.m., cooped up in the studio with only short breaks from playing to listen to play backs and about half an hour for lunch when they crossed the road to the nearest shop and bought themselves yoghurt and cakes.

Next week, Legay play at The Marque in London and members of Polydor's recording staff and artistes and repertoire men will be there. Polydor, in fact, are the people most interested in Legay at the moment. 'Barmy the Policeman' should clinch the matter – and then the record buying public should be given the chance to hear Legay properly.

Last week in Sunderland, Legay were pulled off the stage and mobbed by enthusiastic fans. Heaven only knows what will happen when they get a record in the shops.

The Marquee gig mentioned by David Sandison took place on June 16 1967. The subsequent recordings for Polydor were made under the guidance of Giorgio Gomelsky, who at the time was manager of The Yardbirds. 'Polydor was a demo session,' explains Robin. 'Rod sang "Ringing the Dong", which he wrote, it was about being on the dole. We did a few more songs like that which were a bit obscure-ish.' The Polydor sessions were reported by the *Leicester Chronicle* in 1967:

Rosy Future For The Legay

The Legay, a Leicester pop group, have been offered a recording contract by Polydor on a 12 month basis which could easily become a five year one.

The five – Rob Townsend of Basset Street, Leicester, Rod Read and John Knapp, both from Birstall, Robin Pizer and Dave McCarthy, both from Syston, went to the studios to make a test recording. Everything went so well they eventually went straight on to the master tape from which the record will be finally 'cut'.

Flower Power

It all began for the Legay about a year ago. After four months of practice they landed engagements for small, local venues and haven't looked back. Engagements got bigger and better and they have covered an area of appearances stretching as far north as Sunderland. It should not be long before their first release appears.

Legay have been principally responsible for bringing to Leicester the cult of flower power.

With bookings in the region of in between £100 and £200 a week and the prospect of potential top of the chart records in the offing, it looks like a rosy future for the flower powered Legay.

Legay's popularity was now so high that Helen Garner, from Fleckney, contacted Klock Agency with the intention to start up a fan club. 'I approached John Aston about setting up the fan club in 1967, I'd asked some of the lads in the band and they gave me his contact details. Marilyn, John Knapp's sister, heard about what I wanted to do and asked if she could get involved. I met John Aston in the Klock offices and initially he was all for it. I said that the band had so much potential, so he left it to us to sort out. It never took off though, we just couldn't get Klock to commit to it or support it.' Rumours about the fan club being established, though, were already circulating around Leicester. One night, both Helen and Marilyn were in a Leicester nightclub where Legay were scheduled to play the following week when an announcement was made over the PA system. 'They said that if anyone wanted to join the Legay fan club then to see us at the front of the stage,' said Helen. 'We were bombarded by people, it was unbelievable. Someone asked Marilyn who she was and after she had explained that she was John's sister, they got all excited. One girl even asked me if I could get her a snip of John's hair!'

While initially playing covers, Legay were soon performing their own material, with Robin's writing in particular becoming a key factor at this time. 'David Sandison from the *Leicester Chronicle* was horrified how I wrote our songs because I never did it in the conventional way,' said Robin. 'I'd write something down on a scrap of paper and put it in this plastic bag. Every now and again, I'd go back into the bag, take a look at what was in there and see if I could turn it into a song. If I still had that bag, I'd probably remember where the lines came from.' Mick Reynolds: 'At the time, Robin was really experimenting with his writing. He had an incredible talent but, looking back, I think someone perhaps should have reined him in a bit with the lyrics, not so much with "No-One" or "Banana" but definitely some of the other stuff.'

'Barmy the Policeman', the song that David Sandison predicted would send them straight into the 'hit parade', was the first one penned by Robin with the band and was well received by the public. 'When we played it live for the first time, we were ecstatic because it went down so well,' recalls John Knapp. 'It wasn't a cover, it was one of ours. It was a great moment for all of us.' For John Butler, credit also needs to be given to Rod Read. 'There were a couple of songs that are clearly Rods. They were a little bit more experimental, even lyrically, which may have given them longer life. However, the writing in Legay was exclusively down to Robin, his songs were great, "Vacuum Cleaner Mother" for example.'

The gig at the Sunderland Locarno highlighted by David Sandison (John Aston: 'Legay would have probably got the Locarno gig because we'd booked a couple of Sunderland bands into Leicester or Loughborough University, it was a two way thing') is remembered by Rob Townsend, John Knapp and Mick Reynolds and not just because of the reaction of the crowd. 'When we first played Sunderland, they went mad,' said John. 'When we went back twelve months later, it was completely the opposite, they didn't know who we were. In that short space of time, the scene and audience had completely changed.' Rob Townsend: 'I remember Sunderland, it was great, we got back Monday afternoon and we went to the cinema and watched *A Fistful of Dollars*. We couldn't go back to work because they'd want to know where we'd been in the morning. It was a damn long way to go in those days, there were no motorways, just the A1.' Mick remembers the journey for a different reason – it was the first time the band heard The Beatles' *Sgt Pepper* album. 'They were previewing it on the radio, we all listened to it. It was so obscure, completely different to anything else that had been done at the time. It was unusual for a station to preview an album at the time and it was before Radio 1.'

For John, the drive back to Leicester wasn't just about how long it took. 'I was in the front passenger seat of the van when we drove back. I was asleep but woke up, realising that something felt wrong. Rod had fallen asleep at the wheel and we were driving on an embankment. I woke him up just as we were heading for a concrete wall, we just managed to get the van back on the road. The rest of the band were fast asleep in the back, completely oblivious to what had happened.' Sleep deprivation was a problem that didn't elude Dave Dean, a roadie for the band during the later years. 'We played a weekend in Great Yarmouth, it was a Friday, Saturday and Sunday night plus the Sunday dinner time slot. It was an incredibly long weekend where none of us had a lot of sleep. I was driving back and kept nodding off. Rod tapped me on the shoulder, asked if I was okay and offered to drive. I said no, I thought I would be okay. But I got worse and in the end Rod shouted at me to stop and he took over. I'm convinced that if he hadn't of done that, we would have crashed because I would have gone, no doubt about that. I'm convinced that Rod saved us from what could have been a very dangerous situation.'

During this period, a typical Legay gig would have been packed to the rafters with some of the hottest, and available, women in town. Because of that, inevitably, the guys would follow like puppies on a lead. A hall full of excitable single women, testosterone and alcohol fuelled lads on the pull and a band that wore make-up, handed out flowers and oranges and wore the occasional ladies outfit – what could possibly go wrong? 'We got into loads of fights,' admits John Knapp. 'Mainly because the local guys objected to us pulling their girls. But we looked like girls and the girls liked how we looked. The boys on the other hand would just get angry and want to take us on.' Linda Knapp: 'They got into a lot of fights because guys didn't like the fact that their girlfriends were into them. They were so flamboyant and unique. Rod had long, black curly hair and wore effeminate looking shirts – it was inevitable, especially during the context of the time that they were going to get some grief from the guys in the crowd.' Mick Reynolds: 'They used to get into a lot of fights because of the way they looked, especially when they played at barbeques at a farm or somewhere. The farmers would be taking the mickey after it had finished. There were a couple of scraps because of that.'

After a gig, Legay would often head for the local marketplace in search of a hamburger stall or fish and chip shop. 'On this particular occasion, we'd pulled into this place and it was full of the local townies, or straights as we called them,' recalls Dave Dean. 'The lads were queuing for their chips when they started to get the usual abuse about how they looked like a bunch of girls. Just as we pulled off, John wound down the window and threw what was left of his food into a car that had a gang of lads inside. Well, that was that. They chased us for what must have been the distance between Stoke and Burton upon Trent.' During the chase, Rod told Dave that he wasn't going to indicate and that he was going to take a sharp left but he missed the corner and they ended up mounting the grass verge. If that wasn't bad enough, they'd also ran out of petrol. 'The car that was chasing pulled up behind us,' said

Dave. 'We knew that this might happen so we grabbed the mic stands, opened the van doors and leapt out like madmen and surrounded the car. We didn't hit them but we made it clear that we would have done if they'd tried anything.' However, somehow the car windscreen got smashed and all hell broke loose. 'The police turned up and frogmarched us all down to the local station and interviewed us for a couple of hours,' said Dave. 'However, it turned out that there was a load of stolen cutlery in the boot of the lads' car so we got away with it. I think the police thought it was 50/50 so no charges were brought against us.' John Knapp: 'It must have looked completely bizarre – the van stops in the middle of nowhere and out we all jump, a load of lads looking like a bunch of girls, all heels and make-up, running straight to their car, armed with mic and cymbal stands. The police were really aggressive with us though, because of how we looked I think.'

On another occasion, after a gig at Leicester University, Legay were once again attracting the attention of the girls, much to the disgust of a local rugby team that were in the audience. It ended in yet another brawl, with Rod, Ray Read and John all involved. 'We'd still got our stage gear on and the rugby lads got jealous because the girls weren't interested in them,' explains John. 'One of them picked on Rod, which was a big mistake, and the place went up. I remember this huge guy standing in front of me and I thought if I don't hit him first, he's going to hit me. So I punched him in the face – there was no thought process relating to the fact that he could have punched me back. His mates took him off but he came back, his nose was all over the place and he was covered in blood. He was furious, I thought he was going to kill me. We got away with it though. We were all speeding, it provided you with that extra dose of strength and bravado that was required.'

Because the band had Rod Read in their ranks, they hardly ever lost when it came to a fight. 'He just loved to fight, he wouldn't let anyone push him around,' said John. 'Once, at St Margaret's Bus Station, this guy said something to him, he turned around and head butted him without a moment's hesitation. I remember this old woman shouting at him, "get off you bully!"' Ray Read: 'The tattooed lads, the townies, used to scare me to death. They'd shout a load of abuse at us, we'd square up to them then *smack*, one of them would be on the floor, Rod had sorted him out. We were playing a gig once and there was a bunch of townies standing at the front calling the lads poofters and pansies because they had their faces painted up. One of them, a really hard guy, was giving Rod a load of stick so he hit him with the microphone stand. The guy jumps on stage, it was obvious he was going to smack

Rod. I took a flying leap from the back and got him round his neck and wrestled him to the floor. People couldn't believe what I'd done, they kept saying, "Don't you know who he is?", they were petrified of him.'

Rod's confident ability to look after himself was demonstrated one night at the Palais in Leicester. 'The Palais had glass swing doors and as Rod was coming through, this guy pushed them onto him,' said John Knapp. 'He squared up to Rod saying that he would see him outside. At the end of the night we got to the exit and there was a huge crowd outside with this guy in the middle, waiting for Rod. Rod just casually strolled out, threw this guy to the floor and started punching him, he wouldn't stop. Afterwards, the guy got up, shook Rod's hand and everybody clapped.' Julia Read: 'Rod had another side, you wouldn't want to cross him. He looked slim, had nice hair and clothes but he could really stick up for himself. The fight he had in the Palais was with a guy from Wigston that you didn't want to mess with but he pushed him too far.' For Dave Dean, being able to take care of yourself was an essential requirement of being in a band. 'Rod was such a nice guy, he spoke his mind and knew how to look after himself. You had to do in those days because there were so many idiots around who wanted to take you on.'

....

Rob Townsend's stay in Legay was short-lived. In September 1967, he left the band and joined Family, throwing Legay into yet another drummer related crisis. Both bands at this time were without doubt the two biggest acts in Leicester, if not the Midlands, both contributing to an incredible regional music scene. 'It was a record that got Family the attention, they'd been gigging for about a hundred years to their credit,' said John Aston. 'If they hadn't of had that record and just stayed a local group, Legay would have eventually caught them up with work demands within the 40/45 mile radius of Leicester.'

Whilst the rivalry between the two bands was friendly at first, this was all to change when Rob Townsend left. 'We all got on well with each other to begin with, we had a different sound to them but they were more mature, well respected and better musicians than us,' said John Knapp. 'In the early days though, Legay pulled more people than them and I don't think they liked that. The relationship finally changed when they poached Rob from us, we didn't have much respect for them after that.'

Formed in 1966, Family consisted of the remaining members of The Farinas and later, The Roaring Sixties. The band had a blues/R&B sound that was characterised by singer Roger Chapman's distinct vocals. 'Family were big, they were in a different league to Legay, they'd been professional for about four–five years,' said Rob Townsend. 'When they came along, they were still very bluesy. Jim King, the singer, was playing harmonica and a lot of Sonny Boy Williams.' When drummer Harry Ovenall left the band, unbeknown to Rob Townsend, Family had him on their radar. 'They'd been to see me play with Legay a few times, which I didn't realise. They turned up at a gig, it was a Saturday night, it was open air, and they asked me to join them. Charlie Whitney said, "give us a ring by tomorrow lunchtime and let us know if you are up for it or not." I went home and told my mother and she said, "I've given up hope on you, do what you like."'

On the Sunday morning, Rob went to Leicester Market, phoned Charlie Whitney and told him that he was up for it. 'They said there was a rehearsal at midday the following day up near London Road station, it was a place run by a boxer called Alex Barrow, The House of Happiness.' Meanwhile, Rob had to go to work the next morning and tell them that he was leaving. 'I was late as usual. I said to the boss, "I want a word with you" and he said, "that's good, because I want a word with you." He took me into this little office and said, "right, you go first." I said that I'd been offered a job and he said I'd better take it. So, I left there and then, went for a cup of coffee and then went on to the club and started rehearsing. I think at the end of that first week I'd played my first gig. Legay seemed okay with it apart from Mick Reynolds, who I think had got the hump.' Mick Reynolds: 'When the opportunity arose for him to join Family he jumped at it and, on reflection, you can't argue with his decision as he continues to make a living from music. At the time though, it caused a lot of animosity and bad feeling. We wouldn't give Rob his drums for a while, I remember driving round for days with his kit still in the van.' John Knapp: 'I can remember dropping him off at his mum's house on Bassett Street and that was it, we didn't see him again. We went to the House of Happiness to drop off his drum kit, there was a bit of a hostile atmosphere between us and Family but nothing kicked off.' For John Aston, one of the big differences for Rob Townsend when he joined Family was that he would have been earning a bit more cash. 'He wouldn't have to worry about if he'd got enough money to call in at the service station for ham, egg and chips whereas Legay would have had to have stopped and thought about that.'

In the short time that Rob Townsend was with Legay, he had injected a higher level of professionalism, volume and inventiveness into the band. 'Rob was a great drummer,' said John Knapp. 'After Legay Rogers left, he tightened up the band and we became louder. In the short space of time he was with us, he was extremely influential.' Once again though, with Rob's departure from the band, Legay had to search for yet another drummer. It was a search that would take them to Braunstone and a fifteen-year-old by the name of David Thomas Smith …

Teenage Fair poster, 1967.

Publicity photo with Moth, 1967.

Rod in his bedroom, 1967.

Rod Read, 1967.

De Montfort Hall, 1967.

De Montfort Hall, 1967.

De Montfort Hall, 1967.

De Montfort Hall, 1967.

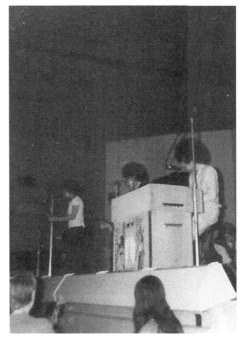

De Montfort Hall, 1967.

De Montfort Hall, 1967.

De Montfort Hall, 1967.

Melton Drill Hall, 1967.

Melton Drill Hall, 1967.

Melton Drill Hall, 1967.

Melton Drill Hall, 1967.

Melton Drill Hall, 1967.

Melton Drill Hall, 1967.

Melton Drill Hall, 1967.

Melton Drill Hall, 1967.

Unknown venue, 1968.

High Flying Around ...

'I was never one for wanting to see somebody every day, I liked to do my own thing as well, which probably suited Rod with him being in a band. We trusted each other, we never felt the need to question each other – although I was a bit worried when they went to Sweden ...' **Julia Read**

Dave 'Moth' Smith was playing in band called Vfranie whilst working full-time at Brown Brothers, a motor parts company situated behind St Margaret's Bus Station. 'I worked there for about three months,' said Moth. 'When I left school I had four jobs in a year. Back in those days, when you got a bit fed up you could leave one job and walk into another. I used to go to where my friends from school were working.' Until Moth's brother started to buy material by The Beatles, there were only three albums in his house – Elvis Presley, The Everly Brothers and Dave Brubeck. 'The latter was my biggest influence,' said Moth. 'My mum and dad were into the musicals so we also listened to the likes of *The Sound of Music* and *South Pacific*. My brother got a set of drums a year before me, I remember going down to his band's rehearsal. They were a suit-wearing straight act who played the working men's clubs doing covers.'

Prior to Vfranie, the band were called Cert X, a mod-loving outfit influenced by Tamla Motown and the Small Faces. 'I was fourteen when I joined Cert X,' said Moth. 'I first played live with them at the King Richard's Girls School Christmas party, we'd changed our name briefly to "It's Hardly British" for the one gig. We'd got hold of a huge Union Jack flag which formed our backdrop, which was quite good for 1965.' Moth, along with the rest of the band, embraced the Leicester mod scene, frequenting most of the cafés, bars and live music venues on a regular basis. 'We used to go down to the mod places and ponce around, drinking our vodka and limes or rum and blacks. We used to have our suits made – it was all about who could have the longest vents put in their jackets and the number of buttons on the cuff.' However, Moth was only a mod for a short period of time, mainly due to the fact he also liked motorbikes and wearing leather jackets. 'I remember going to Scarborough in 1966, I was wearing ice blue jeans, black winkle pickers, shirt and a paisley tie. I was confused though, I ended up in the middle of both movements. The mods and rockers had been jousting on the front, trying to knock each other off of their bikes with their helmets. When the bricks and the bottles started to land, I didn't know which side to go to because I was this "half person". In the end, I took refuge in an ice cream salesman's hut, we were both cowering on the floor together whilst being attacked by both sides.'

....

In September 1967, not long after the departure of Rob Townsend, Moth received the call from Legay to join them. He had been spotted by John Knapp, who had seen him play with Vfranie at The Green Bowler on Churchgate. While the band needed no persuading in letting Moth join, it wasn't so straightforward the other way around. And if at first you don't succeed, you can always try again of course. Or resort to kidnapping. Legay chose the latter. 'I wasn't there that night but I heard the rumour that they'd pulled up in a van and took him away,' explains Vfranie drummer, Paul Coles. 'I don't think I saw him again after that for about six months.' Moth: 'Chris Busby, the guitarist with Vfranie, and I were sitting on the doorstep of Roy Vickers florists on London Road when this blue van pulled up. Legay were all inside, wearing the clothes that you would imagine them playing live in. I was beckoned over to the van, I got in via the passenger side door and was bundled into the back. John used to like to sit in the front passenger seat so I couldn't sit there. I was then bombarded with requests and questions. They sold it to me whilst being tied to a chair and pronged with something sharp.' Chris Busby: 'I'm sure it was a Sunday afternoon, the van pulled over and someone called Mothy over. He had a chat with one of them, came back over to me and said "I'm just going off with these for a bit." And that was it, off he went, I didn't see him again for ages.' John Knapp: 'We picked him up and drove him around Leicester in the van, trying to talk him into joining us. In the end, we said to him, "Look Moth, you get two quid a week, lots of drugs and loads of women." That was it, he said yes and joined us there and then.'

When Moth joined Legay, he was just fifteen. He had seen Rob Townsend play when he was in The Broodly Hoo, The Farinas were also on the bill. For Moth, Rob Townsend was a good drummer who could play a few tricks and who provided Legay with a solid footing. 'They were difficult shoes for me to fill. I was the baby, in a way it was quite a brave move for a fifteen-year-old. I'd made the transition from playing at Braunstone Youth Club to other venues in Leicester and beyond that were always packed. But what I lacked in musical prowess, perhaps my personality and showmanship made up for.' Although initially Moth's style was not as heavy or as proficient as Rob Townsend, it didn't take him long to get into it. 'Moth came out of his shell after he joined,' remembers John Knapp. 'It must have been hard for him to start with, he had to follow both Legay Rogers and Rob so he probably felt a bit of an outsider.' Drumming aside, for Mick Reynolds the arrival of Moth added an element to the band that he feels was lacking with Rob Townsend. 'I was quite upset about it when he left because he gave Legay such a great sound. He wasn't a Keith Moon or anything he was just a really comfortable drummer, he didn't have to work at it. But he didn't fit the image of Legay, something which Moth did right from the start.' Linda Knapp: 'Moth was the baby of the group and because of that, he could be quite naïve. But what do you do when you mention Moth's name? You smile. He had, and still has, that effect on people – he makes you smile just by thinking or talking about him. He's quite a unique person.'

Prior to joining the band, Moth and Paul Coles would watch Legay play live at venues across Leicester. 'I went to one of their first gigs at The Casino with Cert X when I was about fourteen or fifteen,' said Moth. 'They had two quite big PA boxes and I thought blimey, that's professional looking equipment, I was most impressed. Legay Rogers' heavy use of the cymbals reminded me of Keith Moon, which brought a certain amount of excitement to the proceedings. I also went to see them when we changed to Vfranie, we thought they were a little ahead of ourselves, not so much musically but definitely with regards to image.' Paul Coles: 'Rob Townsend blew us away, his drumming was in a different league. I can remember me and Moth standing there, looking at each other, we couldn't believe what we were hearing.' John Butler: 'Moth said to me once that he and Paul Coles, just like me and Geoff Beavan (bass player with Diesel Park West) a couple of years later, used to follow Legay around, going to places such as the Nite Owl on Newarke Street. When Legay asked him to join them, he said he couldn't believe it – there he was in the middle of this room, surrounded by the other members of the band, all looking good. He just couldn't believe his luck.'

Moth left Vfranie and Brown Brothers and went professional with Legay after having an audition at the Nite Owl. 'It took place downstairs,' said Moth. 'I remember that I hadn't done a shuffle on the drums before and one was required for one of the songs so John had to show me what to do.' Moth's first gig with Legay took place at the Nite Owl on a Sunday afternoon, a couple of months after he had joined. 'It was packed,' said Moth. 'One of my school friends, who was also a drummer, was standing right at the front and afterwards he told me how good I was, as if I'd got five times better in the past two months. I think that was because we were all firing off of each other and getting a bit excited by it all.' Paul Coles: 'When Moth joined Legay I think they took him away for a month or so. When he came back, he was like a different person. When I first saw him play "No-One", I thought "what have they done with him", it was brilliant. He said to me, "They've had me working eight hours a day on it."'

The arrival of Moth led to period of stability within the band, allowing them to focus completely on developing their image, sound and writing new material. 'We were pretty oblivious to every other band that were around,' said Robin Pizer. 'We weren't interested in a music scene, we were only interested in playing. It wasn't an ego thing it was just that there was a lot happening. John and Rod had the fashion thing going and we were all learning new instruments. We were just interested in us, we didn't want to copy anybody or anything.' Moth: 'Being in a band is an intimate partnership and you need to be getting on really well so that the ideas can bounce around. There's no point in having an argument with someone one day then getting all mardy arsed about it the next, it isn't very constructive. We all got on well, there was a love between us, the personalities worked.'

So, what's in a name (part two)? 'I'd like to think that the name "Moth" came from a person that was attracted to the bright lights, someone that only came out at night. But it didn't. When I first joined, Mick Reynolds said, "what shall we call him, Smith … Smoth … Moth. That'll do, we'll call him that.'

....

1967 saw the arrival of the 'Summer of Love', with Leicester having its very own 'love-in' on Victoria Park, as reported in the *Leicester Chronicle*.

Flower Power

Victoria Park may be used in the near future for a Sunday afternoon Flower Power concert, for Mr John Aston of the Klock Theatrical Agency, has applied to the Parks Committee for their consent.

'All I want is a corner of the park and enough electricity equivalent to the needs of a washing machine. The groups – The Family, Legay and one other – will play for nothing and the show will be free. We want people to come and enjoy the music and be happy. I'm hoping to get hold of some cheap scent to sprinkle over the grass to add effect.'

He added, 'We will invite a charity like Oxfam to come along with their collecting tins.' Klock are awaiting the Parks Committee's decision.

Leicester's 'happy breed' can find Flower Power in action in at least two centres.

At the 'House of Happiness' (formerly The Roaring Twenties) disc jockey Tony Esquire is in control of the operation of lights and sounds which make psychedelia hum. 'If they don't want to be happy,' said Mr Esquire, 'then we don't want to see them.'

There will be music – much amplified – flashing lights and a free issue of flowers and joss-sticks. Nigerian born Alex Barrow, 27-year-old former heavyweight boxer, is the centre's proprietor.

The scene looks placid enough in murky daylight with murals (in emulsion paint) of embracing couples, intertwined hearts and a young lady in blue tights. But it will look very different in the late evening with the smoke swirling and the music howling.

'Definitely no drugs,' says Tony Esquire. 'We just want to create a feeling of happiness. And we aim to do it with lights and sounds. "Soul" is out, happiness is in.'

Highfields had become the bohemian area of Leicester with people hosting gatherings, events, all night dances and parties within their flats and bedsits. These events were often fuelled by the use of a range of amphetamine-based drugs such as black bombers, blues, dexedrine and purple hearts. 'On a Saturday lunchtime, we'd hang around the Clock Tower and we'd buy some black and greens or purple hearts for a shilling each,' recalls Mick Reynolds. 'The main thing that was around was speed, probably a bit of pot. We knew who could supply them and we'd go into a shop doorway with this guy, get ten, and then share them out. Robin and Mac weren't into it at all, in fact Robin hardly drank.'

As with cocaine, speed is a stimulant that when taken, keeps the user awake and alert, providing the energy to be active for hours without getting tired. The high is generally followed by a long, slow comedown, often causing irritability and depression. 'Speed was an experience, it used to do strange things to you,' said Mick. 'After you'd taken it, we said that you were either "blocked" or "doobed" and you'd be chewing like there was no tomorrow. However, it gave you such a massive confidence boost, you could chat up any girl you wanted. I think we took that in lieu of the alcohol.' Rob Townsend: 'There were a lot of people doing purple hearts because that was the mod thing but I wasn't involved in any of that, not even in the Family days.' John Knapp: 'The first time Rod and I took speed was when we went to The Dungeon in Nottingham, we took them on the train. You took whatever you could get – blues, black bombers, dexies, mandrax, anything. We were the only ones in the band that did it really, you can tell by looking at our faces in some of the pictures. We went to see The Who in Hinckley once and I'd been taking speed. Afterwards, I walked back home to Birstall, which was about fourteen miles away, chewing a handkerchief – there was nothing left of it when I got back.' Moth: 'I'd had a smoke at parties when I was fourteen with some of the other boys from Cert X. Legay was more about speed, uppers and alcohol. We were more "Men of the Midlands", Brew XI and all that.'

Although Legay were becoming tighter as a unit, they were still lacking in direction, vision and an ability to deal with the business end of the band. 'We were all extremely innovative but didn't possess any business acumen,' said Robin. 'We really didn't know what we were going to do the next day as there was no plan, we'd just turn up with an idea and see what happened.' Moth: 'We were naïve and headstrong and we weren't going to be told what to do. If you said something we didn't like, we would ridicule you. But there has to be a bit of arrogance and aloofness in there to make it work.'

Within a couple of months of Moth joining, Legay started to play more established venues, including Blazes, The Speakeasy and The Marquee (they played the latter on 24 February 1968 supporting The Gods). 'I think we sent Legay to the Marquee for fifteen quid,' recalls John Aston. 'It would have cost them that in petrol. That would have meant that margins for the next gig would have gone due to them making up the shortfall from the London gig. As a result, Moore and Stanworth may have had to have waited another week or two for their HP payment. One of the parents used to ring us up and say that so and so hadn't paid this or that but that's how it was.'

Situated on London's Margaret Street, The Speakeasy was a late-night haunt popular with people associated with the music industry, from roadies to members of the bands themselves. Affectionately known as 'The Speak', the venue included a music room, hosting performances from the likes of Jimi Hendrix, David Bowie and King Crimson, and a restaurant. 'The food in there smelt and tasted lovely,' said John Knapp. 'Fillet steak, new potatoes and spinach, really simple. Later on, when Gypsy released *Changes Coming* and we thought we'd made it, we went straight down to

The Speakeasy and ordered loads of it, it cost us a fortune.' On one occasion at The Speakeasy, Jimi Hendrix was in the front row when Legay played a version of 'Hey Joe'. 'He stood up and applauded, he loved it,' recalls John. 'It was a faster version, we were obviously moving into the Moby Grape thing. He'd just had a hit with it and there he was, right in front of us, wearing his purple velvet suit. He looked great, just like a king, he floated around the place.' Helen Garner: 'When Legay played The Speakeasy, my friend and I hitched down to London from the Narborough Road, we left at about 11.00 a.m. Jimi Hendrix was in the audience and they played a version of "Hey Joe", which was amazing. We didn't stay over, we hitched straight back to Leicester as soon as the gig had finished. It was a bit of a dangerous and stupid thing to do in hindsight but in those days, you never thought about it, it always seemed a lot safer than what it was. We were just lucky.' Dave Dean: 'We weren't flustered by being in the same room as the big stars because you were in the zone with them. We were small fry compared to Hendrix and the like but we were still doing what they were doing.' Mick Reynolds: 'I think the gigs at The Speakeasy was the point when I truly thought the group were going to make it. I also remember one particular night there, a couple of us were chatting to these two beautiful girls and we arranged to meet up with them afterwards. They said yes so we loaded the van up and waited for them at the door, just at the bottom of the stairs. My recollection is that we saw them walking out with Ron Wood and Jeff Beck. Mind you though, I don't know where we were going to take them at 2.30 in the morning.'

One particular weekday gig at The Speakeasy would lead to Legay playing abroad, the only time the band would leave the country to perform. 'Rod played the entire gig dressed as a hunchback,' recalls Robin Pizer. 'There were some people in the audience from the Swedish Teenage Fair who liked what they saw and, as a result, we got invited to play.' Moth: 'I remember that Rod was reading poetry from a little red book. There were probably half a dozen English bands there but you had to be from London to get a booking for the Swedish gig. They asked us where we were from and we said Leicester, near London.' Mick Reynolds: 'Legay didn't get off the stage until about two in the morning. After the gig, this Swedish guy had a word with Rod and asked how much we would want to play there. I went to a travel agent shortly afterwards to work out how much it would cost to take the van, the kit and seven people over, I think it came to something like £200 for a week. It was very exciting for eighteen and nineteen-year-old lads in 1967 to travel abroad, we talked of little else on the return home.'

The fact that the Teenage Fair wasn't being held in a tried and tested venue was a concern for the band's manager, John Aston. They were also dealing with unknown individuals and there was always the possibility that they were going to get conned. 'The organiser had no form, we tried to find out more about him but couldn't,' admits John. 'They were asked if they wanted to go, they said yes and came back to Leicester and told us what was happening. They agreed to go for a set figure, we knew it was a loss leader but we said if you want to do it, no problem. The decision was theirs. They had transport and equipment and were in a position to do it if they could get the time off work, which they did. They would either have been paid up front and we would have given them some money, or it would have been up to Mick Reynolds to pick up the brown envelope before the gig. If it had been part of the university or college circuit over here, we would have encouraged them to have gone for nothing. However, if you compare the Swedish gig with that of a village hall, the latter would be more important to us because it paid the bills.'

....

The Teenage Fair was an exhibition for young people held in Gothenburg from 17–22 November 1967. The fair was the first of its type held in Europe and was similar in format to those being held in the USA. Organised by Ted Aspudd and Liz Korallus, the fair showcased fashion, music, furnishings, cars and recreational pursuits. The event culminated in a music festival which, along with Legay, included Traffic, Blossom Toes, The Crazy World of Arthur Brown, Paul Jones, Tom & Mick & Maniacs, Jerry Williams, Vanguards, Young Ideas, Jade Hexogram, May Flowers, Lucas, Thom McJohn and others. The fair drew a large audience but also resulted in protests due to its commercial nature.

Swedish media were active in promoting Legay playing the fair, this from a Gothenburg newspaper, November 1967:

Leagays Doesn´t Believe in Lightshows

Psychedelic pop is now dead, one can hear from well-informed circles in England. A group that are going to prove this at the Teenage Fair is the English group LEAGAYS [sic] from London. Leagay's style is a bit Indian inspired. No Beatles plagiarism but a more melodic and rhythmic music. Leagays doesn´t believe in lightshows and loud speakers/amps. Instead, they try to let the audience enjoy the music more quietly. Fireworks and lightshows are a thing of the past. Leagay's has only one gimmick left and it´s their ankle-length Indian caftans. The style they play they call West Coast. This style was introduced by the American group, The Byrds. Leagay's write their own songs and 'Banana' is their biggest success.

Legay, along with John Aston, took the ferry from Immingham to Gothenburg, a journey that lasted nearly 27 hours. 'I'd just turned sixteen so I was quite excited about the whole thing,' said Moth. 'I shared a cabin with Mac, I had the top bunk and he had the bottom one. When we got there, we were picked up in a couple of Cadillacs or something similar, I think I shared mine with John. In the back of the car was this gorgeous girl with the longest legs you'd ever seen. She was there to meet and greet us.' John Aston: 'I might have been there for one night, I think I stayed there long enough to ensure that they got there for when they said they would and did what they had agreed to do. After that, there was nothing else that we could do, it would have been a waste of time and money being there. In fact, I think I probably went home on the boat we came over on.'

The gig was held in the industrial hall of the Swedish Trade Fair. 'Sweden was a fantastic experience,' recalls Mick Reynolds. 'The venue was a big warehouse with a stage on it, outside were hundreds of screaming girls.' Moth: 'At the venue, there were clothes and candles and all of that kind of stuff on sale, it was all indoors. The mashed potato and frankfurters were marvellous, they sold them from little huts and caravans on the street and in the squares. I was just open mouthed that everyone who walked by was prettier than I was, even the boys were gorgeous. They were sexy, friendly and rich and I wanted to live there.' Robin Pizer: 'One of the bands on the bill that night had a woman dancing around on stage, she was wearing a newspaper dress. Someone cut it off, I think it was one of the band, and it caused an absolute scandal.' Moth: 'I think that's why they were booked. While she was naked on stage, Mick Reynolds rushed round to see if he could help her in any way …'

Legay wasted no time in sampling the delights of the Gothenburg night life. 'We went to a nightclub to see Lucas, who were one of Sweden's top bands at the time, they were supporting The Crazy World of Arthur Brown,' said Moth. 'What a sound, the Swedish PA systems were way ahead of ours, it was incredible. We had 100-watt Marshalls, they had boxes, tweeters and God knows what else.' Mick Reynolds: 'Towards the end of the night, I was chatting up a blonde girl. She asked if we wanted to go to a party, we said yes but we couldn't get everyone in the van, so some of them had to stay behind. I dropped John and the girls off and went back for everyone else. When we got back though, they were all standing outside, they'd been thrown out. Which was disappointing.'

As with a lot of bands during this time, in particular those on tour abroad, Legay were thwarted by a familiar problem – they ran out of money. 'People wanted to take advantage of them when they were in Sweden,' said John Aston. 'We were told that good accommodation would be found and that the lads would be funded but they weren't. When we got there, there was no provision for anything apart from getting the van in and playing. Once the organisers knew they were on site, that was it, they lost interest. They certainly wouldn't have over-eaten, even though getting them a couple of meals every day was agreed verbally with the promoter over the telephone. None of them really drank, which was a good thing, as they wouldn't have had any money for a couple of beers if they wanted to.' Moth: 'We couldn't get anything out of the promoters, they just seemed to disappear. We also asked for money to be sent over but they wouldn't send any, they kept fobbing us off. In the end, somebody must have come up with something but it was difficult, we ended up sleeping in nightclubs and on the floors of village halls.' Mick Reynolds: 'We spent a couple of nights in a nice hotel but they didn't like us. There was a guy over there who had an English mother, he took us under his wing and showed us the ropes. He took us to a village hall where we slept for a couple of nights. Although we were only booked for the one gig, we also played in a college gymnasium as well, although I haven't got a clue who booked us, probably the guy who was looking after us. I had to go after him to get the money though.'

Despite the slightly negative end of the Teenage Fair, the experience left the band feeling quite hopeful. 'That was what it was like being in a band,' said Moth. 'If you were lucky, you'd get spotted and get to play in other countries as well as the village hall so, in a way, it's what we expected. We were fortunate that the chap who booked us for Sweden was in The Speakeasy that night as I think he was looking for the slightly unusual.' John Aston: 'The event that they attended was okay, they were received as well as anybody. It wasn't what I expected but they did well. It was a great experience for them, I know they all had a good time, they would have enjoyed watching the other bands.' Robin Pizer: 'The only thing I remember about Sweden was that it was cold, dark and grey, everyone seemed to be wearing afghan coats, you had to walk through racks and racks of clothes and the girl on stage having her dress cut off from her. And that's about it – most of the time I can't actually remember if I was there or whether someone just told me I was there.'

....

In 1968, Legay had the breakthrough they were looking for when they signed to Fontana Records (Fontana started in the 1950s as a subsidiary of Philips Records). David Sandison, once a journalist for the *Leicester Chronicle*, was working for Phillips and instigated the deal with Fontana (Sandison had previously written about Legay for the *Chronicle* and was a fan of the band).

In total, the band recorded 'No-One', 'Steam Driven Banana', 'In Love Again' and 'Tracy Took a Trip' (John Knapp: 'We didn't want to record "Tracy Took a Trip" so we trashed it from beginning to end.'). The record was produced by Dave Dee, singer with Dave Dee, Dozy, Beaky, Mick & Tich who had a number one single in 1968, 'The Legend of Xanadu'. 'Even though it was all rather exciting, signing for Fontana wasn't a good thing in my opinion and it was only for the one single,' said Moth. 'We were something else when we were in the studio, we couldn't get it together, completely different to when we played live. Dave Dee produced it. I don't think we would have chosen him, even though he was a lovely guy.'

The Phillips recording sessions were also the first time that Mick Reynolds had seen anyone pull out a twenty-pound note which, back then, was probably the equivalent of an adult's weekly wage. 'Dave Dee asked me to go and get some drinks from the Philips canteen and he pulled out a wad of twenty-pound notes from his pocket and gave me one of them,' recalls Mick. 'He was a pleasant enough guy but I just think he was a bit clueless when it came to producing the single. When initially discussing and playing songs to him, we mentioned that at that time Legay were doing a version of The Rolling Stones' "Let's Spend the Night Together" but he dismissed this out of hand. Yet I thought, and still do in fact, that this was a brilliant version, slowed down and sung soulfully by Robin. It used to go down very well wherever it was performed.' Ray Read: '"Let's Spend the Night Together" was fantastic, far better than the Stones' version. They should have recorded that, the fans loved it.'

The end result of the Phillips sessions was the release of the single 'No-One'/'The Fantastic Story of The Steam Driven Banana'. The tracks, both written by Robin, were recorded in one session and went straight to number one in the Leicester charts, beating Manfred Mann's 'Mighty Quinn', which was also released on the Fontana label. 'I can't remember writing "No-One" at all,' admits Robin. 'I turned up with this riff then everybody added to it. The sound comes from a 12-string guitar I had, it sounded like a sitar. John had a fuzz sound on the pianotron which made it sound even more like a sitar, it ran opposite the D string. We recorded a demo of it at Tompkins earlier in the year, Rob Townsend invented the drum beat while we were there.' Moth: 'My memory of recording "No-One" is rather hazy. I remember the building and going down into the studio and the fact that it was Rob Townsend's drum fill. You can play it so that it all looks hard and complicated or you can play it the easier way. It looked good and sounded good though, still does today. The drum sound is quite fitting, quite tribal actually.' The success of the single was mainly due to the huge advance orders it received from fans across the city and county. 'We must have had over a thousand fans at the time,' explains Moth. 'So if everyone went out and bought it, you can understand why locally it would have got to number one. I can't remember hearing it played on the radio though.' For John Butler, the reason why 'No-One' wasn't a success is two-fold: lack of radio airplay and the wrong song choice for the A-side. '"No-One" wasn't a success purely down to the fact that they didn't play it on the radio. It's instant cathartic excitement right from the start and it's quite justifiably got a reputation for being a rare and valuable item. "Steam Driven Banana" is completely different to "No-One", there's some serious musicality in that song, the arrangement, the piano, the vocals are all spot on.' According to John, in 1968 a song such as 'Banana' could have made a connection with the public, probably more than 'No-One'. 'The quirkiness of the title would have probably got them some airplay, it could have been up there with "Pictures of Matchstick Men", "A Whiter Shade of Pale", "Itchycoo Park", et cetera. While I think that "No-One" is fantastic, "Steam Driven Banana" was most definitely the hit that never was.' Clive Jones agrees with John Butler: 'I liked the song but didn't think it would be a hit, something was missing. I preferred the B-side and thought that might have been a better song in my opinion.' Robin Pizer: 'The line in "Banana", "it was started by Henry Morton", was inspired by a tin of Morton's peas I saw in the kitchen. The song itself was based around the concept of the Electric Prunes and the Peanut Butter Conspiracy, American bands who had released a couple of albums. I thought electric prunes/peanut butter/ steam driven banana, that might work.' Moth: 'I get a bit critical about the early recordings, I think we could have perhaps made "Banana" sound a bit bigger, it seems to be a bit thin. Although it pokes you right in the eye, it doesn't seem to have any depth to it.' For Mick Reynolds, 'No-One' sounds better and more relevant now than it did back in 1968. 'It didn't suit the time because the quality of the equipment you had to play it on didn't do it justice. Play it on a contemporary system and it sounds brilliant. My recollection however is that it was originally going to be called "Love".'

Leicester-born Peter Feely used to be in a band called The Psychotic Reaction, which was deeply influenced by the 1960s psychedelic sound. Peter also used to DJ in London before setting up his own club nights in Derby, utilising his own extensive record collection and light system. The nights focused on underground psychedelic bands from the UK and America, including Legay. 'The first time I heard "No-One" was when I listened to it on a compilation album. It's still recognised as a classic throughout the contemporary psychedelic scene. Legay had their fingers on the pulse of some incredible bands – Moby Grape, The Move, The Action for example and you can hear that influence within their music.' For Peter, the unique 'Legay Look', which had been key right from the band's conception, still contributes to today's psychedelic movement. 'A lot of the clothes that people on the scene wear today are quite contemporary, the sixties look is always there, it'll never go out of fashion. That was one of the key factors about Legay – just look how cool they looked, they had something that is still just as relevant today.'

The look that Legay had established, one which would continue to influence four decades later, was being driven by the same two people. 'John and Rod, who were the band's stylists, were creating their own fashion,' said Moth. 'It helped that we all enjoyed dressing up though, I loved to wear make-up. We used to go to The Palais to pose and I thought even then that we used to look different to everybody else. It could have been something simple such as the belt you were wearing or the cut of your trousers, it was probably just a bit more rock 'n' roll to what others were wearing.' John Butler: 'They were a bunch of great looking lads – how rare was that? If you look at the Stones, they had Jagger, Richards, Jones but then they had Wyman and Watts, who looked like a couple of builders. I've never seen a band where all five of them looked so electric. They would go on stage in one set of clothes, during the interval they would come out into the crowd wearing another set. When they went on for the second half of the performance, they'd be wearing another set. For a fourteen-year-old, this was really something else, it was superstar stuff.'

....

'No-One' was released w/e 9 February 1968 along with singles from HP Lovecraft ('The White Ship'), Dave Berry ('Just As Much As Ever'), James & Bobby Purify ('Do Unto Me'), Long John Baldry ('Hold Back The Daybreak') and Dave Dee, Dozy, Beaky, Mitch and Titch ('The Legend of Xanadu'). A review of the single appeared in the *Leicester Chronicle* on 8 February:

> Are local singers Legay making good nationally at last? Tomorrow could be make or break day for the boys because it is then that their first frenzied, hypnotic and wholly undignified record hits the public.
>
> John Knapp, David McCarthy, Rod Read, Robin Pizer and Moth sing as they live – for themselves. Listening to the disc appears in some parts to be an intrusion. There's little pattern – more like a studio work out before a disc is cut.
>
> I hope that doesn't sound unkind, because the sound of 'No-One', which was written by Robin Pizer, will almost certainly attract wide attention.
>
> Of the record itself I would say that I like the African tribal drum opening, diction is atrocious in parts, and the insistent beat has a somewhat hypnotic effect. I cannot see the boys being able to bring out much of this type of material and it doesn't really progress far with the lyrics. But I shan't be surprised if it does well.
>
> It's a long time since a group came onto the national scene with such determination to succeed – no matter who they tread on in the process – as Legay. It has taken time to persuade Fontana to take them in and they are working hard at their trade.
>
> Once Legay have established themselves they will gather round them a fanatic following dedicated to them alone. But older people, and those who lean towards the softer sound, will hate them. Me? I'll give my verdict in six months' time.

Prior to the release of 'No-One', Legay played what many consider to be their seminal gig at The Casino on 4 February, as described here by John Butler. 'I was just coming up to my fourteenth birthday when I first went to see them. I was young, probably a bit too young actually. A friend of mine said "let's go and see Legay", they were playing at The Casino. I'd heard of them, a couple of mates at school had mentioned them, so I was vaguely aware of who they were. I remember seeing Rod Read standing outside The Casino, for some reason he ran down London Road and turned into one of the side streets. He was running at speed but dressed in all of his stage finery. The word was that the drummer, this kid with the strange nickname, was only sixteen, and that was the connection for me. I was fourteen and I knew that the drummer was only a couple of years older than me. The first thing we noticed when we got in was that not only was it packed but it was full of extremely hot looking women. We also noticed these three Marshall stacks, we'd never seen that before, and this peculiar looking Selmer pianotron, in a box, with these strange looking hieroglyphics painted on (Mick Reynolds: 'The hieroglyphics were painted onto a timber frame, the pianotron used to sit inside it. It was only a keyboard on legs so we built a plywood frame to surround it so that it looked like a Hammond organ.') I remember they played "No-One" over the speakers, it was being released that week. Then they came on – I'd never seen anything like it, it was as though they were from another planet, they looked great. Turned out the planet was Birstall, a Jelson Homes same-city connection. They opened up with "Summertime Blues", which they sang with a falsetto chorus line, Robin played an echo 12-string plugged into a Marshall stack, Dave Mac played a Hoffner bass, Moth played on his Ludwig drum kit but the thing that freaked me out the most was the sound of John's pianotron, I'd never heard anything like it. It was great, especially when it was combined with the 12-string. But rising above all of this was Rod's singing and the effect he was having on the girls, he was like a pop star. They played two sets – after "Summertime Blues" they played "Stupid Girl" from The Rolling Stones' *Aftermath* album. I remember Rod saying "we are going to do a new song by an American band called Moby Grape" and they played "Fall on You", which was sung by Mac. They had really sussed out the vocal thing, incredibly tight and professional sounding harmonies. During the break in sets, the conversation turned to the fact that these guys were professional and that they didn't go to work. At the time, I thought it was only John Lennon who didn't have to go to work. We couldn't believe it, everyone in Leicester went to work, we couldn't get our heads around the fact that this was their job.'

The gig was completely sold out with Legay struggling to get access to the stage. 'The fans were crammed in so tightly we couldn't get through,' remembers John Knapp. 'We had to go down the fire escape and through the back door. I really don't know how many people were there but the atmosphere was incredible.' While the weather outside was cold, the temperature inside The Casino was completely the opposite. 'The gig was so hot and uncomfortable, my mascara literally melted and slid off of my face,' recalls Linda Knapp. 'I stood at the back with Julia and Lorraine, the band didn't want us at the front, they wanted the fans there. There were so many people in there, everyone was gasping for air, trying to get near the window and the balcony. You wouldn't get away with it nowadays.' Julia Read: 'I think that most of us girls felt as though we ought to keep out of the way. Because I was Rod's girlfriend, I held back a bit but if I wasn't, I'd have gone mad with everyone else.' For Linda Knapp, and countless others who were following the band, the gig didn't start when Legay took to the stage. 'You'd already got the buzz before you'd even got there, either while you were getting ready or sitting on the bus going into town. Fans would travel to see them, the girls in particular used to pair up and follow them around. They engendered excitement before the gig had even started, people were so hyped up that when they took to the stage, it just exploded. We were young, they stirred you emotionally, you never wanted it to end.'

The Casino gig highlighted exactly what was, at the time, the essence of the band. 'Legay wasn't about musicianship, it was good enough but it wasn't great,' said Moth. 'We were about playing live and you didn't need to be an impresario to do that as long as you projected energy and gave out a good sound. People would get very excited when we played live, we made it memorable because it was also part theatrical. There was definitely a buzz, a tangible atmosphere when we played.' Dave Dean: 'One of the reasons you went to see Legay was the fact that you didn't know what they were going to do next. Everyone tried to get to the front, especially the girls, so you had this situation where the band would play nose to nose with the audience.' Maria Veall, a fan from Sleaford, saw Legay play on many occasions at the town's Mabern Club. 'We small-timers quickly realised there was a different world out there when Legay rolled into our sleepy little town in that white transit van, out of which all these long haired, skinny gorgeous guys got out. They blew us away with their music and style at The Mabern Club later. We loved their gigs so much, we travelled further afield to see them. Legay were so exciting to watch as a live band, it was such a thrill. We were young, it was the sixties and it was happening.'

As Maria points out, the adoration the band received from their female fans now meant that they were prepared to travel to see them. It also meant that rivalries between the fans had started to develop. 'I can remember one particular gig in

Enderby,' recalls Helen Garner. 'There was a group of girls there, one of them had a thing about Moth. Another girl, not part of this group, said that she also liked him. When I went to the toilet with my friend, the girls had got this other girl's head down the toilet and they were threatening her to leave him alone. We couldn't believe it but that's how they affected people, they'd always got girls after them.'

Although Legay were with Klock Agency, the release of 'No-One' highlighted the need for them to also be signed to a London-based agency, allowing further access to venues outside of the East Midlands. On one occasion Legay, along with about eight other bands, auditioned for a London agent. 'We took all of our stuff, set the pianotron up and played about three or four songs, perhaps using the pianotron once for a few notes on one of those songs,' said Moth. 'The first thing this guy said to us was, "why have you brought that thing all the way down here when you've only used it for a couple of notes?"' We didn't like that. The pianotron was in the song, of course we were going to use it. What else were we to do, imagine it was in there?' Robin Pizer: 'All of the other acts that were auditioning were much better than us. They were looking for cabaret bands and we weren't a cabaret band. It was stupid really, we shouldn't have gone down there in the first place.'

....

On 15 April 1968, Legay took part in a 'Barn Barbeque Dance' at Thurmaston in Leicester. Also on the bill were John Mayall & The Bluesbreakers, Fleetwood Mac, Jimmy James and the Vagabonds, The Alan Bown Set, Soft Machine, The Equals, Pesky Gee!, Fairport Convention, Pitiful Souls, Sons and Lovers, and Six Across. All of those great acts for just a quid a ticket! 'The Thurmaston gig was played in a warehouse,' said Moth. 'It had a huge wire cage erected around the outside of the stage. There were a couple of star names up from London and a couple of local bands playing. We had one bucket of water on the stage to show the audience that it was the real thing and all of the others would be full of confetti. And of course, when it came to throwing the contents over them, the audience would duck out of the way, expecting to get drenched. We thought up a couple of tricks like that, sometimes they worked, sometimes they didn't. It was our way of getting the crowd to remember us, just in case the music was shite.'

In May 1968, Mick Reynolds, the 'sixth member' of the band, parted company with Legay. John Aston recalls how Mick was the vital cog in the machine that enabled the band to operate. 'Mick Reynolds was the salt of the earth, he bust a gut looking after them, he was friends with all of them. He organised the transport, looked after it and drove it as well, he was at the beck and call of all of the lads.' Mick was eventually replaced by Dave Dean, who went to school with Moth. Dave was eighteen when he joined Legay. 'The main reason I became a roadie was the fact that I had a driving licence and I was such a big pal of Moth. I can't recall how it actually came about, whether they asked me to do it or I just slotted in but it just seemed the natural thing to do.'

Dave first saw Legay in late 1966 when they were still playing the school halls and were just starting out at The Casino. 'It sounds a bit daft coming from a chap but the main thing about them as far as I was concerned was how attractive they looked,' said Dave. 'The girls used to go mad for them, they just seemed to be drawn to them.' When Dave started to work for Legay there wasn't any money available to pay him. 'I think it was John who came up with the idea of paying me a wage. I got the grand total of five pounds a week. If we were gigging, the band would pay for our meals and accommodation as well so we didn't have to worry about that. It didn't seem like a lot of money at the time but I was grateful for it as I wasn't getting anything else.'

Being a roadie can mean taking on several different jobs, but essentially it's all about setting up and dismantling the stage at each venue, carrying equipment back and forth, and setting up the lighting and even restringing instruments. It didn't take long for Dave to witness first-hand a problem that blighted a lot of bands – their valuable equipment being stolen. 'On one occasion we played with Chicken Shack. They were just the same as us really, trying to make their way. It was a shared dressing room so all of the guitars would have been lying around. As they were leaving, one of their entourage picked up Mac's guitar and walked out with it so we had to stop them. I don't think it was an accident, it was just a bit out of order – it was like stealing the tools off of your mate, you just don't do that sort of thing. Another time was at The Marquee, some of our mics went missing. You don't pinch mics unless you're a musician and even though there was a few of you packing stuff away, there was always the opportunity to steal from you.'

Dave was also in charge of the transit van, driving the band, and the equipment, from venue to venue. It goes without saying that an essential part of the job was to avoid colliding with other vehicles. Or people. Or cows. 'I can remember one night in 1968 when we were coming back in the van. It was foggy and we were driving down a country lane. We whipped around this corner and hit a herd of cows, they were bouncing off of the side of the van. We were bricking it, in those days you could get hanged for killing a cow.'

Today, Dave can still critique the band members and highlight what each one brought to the band. 'Moth will always be favourite because he was my pal. When he's drumming, he gives everything. He wasn't as good as Rob Townsend but he looked a lot better. Robin was the most talented in the band, he was the musician, he had, and still has, a great voice. Mac's a bit of an enigma – he played his part and looked great on stage. John was a mixture, he was the pianist, the guitarist, the singer – he did a lot of the harmonising work. To me, though, Rod Read was the essence of the band, his mannerisms and voice were Legay.'

By 1968, John Butler had seen Legay play live on about twenty occasions. Forever gigging, Legay became his favourite band. 'I went to see them a lot with Geoff Beavan, we were hooked on the sound and their underrated musicality. Robin was writing, you could hear these great things coming from the pianotron played by John and Rod was just a pop star. I remember there was a big gig on at the Granby Halls and Legay were on at St George's Hall, just behind the old police station on Charles Street. I went down there and they were great that night, it was only a small hall but it was still full, loads of women, and I remember thinking, "I'm in the best place tonight, I don't want to be at the Granby Halls, this is where it's at."'

In between recording *Tommy* at the IBC Studios in London, The Who played Leicester's Granby Halls to promote their album, *The Who Sell Out,* and the single, 'The Magic Bus'. Legay supported them along with Family, Joe Cocker and Spring. 'We got the gig through Klock Agency,' said Robin Pizer. 'There was a stage on the right where The Who played and then one on the left where the other bands played. We played on the same stage as The Who.' Mick Reynolds: 'The Who's management would have got in touch with Klock and asked them for local fillers, bands that were big in their own area that would have helped sell tickets and add to the atmosphere of the gig.' Moth: 'It was fantastic just to see The Who, never mind support them, they were the most exciting band around.'

Since the early days of playing Motown, Legay were heavily influenced by the look and sound of The Who. 'We really wanted to sound like them, in fact, we went to see them live quite a lot during the early sixties,' said John Knapp. 'We weren't really a band then, we were still in the early stages of being one. In 1965, they played Leicester and Hinckley eight times, we saw them at the Il Rondo and the St George's Ballroom on many occasions during that year. They were by far the most exciting live band to see, nobody else touched them. They were incredible, they had so much energy, the atmosphere was always fantastic.' Mick Reynolds: 'Robin went to see The Who in 1964, he came to school afterwards and said that he'd just seen this incredible band, he was completely blown away by them.' It was at a gig by The Who at the St George's Ballroom, Hinckley, in March 1966 that one of Rod's unique shirt designs caught the attention of Roger Daltrey. 'Rod was wearing a new purple and white shirt, it really was a striking design,' recalls Mick. 'Daltrey took a fancy to it from the stage and offered to buy it for £4. He bought it but he had to give Rod a grey crew-necked jumper in which to go home. Daltrey was photographed on a number of occasions afterwards wearing that shirt.' In the years to come, Legay would often bump into The Who at motorway cafés after gigs and have a cup of tea and a chat. 'We saw Roger Daltrey once at a café on the M1 and he still remembered acquiring Rod's shirt,' said John. 'We supported them a couple of times during the early days but they were huge by the time we played with them at the Granby Halls. We didn't even see them backstage, never mind talk to them.'

On 5 February 1969, Legay played the Leicester Arts Ball at the Top Rank Suite, Leicester. They were on the same line-up as The Moody Blues, The Nice, Fairport Convention, Alan Bown and The Gun. Problems arose when, because of illness, The Nice and Fairport Convention failed to play. And The Gun were in a collision with a bus by the Clock Tower. And The Moody Blues' van broke down on Narborough Road. And Legay's amps weren't working properly. This from the *Leicester Chronicle*:

Pop Go Top Groups, But Arts Ball Swings On

Students and guests at Leicester Arts Ball last night were disappointed by the non-appearance of the two top groups. But there was a behind-the-scenes battle against adversity to provide a show.

The 'Nice' and the 'Fairport Convention' – two of the best groups on the college circuit – phoned during the day to say that, because of illness, they could not attend.

At 2.00 p.m. both 'The Legay', Leicester's own group, and 'The Gun' were asked to take on the job.

The Legay had their van in for servicing and two amplifiers as well. One came back from servicing and was making a buzzing noise all night, which in turn, set the other amplifiers off, producing a harsh discord throughout their act.

Broke Down

The Gun came from Ilford for the ball and were in collision with a bus at the Clock Tower. Luckily, nobody was hurt.

The Moody Blues, scheduled to appear at the end of the show, arrived early but their equipment van broke down on Narborough Road South.

The road manager of the Moodies said 'An AA man towed us to a garage and tried hard to get another van while ours was being repaired. In the end all the road managers of the other groups took out the two vans and moved our stuff in for the sake of the dance. We were just in time.'

Sympathy

The Legay were in a difficult position, because they were expected to take over from the Nice and were on stage as well. This meant that, besides doubling for one of the top groups, they had the unenviable job of trying to warm up a crowd annoyed by the changes.

Ignatius Read, lead guitarist of the group, said; 'They seemed to hate us at first. The crowd were annoyed that the groups they had come to see were not on. Luckily, they grew more sympathetic. They were older than the usual set who go to dances and because of this we gained their sympathy when they saw what we were up against.'

Co-chairman of the entertainments committee of the Leicester College of Arts, Stan Grant, said; 'We sold 1,500 tickets in advance and not many people asked for their money back. I suppose they thought it would probably be a good dance anyway. We were the victims of a set of unfortunate circumstances and it was just one of those things.'

Terry Gannon remembers the gig well. 'My brother Jim was home so we walked into town from the St Matthews Estate, stopping for a drink at each pub en route. There were so many in that short distance, we'd have a whiskey in one then a half pint of mixed in the next and so it went on. Needless to say, we were as full as a catholic school by the time we floated through the elevator doors. A great night, I still don't know how I got home.'

On 15 March 1969, Legay, along with Van der Graaf Generator, supported The Moody Blues at Loughborough University as part of the 'To Our Children's Children' tour. The album, The Moody Blues' fifth, was released in late 1969 and was the first on the band's newly formed Threshold Records label. 'There was a stage in the gym area and then one in the main hall,' said John Knapp. 'The Moody Blues were on the latter.' Mick Reynolds: 'In those days it was often the case that there were two stages as it meant the changeover was quicker. You'd watch a band on one stage and when they had finished, you watched another one on the next stage straight afterwards. In the meantime, the roadies would be clearing the other stage for the next band and so it went on.' Unbeknown to the band's fans, the gig with The Moody Blues would prove to be the last under the name of Legay. Since the summer of 1967, a transformation had been taking place with regards to the band's look and sound. Now, in March 1969, it was time for Legay to wave goodbye to their Tamla, mod and psychedelic roots, and say hello to the harmonious sound of West Coast America …

Changes Coming ...

'We want to leave and base ourselves in London as soon as possible, where people will listen to our music without us having to compromise. As far as Leicester is concerned, we never want to go back and play there unless we've made it and people really want to hear Gypsy and not Legay ...' **Rod Read**

By the summer of 1967, Legay had become increasingly aware of the West Coast sound that was emerging from the USA. This new influence on the band triggered yet another dramatic shift in their sound. Slowly, they began to drop their psychedelic persona in favour of the West Coast bands. 'We were in the offices of Klock Agency and the guy who was in charge of the bookings for Leicester University happened to be there,' explains Mick Reynolds. 'He had just returned from California and had a bundle of LPs by groups we had never heard of – Jefferson Airplane, Buffalo Springfield, Moby Grape, Captain Beefheart to name but a few. We borrowed half a dozen of them, Robin taped Moby Grape and a couple of others on my Grundig recorder.' After listening to those albums, Legay's sound began to change and Robin's writing began to reflect these new influences. 'We'd heard The Byrds but these bands took it to a new level,' adds Mick. 'It wasn't hard for the band to adapt to this new style as they already relied on harmonies – the West Coast sound was dominated by the same harmonious sound.' Moth: 'When I joined Legay, they were full-on psychedelic. Robin was handing out oranges and painting his toenails and people were dressing up as Red Indians. The songs we were writing, "Television" for example, were quite weird. We had intros that were nothing like the rest of the song and outros that were a little piece on their own. We were also starting to become influenced by some of the albums that were coming over from the USA, in particular those by The Byrds, Love, The Electric Prunes and Jefferson Airplane. West Coast music was being imported into the country but it wouldn't be played, apart from The Byrds. We loved singing and we loved guitars and at the time, that was the way we wanted to go.' Paul Coles: 'I loved the new stuff when they brought it in. I was round Moth's house when I first heard a HP Lovecraft album, I thought "wow", I'd never heard anything like that.'

In the summer of 1968, Legay played a gig at Winstanley School in Braunstone. For John Butler, it was a significant moment, in particular due to the way the gig was structured. 'It was the first time I'd seen them where they played two different sets, the first was as the "old" Legay, with John playing the pianotron, the second set was the "new" Legay with the three guitars. So, in effect, they started to introduce this new look and sound by performing them in two sets. I remember Robin and Rod sang "Temptation" by the Everley Brothers which was incredible. The combination of those two voices was something else.'

On New Year's Eve 1968, Legay played the County Arms in Blaby. By then, the process of Legay morphing into an English version of an American West Coast band was well under way. 'They'd turned into a three-guitar band but John was also still playing the pianotron,' said John Butler. 'He would stand up to do it. I can remember he played "Wayfaring Stranger" by HP Lovecraft on the pianotron with his guitar tossed around his back. I went up to Rod at the interval and asked him why they had changed their image and he replied, 'Don't you like it either?', as if to suggest that a lot of other people had asked the same question. But we liked the new image, that was the point of asking him.' Paul Coles: 'I can remember they played one of the Nottingham clubs when they'd just got into their new sound. The powerhouse Motown was the first thing to go and we thought, no, the Motown was great, nobody was doing it like you, where are you going with this?'

Changing the sound of Legay was one thing. Now, inevitably, the band had to concentrate on the look. 'Rod didn't find it hard to swap the "mod" look for the hippy look because as the fashion changed, he went with it,' said Julia Read. 'If you looked at us girls, we all had this smart Mary Quant look but when flower power came in, we all had messy hair, the complete opposite.' Dave Dean: 'Leicester had never heard of the West Coast sound when Legay first started to cover it. It was all about harmonies, which they were very good at. They tried to look casual with leathers and clean jeans, which were what Moby Grape were doing. You look at how Moby Grape dressed and that was how they looked.' Moth: 'Moving to the West Coast sound meant that we couldn't look like girls any more. We had to consciously make a change in direction with regards to image so we started to wear Levi's, looking a bit drab. We also stopped connecting with the audience so much, opting to be cool and musical instead. But we weren't good enough to be musical, we couldn't compare with Buffalo Springfield or Moby Grape, they were bands who, as individuals, could have all been solo artists in their own right. We were writing our own material that was influenced by that sound. But we weren't from the West Coast of America, we were from Syston, Braunstone and Birstall so we tried to sound like an English version of those bands.' John Butler: 'The funny thing about Legay was that while they had this great style and charisma, when they used to come off of the stage and talk, which wasn't often as they weren't a "loud-mouthed" band, they were incredibly Leicester. The dichotomy was there – you had this great band from a planet where only groovy people lived but when they opened their mouths, they were so obviously from Leicester.'

The final act of the Legay transformation took place at The Nite Owl on a Sunday afternoon in early 1969, when John swapped keyboards for guitar and Rod dropped the role of lead singer and also took up the guitar. This switchover of roles created a unique four guitar/ vocals sound. 'We went out of the pop scene and into an underground, West Coast hippy scene,' said John Knapp. 'This was the first time I played "Rock n Roll Star", it was the first of the set. We were still called Legay but we didn't play any of the old songs. It must have been a bit weird for those watching though because I'm playing guitar, the pianotron has gone, Rod's not the frontman any more and we've dropped all of the Tamla and psychedelic stuff. Nobody made the decision to drop Rod from being the lead singer though – if you wanted to play in the same style as Moby Grape, The Byrds and Buffalo Springfield then the decision is made for you. Everybody did a lead vocal on whatever song it was.' Moth: 'We wanted to have harmonies and guitar parts and I think we turned, maybe mistakenly, from a pop band into one of those that like to invite you to discover them and "look at how clever we are with the twin leads". Sometimes, when it worked well, there wasn't the space for another guitar. It was like giving Mick Jagger a guitar, it turns into a five-piece without a frontman.' Dave Dean: 'I don't think the changeover in style affected the fan base too much, they may have lost some of the female following but it wasn't a lot, I think most of the fans went with them. What they did lose though was that "frontman" feel, they all just stood there in a line.' Legay fan, Maria Veall: 'When they changed we just had to get used to it, we were just thankful the line-up was the same. We loved their music and vocal harmonies, Robin had such a strong voice. The three lead guitars sounded so good, like the ringing sounds of The Byrds, and the bass and drums were awesome too. They were so friendly and mixed with everyone and of course, they looked so cool.'

As the look, sound and feel of Legay had all but disappeared, the next obvious step was a change in name and identity. On 19 March 1969, the band visited the London home of David Sandison, their long-time friend and supporter (Moth: 'David Sandison was a big fan of the band and did everything in his capability to get us noticed.') 'I was sitting in the window at David's place,' said John Knapp. 'We were talking about how the Legay thing was going a bit sideways and trying to think of a new name. We were becoming aware of the "gay" connotation of the name and that was one of the reasons why we changed it. Looking back, it was ridiculous really as it was such a great name.' Moth: 'Gay didn't mean anything in those days apart from to those in the know. The word used was "queer". If we had called ourselves The Queer, everyone would have known what it meant. Certain people within the music business at the time, however – producers, promoters, agents – who were gay wouldn't let a chance like that pass them by so we were hunted, shall we say, until they got the right idea that we were in fact very masculine underneath our make-up and flares.' Robin Pizer: 'We were talking about what we were going to do. We weren't Legay any more, we were different, we were changing. David had this huge paper light shade which Moth was playing around with. He said, "What about Gypsy Moth?" We liked it and, eventually, shortened it to Gypsy.'

It was during this time that David Sandison introduced the band to Peter Swales, who at the time was working with The Rolling Stones. 'Peter used to write us long letters about projection, rhythm and performance, he used to tap the table to the beat that he was talking about,' said Robin. 'He said that our songs had to make a connection with the audience, that we should try this thing or that thing. He was quite an iconic figure, he was like the Rolling Stones' office whiz kid.' The idea was that Peter Swales was to manage Gypsy. He later set up Sahara Music with the purpose of managing and promoting Gypsy and two other acts, BBBlunder and Reg King. 'We used to go to these solicitors' offices, it was completely not our environment,' recalls Robin. 'We used to drink tea out of these lovely china cups. The discussion was about us – we formed our own management company called Romany. Romany's contract was with Sahara, which was split into Sahara Publishing and Sahara Records. Sahara then signed us to United Artists. We had our own company within our own company. There was five of us in the band but there was six parts to the contract so if somebody wrote a song, they would get the extra part. That way, we were sharing the royalties to everyone in the band, not just the songwriter. If something disastrous was to happen, Romany would go bankrupt and not us.' An advance was negotiated from Sahara Records and Publishing which then went into the Romany account. 'The reason why we don't get any royalties today is that we have had so much up front in non-returnable advances,' explains Robin. 'The deal was that any incoming money would pay for the advances before we got any of it. We were paid about £40,000 up front (the equivalent of £460,320 today) so it's no surprise we didn't get anything back. Had we made any money it would have been quite a lot, but we didn't. We spent the advances on recording, we laid out a fortune at Olympic Studios and only a few songs came out of there. We would spend about ten hours in the studio, mostly working through the night.'

....

Under the management of Peter Swales and Sahara (which boasted Mick Jagger and Prince Rupert Loewenstein as their advisors), Gypsy played their first official gig supporting Led Zeppelin at Klooks Kreek on 1 April 1969. Klooks Kreek was a jazz and rhythm 'n' blues club based at the Railway Hotel, West Hampstead, London. The club, which was essentially an upstairs function room, opened in 1961 and played host to the likes of the Rolling Stones, The Yardbirds, The Animals, The Who, Eric Clapton, Cream and Rod Stewart. According to LedZeppelin.com, songs performed during this period include 'Train Kept A Rollin', 'I Can't Quit You Baby', 'Dazed and Confused', 'As Long As I Have You', 'Killing Floor', 'White Summer/ Black Mountain Side', 'Babe', 'I'm Gonna Leave You', 'You Shook Me', 'How Many More Times', 'Communication Breakdown' and 'Moby Dick'. 'I remember Jimmy Page had got these bloody great Rickenbacker speakers,' said Robin. 'We said to make it easy, could we just plug into your speakers? No way. And they wouldn't shift them either so we had to put our stuff in front of theirs.' John Knapp: 'It was such a tiny place, I think we played for about an hour. We'd just got off the stage and were heading back to the dressing room when Zeppelin arrived. You could feel this thing with them, you knew they had something. The DJ played some tracks by The Who and one of them said, "Here's the boys", they were obviously big fans of theirs. Zeppelin were heavier than The Who though, more rock and blues based.' Moth: 'When they walked into the dressing room, they looked really affluent wearing their leather coats. We thought bloody hell, who are these guys? They already looked like stars. We went out to listen to them and it was deafening, mainly because of John Bonham's drums. I think we got a better reception than what they did though, they cleared out half of the audience.'

The band were now living in a flat above a Wimpy Bar/curry house on the Finchley Road in London. 'When we used to live on Finchley Road, I used to watch the drug addicts walk by in the early morning from our window, begging for food,' recalls Robin. 'They used to sleep in the railway sidings at the bottom of the road and they'd come out, covered in coal dust, begging.' Gypsy went on to perform at the 1969 Isle of Wight Festival, becoming the only band to play there twice in the same year, performing alongside the likes of Bob Dylan, The Who, Free, The Band, Joe Cocker and The Moody Blues.

Not long after the Isle of Wight Festival, Gypsy signed to the United Artists label and released two albums. The eponymously-titled first album was released in 1971 (John Peel: 'The Gypsy's first and so far only LP is one of the best debut LPs I can remember hearing.') and *Brenda and the Rattlesnake* in 1972. Gypsy also released four singles of which one, 'Changes Coming', was banned by the BBC for being 'too political'. However, the band managed to perform the track on *Top of the Pops* in August 1971 before it was pulled from the playlist.

Shortly after the release of the first album, which despite extensive gigging only managed modest sales, Rod Read left the band. He was replaced by Ray Martinez who was formerly in Spring. 'Rod had had enough, I don't think he got the recognition he deserved,' said Julia Read. 'He got really disheartened with things after the first album. In 1971, they toured a lot around Europe so in the summer I went to work in Jersey because I knew they weren't going to be around. In August, when they were on *Top of the Pops*, we watched it with the lady whose house we were staying in. Shortly after that, Rod came over and stayed with us for a couple of weeks. He left Gypsy towards the end of that year. When he said he was going to leave, we decided to get married in March the following year. After that, he took a break from music for a while then at the weekends, he'd go and work the clubs with Rich Priestly in a band called Star.' John Knapp: 'Rod wasn't into it any more, he wasn't working properly. It was a sad time, we knew he wasn't happy, he wasn't the frontman any more and that's what he wanted to be.' Linda Knapp: 'There was a falling out and a lot of bad feeling when Rod left because the band didn't want him any more. He was the frontman who was pushed to the back. I really felt for him, he'd given so much and there was this huge feeling of rejection.'

In 1973, Gypsy returned to Rockfield Studios in Monmouth, Wales, to record their third album. Unfortunately for the band, however, oil prices, and consequently the cost of vinyl, were sky high and United Artists were under pressure to reduce costs and make savings. As a result, the third album, which is known within the band's circle as 'The Orange Album' due to its plain cover, was shelved and to this day remains unreleased, although most of the tracks can be found on both YouTube and the Gypsy Facebook page. 'United Artists were only releasing albums by their major artists,' said Robin Pizer. 'Loads of albums were shelved and then forgotten about. The version that's around today hasn't been mixed, it needed a lot more work on it at Trident, one or two of the vocals need redoing. We never got as far as a title, that always came at the last minute.'

After eight years rehearsing, gigging and recording as both Legay and Gypsy, the band eventually split up in 1974. All of the band members went their separate ways, most remaining in music until eventually moving on to other careers outside of the industry. The most notable development from the band split was John Knapp teaming up with John Butler and Moth in 1979 (along with Lee Strzelczyk and Tommy Willis) to form Flicks, releasing one album, *Go for the Effect*. Legay fans John Butler and Geoff Beavan would later go on to form Diesel Park West with Moth and Rick Willson.

In 2009, Circle Records purchased tapes and acetates of Legay's Kettering and Polydor recording sessions. The recordings are raw and provide a fascinating glimpse back to the essence of Legay, their own take on tracks that would have stirred a live audience into a frenzy. Four of the tracks – 'High Flying Around', 'Minstrel Boy', 'You're On My Mind', 'Impartial Judge' – have now been released as an EP. For further details, visit www.circlerecords.co.uk.

....

Rod Read, founder member and enigmatic Legay frontman, passed away in 1985. His death still has a lasting effect on those that knew and remember him. 'Rod was a really gentle person and I don't know anyone who didn't like him,' said Rod's wife, Julia Read. 'He had a certain look about him, which was what attracted me to him in the first place. Sometimes though, you don't expect them to be nice with it, it doesn't always work like that, but he was.' John Knapp: 'Rod was my best friend, he was the inspiration for me to express myself and not to be afraid of standing out in a crowd. He inspired me to design and make clothes, to join Legay, to write music, which I still do, and of course, to get into loads of fights! When he left the band it had a huge effect on me, I'd lost my best friend and deep down I knew Gypsy would never be the same, or as good, without him. He was, and always should have been, our lead singer/frontman.' Robin Pizer: 'Rod was an innovator and brought lots of ideas in terms of dress and music to the band. He also had a great sense of humour, he used to send up some of the most eccentric dancers in our audience. It wasn't malicious just funny. He had a character we called Count Scissor, he would run backwards, clapping out of time in a sort of exaggerated Mick Jagger fashion. A sad loss in many respects.' Mick Reynolds: 'He was a lovely guy, very proud of his appearance. He could be moody and an introvert but generally he was quiet, somewhat shy and a very good friend.' Linda Knapp: 'Rod was not only a showman and the frontman for the band, he was a lovely guy. It was a sad day when he died. He was very handsome and soft spoken and I always thought that if Julia was with him, then he must be a really nice guy. Although we didn't know at the time, when he was dying he came round to say goodbye to everyone, even though he'd been the one that had been hurt. In his own way, he said goodbye to us all.'

Legay Rogers, founder member and instigator of the band, passed away in 1997. As with Rod Read, for those that knew him, Legay will always be remembered with great fondness and affection. 'Legay was such a funny guy,' said John Knapp. 'Some of the things he said and did were incredible. If he could find a shortcut to achieve something, he'd do it. He drove a three-wheeler Reliant Robin because he couldn't be bothered to pass his driving test! He wasn't just a drummer, he was a fantastic showman and a good friend. He always went on first and got the crowd going. We missed that after he left.' Robin Pizer: 'Legay was a lovely guy but he was born an old man. He acted old, talked old, walked old – his entire demeanour was old! He kept calling us "you young 'uns" but he was only about a year older than us. Just like Rod, he's still greatly missed.' Mick Reynolds: 'He was a nice guy, very proud and conscious of his appearance which he modelled somewhat on his hero, Brian Jones, as their hair was similar. One lesson that he taught me was as a young lad of sixteen/seventeen, we were unable to grow proper sideboards so we would grow our hair down by the side of our ears. The problem was that our hair would then curl up when we were asleep. Legay had a cure for this that we would all use – stick your hair to your face using Sellotape before going to bed! I will never, ever forget that, just one of many wonderful memories.'

....

'I met a couple of the Legay lads many years after both bands had finished,' recalled the late Clive Jones, band member with Pesky Gee! 'I remember bumping into Rod Read on the market where he worked, we had never spoken before and now all of the posing was finished, we spoke about the bands. I remember thinking what a really nice guy he was and what a pity we had never spoken before. Later on, I was playing a gig as Dr Pesky, a sort of comedy act that I played in the pubs and clubs, when a guy came up and spoke to me. It was Legay Rogers and, like Rod, I had never spoken to him before. We reminisced about the bands and later on, he jumped on stage and started to play the tambourine. A nice memory and another great guy who I had missed speaking to in the past. Both of these people have passed on now but the memories will be with me forever.'

Looking Back ...

'We all thought they'd be huge, they were so dynamic they couldn't possibly fail ...'
Paul Coles

Nearly fifty years on and the jury is still out with regards to the Legay/Gypsy debate. While there is no doubt that Legay had something quite unique, there is also an opinion that the times were changing and they simply went along with that change – we'll never know what would have happened if they had continued as they were. One opinion that is consistent throughout though is that Legay certainly should have achieved more success as a band regardless of the changeover to Gypsy. Options are plenty as to who should shoulder the blame for that – the agents, the record company, the band themselves …

'When we started changing our music, the people in Leicester who'd followed Legay kept asking us to play all the old numbers. A few of them liked what we were trying to do but it was all a bit of a bring down. What made it worse was that our agency wanted us to play all of the old stuff as well because that's what sold. They weren't interested in trying to promote anything new, they just wanted to keep all of their promoters in the surrounding towns and villages happy, so we found ourselves doing less and less work. The thing was that we had to move forward musically, we could have gone on playing Legay music till we were in wheelchairs and we had a lot of things that we felt we ought to be doing. As it turned out, we're glad we stuck at it and did what we wanted.' **Rod Read (1969)**

'Those times for me were the best anyone could have ever wished for – creative, exciting, emotional and dangerous. But best of all, I was in a great band. I was with my best friends doing something most kids would die for. I take great pride in knowing we brought a lot of joy to people and, maybe in a small way, changed some of their lives.'
John Knapp

THE EMBI
MARKET HARBORO'
HARBORO' HOP
Tonight
Mick Poulton's M.Ps.
The Plague
First time in the midlands
death defying t.v. muscleman
SILVER STATUE
8—1 a.m.   6/- at door
Licensed Bar
EMBI
SUNDAY
DYNAMITE
LEGAY

— CASINO —
LONDON ROAD
(Nr. Victoria Park)
SATURDAY
8 p.m. :: 5/-
LICENSED BAR
LEGAY

★ PELICAN ★
TONIGHT
SOUL EXPRESSION
SATURDAY 12—2.30
MOZZLETOFF
SATURDAY 8 p.m.
LEGAY
GROUPS SUPPLIED BY
P.S. PROMOTIONS
Tel. THURNBY 5696

THE BIG "SCENE"
as always
TONIGHT — FRIDAY IS AT
The
★ COUNTY ARMS ★
Blaby
The "Fabulous"
★ JIGSAW ★
plus
★ LE-GAY ★
Groups by Friars Promotions Ltd.
Tel. Cov. 72908   Saprcote 685

HOUGHTON CRICKET CLUB
★ BEAT DANCE ★
to
★ LE-GAY ★
VILLAGE HALL
FRIDAY, OCTOBER 23th
9.0 till 1.0 a.m.
Adm. 6/-   Bar applied for

★ PELICAN ★
TONIGHT
COMMANCHEROES
FRIDAY
SOUL EXPRESSION
SATURDAY 12—2.30
MOZZLETOFF
SATURDAY NIGHT 8 p.m.
LEGAY
GROUPS SUPPLIED BY
P.S. PROMOTIONS
THURNBY 5696

PS Promotions   SUNDAY
casino
THIS SUNDAY
SOUL EXPRESSION
HERMITS, LEGAY
6-30   BAR   5/-

TONIGHT
THE RED SPOT
CAMBRIDGE ROAD
WHETSTONE
THE LEGAY
PLUS
THE INVADERS
PLUS
SPECIAL GUEST APPEARANCE
T.V. RADIO & RECORDING STA
UNIT 4 PLUS 2
Adm. 7/6 : 8 p.m. till 12.30
LATE BAR — LATE TRANSPO
— LIMITS IN OPERATION —

P.S. PROMOTIONS PRESENT
new sunday scene
Casino Every
Sunday
NOW OPEN 6·30 PM
THIS SUNDAY
MATADORS
LEGAY
MIKE & THE PLANETS
BAR & BUFFET. ADM. 5s

CASINO
LONDON ROAD
Friday •DISC-A-DO•
Bargain 2/-Night 8.0p.m.
SATURDAY at 8 : 5/-
★ **LEGAY** ★
Sat. Next BROODLY-HOO
LICENSED BAR AND BUFFET

ST. GEORGE'S BALLROOM
HINCKLEY
SATURDAY, JULY 30th, 8-11.45
Holiday Special
FROM THE BRIAN EPSTEIN
STABLE
TONY RIVERS
AND THE CASTAWAYS
PLUS
LEGAY
Licensed Bars   Admission 7/6

ST. GEORGE'S BALLROOM
HINCKLEY
8 p.m.—1 a.m.   8 p.m.—1 a.
New Year's Eve
Carnival Dance
with
THE DOWNLINER
SECT
plus
THE RENEGADES : THE SHEL
8/6 Tickets on sale now 8/6
at door 10/-
LICENSED BARS UNTIL 12.30 p

THURSDAY, JANUARY 5th
8.0—10.30   8.0—10.30
TEEN-BEAT NIGHT presents
LE GAY
Licensed Bars   Admission
SATURDAY, JANUARY 14th
THE PEDLERS

FOR THE MEMBERS AND FRIENDS
OF THE
* PORT ANTONIO CLUB *
64 UPPER CONDUIT ST., LEICESTER
A.B. Promotions presents a great
ALL NIGHTER
WITH THE LEICESTER MOD GROUP
THE LEGAY
PLUS D.J. CHOP CHOP
— FRIDAY NEXT FROM AMERICA
CLARENCE 'Frogman' HENRY
— COMING SOON —
★ **JOE TEX** ★

LAUNDE YOUTH CENTRE
NEW STREET, OADBY
★ **DANCE** ★
TO LEGAY
Friday, Dec. 16th
8.30   5/-
REGENT   106 Belgrave Gate
(opp. Kingstone's)
Tonight and Friday, Beginners 7.45
CHILDREN'S CLASS
EVERY SATURD

Husbands Bosworth
Town Hall
INVADERS
TONIGHT :: 8.30 p.m.-1 a.m.
★
E.M.B.I.
Market Harborough
ultra-violet flashing cine
screen psychedelic pop
Happening this Saturday
join the crowds flocking
to this out-of-town scene
LEGAY
to miss is tragedy
Licensed Bar
SUNDAY at swinging
market harboro'
Embi : mods galore
CONCLUSIONS
★
HARBORO' HOP
LEO SABOLI (fire eater)
INVADERS :: SISSY
FRIDAY NEXT, 24th

THE CHICANE CLUB
109-111 HUMBERSTONE ROAD
★ TONIGHT ★
LEGAY
OPEN 8 p.m.-3.0 a.m.
Licensed 8.0 p.m. to 10.30 p.m.

Latin Quarter
CELLAR CLUB
28/30 Belgrave Road
TONIGHT
A return visit of the popular
LE-GAY
SATURDAY
ALL-NIGHTER
with
The Lemon Line
and
The Boss

CASINO : SUNDA
New Year Carniv
WITH
★ **LEGAY**
AND
WOT DAT DAR
6.30 — BAR — PRIZE
NEXT SUNDAY
MOZZLETOFF
★ P.S. PROMOTIONS
THURNBY 5696

GRANTHAM Drill Ha
SATURDAY, OCTOBER 1
GENO WASHINGTON
& THE RAM JAM BAN
BROODLY HOO :: LE-G
ADMISSION 10/-
BUFFET   7.45 till 1

'We just had so much fun we thought this is going to happen, regardless. We had no leader and were very insular, it was almost like a marriage. Maybe if one of us had been a leader, things might have been different. All in all, I look at it as a bit of a mixed blessing because I think some of us wouldn't be here now if we had been successful.' **Robin Pizer**

'It's difficult for me to judge how successful we were because by the time I'd left, we'd just started to spread a bit, that's why I remember the Sunderland gig because it was a long way to go. I remember that it was reasonably well contained, we were well known but only within Leicester, Leicestershire and touching on the Midlands. I can remember the gigs at the Nite Owl and The Casino, I used to enjoy playing there. They were nice guys and it was fun. We were all teenagers doing what we wanted to do, be in a band. If you wanted to pose, you could pose, if you wanted to play a song, you could play it.' **Rob Townsend**

'The main reason why I think Legay didn't make it was managerial, they didn't play the right places. They definitely had the fan base, girls would follow them from Leicester and other places all over the country. My favourite memory of them however is of the first couple of times I saw them, the shock factor that they were so good. It took off so quickly, it all happened within a couple of months. They were brilliant live and to this day, I can't believe how they didn't make it bigger. Most of the other bands that were around at the time were copies of other bands. Legay were completely different. They had this aura about them and a sound which you'd not heard before, they took it to a new level. It was quite breathtaking really.' **Julia Read**

'What a wonderful experience growing up with great friends, listening to and replicating brilliant music. We shared so much excitement, those hours in the van, the humour, the serious talk of "making it". It was just so very good listening, watching them grow their repertoire, from Tamla based to a West Coast America sound. If ever a band deserved to make it then Legay did, they just needed that elusive break.' **Mick Reynolds**

'It was a pity that they couldn't have carried it through because they had a really good, solid fan base. They tried to get into London, which is where it was all at. It nearly worked but they needed a good song.' **Dave Dean**

'The music scene had changed and I don't know how long they could have rode on the back of the Motown influence. Nothing stays forever and you either change or sink so I don't think they had a choice in a way.' **Linda Knapp**

'We just needed to find a round hole for Legay, not a square one. Maybe they were just before their time, they were a good looking bunch of lads, in the right quarter they might have stood a chance. I can remember thinking at the time that all they needed was half a paragraph in the Melody Maker or the New Musical Express, that was all that was needed, just to be spotted by someone. It had to be from one of the correspondents, just saying that they'd seen the band, enjoyed them, look out for them – that was all that was needed.' **John Aston**

'Legay were a big influence on me. If you listen to "Like Princes Do", off of our first album, the opening riff is definitely a nod towards "No-One". I realised straight after the first time I saw them at The Casino that this was my scene, they were playing my kind of music and it didn't belong to the older generation of musicians who were incredibly jealous of them. They had chicks who looked fantastic and they packed them in wherever they played. Rod Read remains one of the greatest front men I think I've ever seen, he was the soul of the band with a velvet voice. He was definitely the "magic" of the band for me.' **John Butler**

'I think you have to be in a band to have some idea about why you never made it. Certainly, they had everything on their side with the looks, image and good songs but I'm wondering if they were difficult to handle and to take direction? I read that Rod deliberately sang a song not very well so it was not released. If that was true, who knows, maybe that song might have broken them into the big time, even though they didn't like it. Bands didn't always know what was best for them and there was an attitude from certain members. Maybe that also came across off-stage and put managers, promoters and record labels off.' **Clive Jones**

'We all thought they'd be huge, they were so dynamic they couldn't possibly fail. They could have played two–three weeks in Leicester and they would have sold them all out. I think they should have carried on with Legay and gone a little bit more psychedelic but they didn't, they went really serious instead. When the West Coast albums started to come though, the songs they took were brilliant and they still kept a bit of Motown

ST. GEORGE'S BALLROOM
HINCKLEY
66 – WINTER SEASON – 66
REOPEN THURSDAY, SEPT. 1
TEEN-BEAT presents
LE GAY
Licensed Bars   Admission 3/-
*
SATURDAY, SEPT. 3
THE FORTUNES
8/6   Tickets on Sale Now   8/6
*
SATURDAY, SEPT. 10
THE SMALL FACES
/-   Tickets on Sale Now   16/-

.LL NIGHTER
TOMORROW NIGHT — FRIDAY
at the
LATIN QUARTER
28 Belgrave Road
SOLOMON ★ BURKE ★
(U.S.A.)
AND THE SENATE
Plus! Plus! Plus!
LEGAY
MEMBERS 10/-

CASINO :: SUNDAY
LEGAY
Midland Beat Championship
THE STRAY (KENT)
v
THE NEW OPPOSITION
6.30 — BAR — 5/-
P.S. PROMOTIONS
THURNBY 5698   (ONLY NUMBER)
For all GROUPS : BANDS, etc.

JACK GARDNER'S FARM
EAST LANGTON
Signposted off A6 between
Kibworth and Market Harborough
BAR 'N' BARN
★ BARBECUE ★
EXECUTIVES BIG BAND
★
BROODLY-HOO
★
LE-GAY
TONIGHT
BAR TILL 12.30

P.S. PROMOTIONS
PELICAN HOTEL
TOMORROW
LEGAY

THE ★ LATIN ★ QUARTER
28 Belgrave Road
*
TONIGHT 8 p.m. to 3 a.m.
FIRST TIME IN LEICESTER
SANDS
FROM LONDON
LEGAY
FROM LEICESTER
ADMISSION 5/-
*

Latin Quarter
CELLAR CLUB
28 BELGRAVE ROAD
THE WEEKEND SPECIAL
STARTS WITH
LE-GAY
8 p.m. till 1 a.m.
- - - - - - - - -
SATURDAY
* **ALLNIGHTER** *
From London
THE LIGHT
also
THE TRAX

IL RONDO SUNDAY CLUB
MEMBER 1965
THIS CARD IS NOT TRANSFERABLE

P.S. PROMOTIONS PRESENT
new sunday scene
Casino Every Sunday
NOW OPEN 6:30 PM
THIS SUNDAY
SOUL EXPRESSION
HERMITS
LEGAY
BAR & BUFFET. ADM. 5s

"AWAY IN A MANGER"
Marmalade, 10 Years
After, Legay: 9.15 pm
Wed 13 Dec : New Hall
(bar till 11.30) : 6s

Casino Ballroom
SATURDAY :: 8.0 p.m. :: 5/-
LEGAY
Licensed Bar, Buffet, etc.
*
TUESDAY 7.30 p.m :: 2/-

in there as well. It started to go wrong when they began to write their own songs and stopped doing the Moby Grape and Buffalo Springfield stuff. It just wasn't strong enough in my opinion. They didn't look or sound the same, before they were at you and in your face.' **Paul Coles**

'Legay had far more opportunity to make a name for themselves than Pesky Gee! We were just another soul band, a good one, but one amongst many. Legay had broken away and were creating this different sound. Rod Read should have made it by himself, he had such a great talent. He should have been up there with the Steve Marriotts of the world.' **Chris Dredge**

'They had the talent, the ability and the looks. They had everything apart from somebody to take them and promote them properly. They needed a break, which was all it took, and they didn't get it.' **Chris Busby**

'Legay were very good. Great sound, great singing and great songs. I'd never heard a band play what they were playing but as soon as I heard the music, I could see their influences, it was like me and the blues. We followed a tradition, it was how we learned to play our instruments and play great music.' **Mick Pini**

'The music was fantastic, it was so different to anything else that was around, it made you feel really good. They had a definite presence about them, something which the other bands didn't have. They even used to walk different! But they didn't get the support or the help they needed to take them higher, I got the feeling that Klock didn't want them to get any further than where they were. I drifted away from them when they turned into Gypsy, it just wasn't the same any more. It was a shame, the excitement went.' **Helen Garner**

'My only regret is that we should have made it, we should have left a bigger footprint than what we did because at the moment, it's just a little mouse print. Locally, I think we were in the Premier League but not so nationally. It was nice to be recognised, it was only on a local scale but when we used to travel around in the van, people used to see us and give us a wave, it filled you with a huge sense of pride. We always tried to entertain, do something different and that made a lot of people happy. You can't blame Klock Agency for us not making it, they were a little outfit in Leicester, a local

agency. We needed to be with a London agency as well, then perhaps things would have been different and happened faster. They might even have pointed us away from being a four-guitar band. Looking back though, I think we should have remained a little psychedelic, a bit off the wall and stayed as a pretty pop band, perhaps then we wouldn't have been banned by the BBC. If "No-One" was a hit, who knows what would have happened. However, you could say that perhaps it was a good thing that we didn't make it, I personally can be a little excessive in what I do. I might have survived though and be living on a little farm somewhere, gardening and whatever, but having a little bit more money in my pocket. Perhaps this was God's way of protecting us all, twenty-seven appears to be the age when you drown in your own vomit so who knows.' **Moth**

Part Two:

Brief Encounters

Memories of the Leicester Music Scene

Introduction

'The sixties was a great time for music and communication – we were in contact with each other more than today, even with all of the technology available. It was really happening, there was something in the air, a kind of rebellious feeling for change, a feeling for a freedom to do or make something happen.' **Mick Pini**

Leicester's music scene during the 1960s was very much like any other similar-sized city – it had its eclectic mix of aspiring bands, venues, musicians, agents and promoters. It saw the arrival of Beatlemania, mods and rockers, the rise and fall of a psychedelic scene and its very own 'summer of love'. The city was awash with pubs, cafés and bars, some of which can still be seen today, though the majority of them have long since disappeared. It had its creatives – the artists and graphic designers, the adventurous independents who shrugged the high street look and designed their own clothes and those who, well, just wanted to look like everyone else. Leicester had a drug culture – purple hearts, LSD, cannabis and more – which were freely available if you knew where to look. The one thing that differentiated Leicester from any other city, however, was, and still is, its people and the individual memories that each one of them holds.

A musician stuffed full to the brim with such memories is Leicester blues guitarist, Mick Pini. 'I went to Sparkenhoe Primary School, Gospel Street School and then on to Dale, probably one of the roughest schools on the planet, where I met Romeo Challenger, my old drummer from Nedd Ludd. He left to join Pesky Gee! and then Showaddywaddy. I knew all of the West Indian guys up there and used to go to some fantastic blues parties on Laurel Road. In those days, if you wanted a rare blues LP, Sonny Boy Williamson or Howlin' Wolf for example, you'd go to Advance Records on Silver Street. You had to wait weeks for it to arrive and you'd pay a lot more than normal LPs but it was worth it. I started the hippy thing on Victoria Park with some close friends and played at the free festival on Welford Road Reccy as a part of Nedd Ludd alongside Arnham Bloo, Pete Biblokto and Spring. Nedd Ludd used to practise at Glenfield Village Hall, we played quite a few gigs. We used to play a lot of village halls – Kibworth, Enderby, Evington for example – and schools. I remember we played at Evington Hall Convent School once. The House of Happiness, which was run by former boxer Alex Barrow, was just around the corner from Landos Café and where I was born. John Mayall couldn't get his Hammond organ up the stairs of the House of Happiness once so the gig was cancelled. The Il Rondo was a fantastic venue – I saw Cream play there and John Mayall's Bluesbreakers which included Eric Clapton, Peter Green and Mick Taylor. If I recall, the third time Cream played there the gig was cancelled because someone nicked their kit. King Crimson were another band who played there and to this day I've never heard or seen anything like it. Friday night was blues night at the Rondo, you'd meet up with friends and afterwards go to a party somewhere. There were no apps to download in those days to organise a night out, we just used to talk to each other, it was all done via word of mouth. It was a lot more exciting than knowing where you were going, it was fun and so unpredictable.'

In this part of the book, more memories unfold when we tell the story of bands and artists, discover the lifestyle of a mod and revisit four of Leicester's most iconic venues. We will also hear about the intricacies of making your own clothes, getting ready to go out and discover how a booking agency and a graphic designer worked.

The Il Rondo & The Palais

'I remember the Rondo girls, many of whom spent their days in a hosiery factory, then on Friday nights morphed into Grace Slick and Sonia Kristina lookalikes ...'
Chris Lewitt

Apart from the De Montfort Hall, three of the most popular venues in Leicester during the 1960s by far were The Nite Owl, The Palais and the Il Rondo, each one offering an incredible variety of acts and different experiences for its clientele. Whilst the Palais was seen as quite mainstream and more for the older generation, the Il Rondo on the other hand was consistently eclectic with its choice of acts. It also had a reputation of being the preferred choice of venue in Leicester for certain artists as its atmosphere was deemed to be far better than that of the De Montfort Hall. Higher ticket receipts usually won regarding that particular debate, though. Despite there being no way of verifying, a quick search on the Internet produces a 'who's who' of acts that performed at the Il Rondo – here's just a handful: The Who, Howlin' Wolf, Genesis, The Action, Jessie Fuller, John Mayall, Eric Clapton, Mick Taylor, Peter Green, Cream, Steam Package, Long John Baldry, Graham Bond Organisation, Shotgun Express, Brian Auger Trinity, Gary Farr and the T-bones, Jimmy James and the Vagabonds, Spencer Davis Group, King Crimson, Savoy Brown, Ten Years After, Mighty Baby, Pretty Things, Downliners Sect, Chicken Shack, Geno Washington, Sonny Terry and Brownie McGee, Chris Farlowe and the Thunderbirds, Sonny Boy Williamson – the list goes on. Legay roadie, Dave Dean, adds: 'All of the big acts played at the Il Rondo. Back then though, you didn't think anything of it.'

Situated on Silver Street, the Il Rondo was an insatiable magnet for Leicester's teenage population. Present day music promoter and Il Rondo regular, Chris Lewitt, takes us on a tour of this iconic venue. 'Just a short stagger from the Clock Tower, this area became the hip place to hang out in Leicester. The rather shop-like entrance led us to the kiosk box office where between six shillings (30p) and the top price band of eight shillings and sixpence (42.5p), we could get to see a complete cross section of the British music scene. Next stop was the cloakroom, which I thought was quite grandiose considering everyone wore duffle coats or greatcoats. After the cloak room, we would move up the stairs where, only hours earlier, organs, mellotrons, drums, amps and guitars had been dragged up by exhausted roadies. Two flights of steps would take you past the ladies' cloakroom and straight onto the dance floor. Making all of this so memorable was the huge wall mirror facing us. It prompted desperate last-minute alterations, a tug here and there to our ridiculously long hair. Actually, that mirror could be a nuisance for couples sneaking out to seek privacy at the top of the stairs as they were blissfully unaware that the entire bar, including those that they should have been with, could be watching. I also remember that if you wanted to avoid someone, you were spotted in that mirror by the very people you were trying to avoid as you entered. The only diversion was to turn around and go out again.' All of the floor was allocated to dancing except for bench seating which went down both sides. Approximately 30/40ft square, the dance floor could accommodate 250 people, if not more. A bar was angled across the corner of the downstairs dance floor and, after climbing up a couple of steps, another small bar area with tables and chairs provided a good view of the stage. 'Once inside, the pale blue light show and exotic aura of patchouli oil and incense made for a heady cocktail,' remembers Chris. 'At the front of the dance floor was the cramped stage which was raised about four feet above the floor. Behind the stage was the smallest, most uncomfortable dressing room imaginable. Just a few steps up at the end of this seating area was the upstairs bar, which had a few more tables in a small balcony type area. I remember the pattern design of the floor tiles upstairs had a kind of resemblance to the bubble writing type of design on the cover of Cream's *Wheels of Fire* album. Or that's how it looked to me on a Friday night in 1969.'

The places to go pre-show before heading to the Il Rondo were usually self-contained around the Silver Street/Loseby Lane area. The Crown and Thistle and The Globe were popular haunts but the absolute pre-gig hangout was The Churchill, which was directly opposite. Churchill's, along with The Nite Owl, was the place were members of the local drugs squad would mingle in a very conspicuous fashion with the Friday night revellers. (Terry Gannon: 'Churchill's was the place to buy smoking materials and any other stimulants as an aperitif for the gig over the road at the Rondo.'). 'Just past Churchill's, moving down Silver Street towards the Clock Tower, were wonderful and seedy old town pubs like The Antelope,' said Chris. 'Further down was The Eclipse, one of Leicester's most notorious pubs. People from our crowd only ever went in there if you were dared by your mates with money as a reward for being mad enough to go in. I remember police vehicles providing an escort just behind the last bus at weekends. Luckily the Rondo went on a bit later and we were happy to walk home or go to one of those parties that seemed to be on somewhere every week.'

The Il Rondo obviously has a special place in Chris Lewitt's memory. 'As the years rolled on this place became symbolic of so much more than a night out. Teenage angst, stumbling relationships, spectacular break-ups were all fuelled by copious amounts of what by today's standards would be fairly medium-strength beers. I remember the Rondo girls, many of whom spent their days in a hosiery factory, morphed into Grace Slick and Sonia Kristina lookalikes on a Friday night – they looked amazing. And despite the backdrop of our working lives and trying to mould our own social groups, the one constant offering on the Il Rondo menu was the music – the King Crimson show in August 1969 was for me a seismic event and one of those "I was there" moments for all lucky enough to attend. The Rondo provided us with music that we, of a certain age, were privileged to absorb, witness and make judgements on each week for a very long time.'

....

Originally from Dublin, Jim Gregan moved to Leicester in 1959 aged thirteen. Leaving school two years later, Jim went on to become resident DJ at two of the most popular venues in Leicester – the Il Rondo and the Palais – and is now a steward at De Montfort Hall. Jim started to learn how to dance when he was sixteen. 'In those days, you didn't have so many discos or nightclubs as you have now, most places were dance orientated – waltzes and foxtrots, et cetera. I didn't know how to do any of that so I decided to learn. My dad was a drummer in a dance band in Ireland and he taught me the waltz at home but he couldn't teach me the quick step. So he advised that I went to a dance school.' Along with a school friend, Jim joined the Granby Dance Studios which was situated above Burton's on Church Gate. 'It was run by a lady called Isa Cooper. I did so well there that the principal asked me firstly to help with the beginners and then the children on a Saturday morning. Eventually, I moved on to playing the records as well on a Saturday night.' Richard Furness, who used to run the Il Rondo, and Isa Cooper were a dancing partnership. In 1963, Richard asked Jim if he wanted to play records at the Il Rondo during the intervals. 'I'd go over there once I'd finished at The Granby,' said Jim. 'And that's how it all started. I left the Il Rondo in the mid-sixties and became resident DJ at the Palais. Officially, I was there until 1970 but I used to help out covering holidays and suchlike until about 1972. I was neither a mod nor a rocker, I was just the guy that played the records.'

The Il Rondo was an established venue for live acts, hosting a wide variety of bands and artists. 'When I first started, I thought the Il Rondo was just a pub place,' admits Jim. 'The first couple of bands that I saw there were those that would enter the charts at number 12 or 15 for example but we would have bands that were further up the charts. It was strange, sometimes we would book acts that you'd expect would sell out but didn't and then we'd have pub bands that you thought would draw a handful and the place would be rammed.' Once a month, the Il Rondo would host specialist nights including jazz, blues and folk. 'I saw Howlin' Wolf and BB King there,' said Jim. 'They were great nights, I saw most of the big jazz bands there too.'

Jim was based on the left-hand corner of the stage. 'I had the best view in the venue – I could see the stage, backstage and the dance floor. My job was to not only play the records but to announce the acts and to dim the lights in the hall. We only had the one deck so by the time I'd taken one record off and put another one on, there would be a pause. So I used to ad-lib in between each record and hope to God that when I put the needle down on the next track it hit it straight away.'

Jim would also play records before the acts came on, during the interval and after they had finished. 'In the early days we were known as "record presenters", we just used to play records, we never used to talk in between. After a while, Richard decided to put a mic on and I'd link the tracks up by saying stuff like "here's the number 10 in the charts". It never used to phase me talking over the mic, I was pretty fearless in that respect.'

At the Il Rondo, bands would usually have been on stage between 7.00–10.00 p.m., sometimes later. To give the bands a break, most gigs would have accommodated a fifteen or twenty minute interval halfway through. Band members would either go to the bar and have a drink with the fans or take one backstage. 'I'd announce that it was five minutes before the second half of the show and they'd get themselves ready,' said Jim. 'Then I'd announce them again and off it went. Most bands would play a mixture of covers and album tracks but you would have to wait until the end of the show to hear the songs that were in the chart, that way you had to stay.'

The difference between the De Montfort Hall and the Il Rondo wasn't just about size. Bands such as The Who would play the Il Rondo because at the time, they would have been classed as up and coming. After their chart success, they would have moved up to the bigger venues. 'If you look at the names of the bands that played the De Mont, most of them would have played the Il Rondo at some point,' said Jim. 'A lot of promoters may have preferred their bands to play the Rondo because it would have been a better atmosphere than a larger venue, even though the latter would have generated more money. But the Rondo was always a fantastic gig.'

Name the bands of the day and the majority came to play the Il Rondo. A lot of them would release two albums a year, which meant that they would also tour twice a year. 'I saw The Who a couple of times there,' said Jim. 'The record charts came out on a Friday and on this particular occasion, they were booked in to play just as one of their singles charted. Richard had already got a contract with them and their promoters but they asked for more money because of the success of the single. Richard refused, there was a bit of a stand-off but there was a signed contract so they had to play. They weren't very happy. They were a great band but, because their singles were charting, they had become hard to work with. Other bands who had had similar success weren't like that at all.'

Apart from The Who, three bands that stick out for Jim that played the Il Rondo were Steam Packet, Chris Farlowe and the Thunderbirds and The Spencer Davies Group. 'Chris Farlowe always looked like a boxer when he was on stage. He looked like he was shadow boxing with the mic stand. He recently played at the De Montfort Hall so I took my autograph book in and asked him to sign it. He said okay, not a problem. Then I said I was wondering if it had changed since the last time he signed it and showed him an autograph he had given me back at the Il Rondo. He was amazed, he kept saying, 'He's got the Thunderbirds' autographs!'

The Steam Packet were one of the most popular acts to play the Il Rondo. 'They were brilliant live, a fantastic band,' said Jim. 'They would play with different line-ups, it all depended on who was available. When they played the Rondo, the backing band was Brian Auger and the Trinity and they were fronted by Rod Stewart, Julie Driscoll and John Baldry. I'm not too sure if Steve Winwood was there also.'

One night at the Il Rondo, Jim was having a drink backstage and a chat with members of the Spencer Davies Group. 'They wanted to know where the best place was to go after the gig so I told them to try the Latin Quarter,' said Jim. 'I thought about the Nite Owl but I didn't want to send them there. When I'd finished, I went down to the Latin Quarter with a girl I was seeing at the time and was amazed when Spencer Davies asked us over to sit with them for a drink. The girl I was with was over the moon, they were quite a big band at the time.'

When a big name band came to the Il Rondo you had to literally push your way forward to get close to the stage. If the people in front of you knew you were only trying to get a better view however, you had no chance of moving. 'If you were someone who had come to see the band, you wouldn't have got very far,' said Jim. 'If they knew you had a job to do, however, they'd let you through. I could stand at the back and make my way towards the record deck without any problems.' Whether you could dance to a band depended on who was playing and how much space you had around you. When The Who came, for example, the only space you had was where your feet touched the floor. 'When acts such as Chris Farlowe came, you had a bit more space and could move about a bit more,' explains Jim. 'A lot of the time though, people would just stand around and watch as they do today. Most of the dancing took place when the jazz bands came, Kenny Ball for instance.'

The Il Rondo was a favourite venue for Leicester's mods with most of the related bands playing there. Bands would mostly play the weekends with the big names, such as The Action, playing either a Friday or Saturday night. The local, or up and coming bands such as Legay, would usually play on a Wednesday night. Inevitably, where there were mods, there would be amphetamines. 'Churchill's wasn't the only place where you could pick up drugs, the Rondo had its moments,' said Jim. 'It wasn't a drug den but every now and again somebody would say that there was something going on in the gents' toilets and we'd get down there and fish out plastic bags full of pills from the cistern.'

The Il Rondo dance floor was where you would hear the buzz that something was going off outside. On one particular occasion, everyone rushed to the windows – rockers had ridden up to the outside of the Rondo and had tightly parked their bikes across the street at the Royal Arcade at what was then Swears & Wells, effectively blocking off Silver Street. 'All of the mods were inside, their scooters were parked neatly outside,' recalls Jim. 'They hadn't got a clue how they were going to get out. Then one lad decided that he would ride his scooter at the rockers, he thought that they wouldn't want their bikes damaged and they would let him through. Wrong move. He hit their bikes, the scooter ended up in pieces and he landed on his back on the other side of the bikes.' By now, along with the mods inside, Jim was concerned about how he was going to get out in one piece. With a case of records in one hand, he walked out of the Il Rondo and down towards the rockers, wondering if he was going to get through. 'All of a sudden, I hear, "Jim, Jim". It was a guy I used to work with during the day. He said, "Come through here mate," and four bikes parted. I walked through and they joined back again. At the time, walking towards those bikes was probably the scariest moment of my life because I didn't know if they were going to let me through or not. I can't remember how it all finished, I never looked back, and I just got out of there.'

Fights between the mods and the rockers wasn't restricted to Silver Street. Bread Street used to be located near to where the entrance to the Haymarket car park is today. It ran through to Charles Street and had an Italian coffee shop on the corner. Fights would often take place there between the mods and the rockers. 'The buzz would get round the Il Rondo that it was going to kick off there at the weekend,' said Jim. 'It was the place to go if you wanted to join in or watch. If it was the latter, you never actually went into the street as you could get embroiled in the fighting. Once it started, you couldn't get out.'

Jim left the Il Rondo in the mid-sixties to become the DJ at the Palais on Humberstone Gate. 'I used to be friendly with the guy who ran the record bar in the Co-op on High Street,' recalls Jim. 'He was also a record presenter at the Palais. Unbeknown to all the other DJs in Leicester, I knew he was leaving to become a priest. The Palais were sending people down to the other venues, including the Il Rondo, to check out the DJs and they asked me if I wanted to do it. My name at the Palais was "Gentleman Jim Gregan" because I always wore a bow tie.'

The Palais was a dance hall that had two resident bands and a 'record presenter'. The bands were The Ivor Kenny Band and a trio called The Mike Miller Set. When Mike Miller left the Palais, a band called The Magic Roundabout took over. Ivor Kenny would play a variety of music including pop, waltzes, quick steps, the barn dance and even the Lambeth Walk, but on Friday and Saturday nights it would be mainly 'pop' music. Mike Miller and The Magic Roundabout would play more 'pop' than anything else. 'The Palais has always been a dance venue, even during the war,' said Jim. 'There used to be a fountain in the middle of the dance floor, apparently the pumping system was still there when I was a DJ. The actual dance floor itself was a sprung floor and you could really tell the difference when you were dancing on it.'

To most people, going to the Palais would be a night out in itself, sometimes it would be full as early as 9.00 p.m. 'You'd get people coming in after the pubs had closed but most would be there quite early on,' said Jim. As with the Il Rondo, the Palais also used to have themed evenings, with record nights being held on Sundays and Tuesdays. Although you wouldn't have to queue to get in to these nights, they were extremely popular. The floor held around 900–1,000 people and was usually full by 7.30 p.m. 'At the end of the record night, I would play a track called "Swingin' Shepherd Blues",' said Jim. 'I would have to play that between 10.40 and 10.45 p.m. so that people could leave and get their last bus home. If I was running late or my mind was elsewhere, the manager would come on stage and say "swing that shepherd" and I'd put it on.'

Jim always ensured that he had the top twenty available for the record nights. 'I tried hard not to let anyone down. If someone came up and said can you play so and so, it's at number 15 in the charts, I wanted to play it. Cowlings used to give me records, I used to go in there and ask for a particular track and they would say, "By the way, have you heard this one, would you like it?" In return, I'd play the single and say that it was available at Cowlings on Charles Street. It must have worked otherwise they wouldn't have kept giving me the records.'

Cowlings wasn't the only business in Leicester to offer Jim a selection of freebies. The Irish turned Jim into a part-time model. 'I was friends with the guy who ran The Irish, which was in Humberstone Gate at the time, and every now and then I'd go in there and he would ask if I was working the weekend. If I was, he'd pick up some clothes that had just arrived and ask if I would like to wear them. He'd lend me them and I'd wear them down the Palais for a couple of nights. They once gave me a pair of blue army trousers which had a black stripe down the side, I think they sold fifteen-to-twenty pairs after I wore them. I asked what would happen if the ones I was wearing got dirty and he said he'd get them dry cleaned and sell them.' On one occasion, Jim borrowed a psychedelic-inspired waistcoat from them, a natty little thing which had small mirrors incorporated into the design. 'That evening, I was sitting on the stage and the spotlight fell on me. My boss told me I couldn't wear it again because I nearly blinded him. It was like wearing a glitter ball, the light reflections were bouncing all over the place.'

Building on the success of the record nights, the Palais introduced a revolutionary new concept to brighten up Monday evenings: Disco-vision. 'I'd be playing records and then, all of a sudden, a screen would come down, it was about 4ft wide by 3ft high,' explained Jim. 'On the balcony at the back of the stage, a projector would show Pearl & Dean adverts, the same that you would see in the cinema. I'd be playing the records and Pearl & Dean would provide the vision!'

Whilst at the Palais, Jim was the first DJ in Leicester to mix using two songs, 'My Lady' and 'Breaking Down the Walls of Heartache'. 'It wasn't the greatest of mixes, you could hear the join, but it got better as it went on,' admits Jim. 'And you could only do it if the two decks were working, very often one would break down. I think we were also the first venue in Leicester to have flashing lights, we were literally flicking switches on and off to the music. On dance and record nights, the lights were lowered on the dance floor and the stage was lit. But on record nights, previous to when I started, the lights were full up on the dance floor and the stage.'

At the Il Rondo and the Palais, Jim was in the best position to witness the music scene in Leicester, with its changing fashions, trends and technology. The two venues were being used by different audiences for different reasons. At the Rondo, it was to see live acts whilst at the Palais, it was to dance and to have a good time. While fights inside the Il Rondo were quite rare (they would usually take place outside), it was a different story at the Palais. 'You could go a long time without seeing a fight inside the Rondo, I could probably count them on one hand,' said Jim. 'You couldn't say that about the Palais though. The Il Rondo was respected as a venue, the Palais wasn't. If you spilt a drink in the Rondo, you'd get a mop and bucket and clean it up. In the Palais, you'd be walking in it all night. And the fact that it had been spilt would have probably led to a fight. It was completely different.'

One of the good things about being a DJ during the 1960s was the comradery between colleagues. 'Once your shift had finished at one venue, you could move on to another and cover for half an hour or more while the resident DJ had a break,' said Jim. 'All of Leicester's DJs got in for free at the venues. Once you were known as "The Palais DJ", everyone got to know you and you'd get to know everyone else.'

Today, Jim still takes time out with friends to reminisce about the sixties and the two iconic venues he worked at. 'I'm still in touch with some of the other DJs and we meet up occasionally for a chat about the old days. I never used to take drugs, none of my friends did either, and that's probably why I can remember everything. The closest I got was taking an aspirin and a bottle of coke, they reckoned it could give you a bit of a high but it never worked. You could have a really good night just going out and having a couple of pints. And you'd remember it the next day, which was the difference if you'd taken drugs.' And of the venues? 'I walk past what was the Il Rondo quite a lot and I think how good the building still looks. However, I walk past what was the Palais and I think what a dump, it's awful and a real shame. Everyone used to meet there, speak to people who were teenagers or in their early twenties during the 1960s and you'll guarantee that they would have met at least one boyfriend or girlfriend there. It's a real shame, it's lost all of its charm, character and charisma, something that won't ever be recaptured.'

Cert X & Vfranie

'Our favourite coffee shop was The Medina on Hinckley Road. We used to just sit there with the girls, Motown blasting out on the jukebox, sitting on a bottle of Coke for three hours. It didn't matter, you were with your gang and everything was great ...' **Paul Coles**

Vfranie were Paul Coles (drums), Graham Morris (guitar), Jimmy Rose (vocals), Chris Busby (guitar) and Paul Wolloff (bass). Paul Coles replaced Dave 'Moth' Smith as drummer in 1967 when he left to join Legay. Formed in 1965, prior to Vfranie the band were known as Cert X. 'When Graeme and I formed the band, he said that he knew a good lad who could play bass for us so we went to Aylestone Park and he introduced me to him,' remembers Chris Busby. 'Paul Wolloff was on the swing, playing the harmonica and I thought bloody hell, you're a bit of a show-off, you're good. We knew Jimmy from school, he said that he could sing, so all we needed was a drummer. When we were practising, Moth would use the radiator as a drum. I remember Graeme said to Moth's dad, "Are you going to buy him some drums then?" It just blossomed from there really.' Moth was just fourteen when he joined Cert X: 'We loved the mods, Tamla Motown and the Small Faces. We were very similar to Legay and R&B bands such as The Impressions but we mainly played Motown covers to start with. We started writing our own stuff though near enough as soon as we got together, "It's Got To Be My Wall" was one of them.' Chris Busby: 'We used to practise in my dad's workshop on Evesham Road on Saturday afternoons, he had his own painting and decorating business. We started off by playing covers of The Beatles, the Stones, The Who and Small Faces, it was mod related stuff at first. Then we started to play a lot of Tamla. Moth would play songs such as "Wipeout", he used to love doing his drum solo.'

Moth and Paul Coles had known each other since they were twelve years old. Moth used to live in Braunstone while Paul lived on Gooding Avenue, not far from the Roxy Picture House. 'We knocked about together on the Narborough Road for about six months,' said Paul. 'Then we didn't see each other again until September 1966 when I saw him playing with Cert X at Glenfield Youth Club. He said that they were playing Winstanley Youth Club the following Saturday and asked if I wanted to go. I was hanging around with a gang of lads at the time but I went up there on my own. After that gig, I blew everybody else out because I knew these were the boys I wanted to be with.' In November 1967, both Paul and Moth started work at Brown Brothers, a motor parts company near St Margaret's Bus Station. After work, the two friends would often visit the Green Bowler on Churchgate or take a stroll over to New Walk for lunch. 'We used to go to a little restaurant at the bottom of New Walk nearly every week,' recalls Moth. 'I'm sure it was called Edwards. We used to have duck and the waiters wore straw boaters, it was marvellous.'

Cert X changed their name to Vfranie in 1967. 'I haven't got a clue why we changed the name,' said Chris. 'I remember that Paul Wolloff's girlfriend's sister was called Vfranie, that's where we got it from.'

When Moth left to join Legay, the band didn't have to look too far for his replacement. 'I used to go and watch Vfranie practise and generally hang around with them,' said Paul. 'It was just a natural thing after Moth left. I'd drummed a bit before with a couple of outfits, I knew the band and how it worked, so I just slotted in.' Moth: 'I suppose when someone leaves to join another band it's always hurtful. We were all friends though so when I left, Paul stepped straight into my shoes.'

Paul Coles' first gig with Vfranie was at The Coronation, Leicester, in August 1967. 'We all wore Arthur Brown make up, Legay were wearing it as well,' said Paul. 'I remember seeing them at The Redspot in Whetstone in the summer of '67 and we thought wow, they looked great.' Vfranie were similar to Legay regarding influences. Once the psychedelic era had arrived, Graham Morris started to write his own material and the band slowly phased out Motown and began to take on board the emerging sound that was emanating from the West Coast of America. 'In that respect, we were on a parallel with Legay really,' admits Paul. 'We actually wanted to be the second Legay. When they moved onto the Moby stuff, we'd look to see what was left that we could do. They'd always get the best tracks though because they got the albums first.' Chris Busby: 'We were big fans of Legay, we were influenced by them with regards to direction because we enjoyed watching and listening to them. We loved them, the image, the sound, everything. The essence of Vfranie was mod and Motown and then like a lot of bands, including Legay, we evolved into a psychedelic outfit.'

As with Legay, and a lot of other bands from Leicester, Vfranie made the short trip to Tompkins Studios in Kettering to record some tracks. 'We went there once to record two or three numbers because Graham Morris's brother's friend was a producer at Yorkshire Television,' said Paul. 'They were making a kids' programme that showcased new bands. He said that if we could get some tracks down, he'd hand it over and see if he could get us on there. Nothing came of it but that was one of the reasons why we recorded.' Chris Busby: 'They were recorded onto an eight-track, Graeme Morris still has them. We also went down to a studio in Shepherd's Bush, there was a band competition on. I think the prize might have been a contract with an agent.'

The music scene in Leicester during this period was a varied one, with lots of opportunities for bands to play. People wanted to see live music and the promoters made a lot of money. 'We were signed to Klock Agency on Market Street, an agent in Derby and Friar's Promotions, the latter would get us gigs at The County Arms and in the West Midlands,' said Paul. 'In February 1968, after we had signed to Klock, we worked about twenty days in venues across the region, which was incredible really. The school halls and youth clubs were brilliant to play, always packed. We would also team up with a few other bands and hire a hall on a Wednesday night for a tenner just to get a gig in the week. It didn't matter if there were only a few people there as long as it paid for itself.'

Band members would go to The Casino every Sunday, where sometimes there would be three bands on throughout the night. 'It was a real mix of people,' said Paul. 'We played there once, we took a television and put it on the stage, wrote "condemned" on the front of it and put an axe on the top. Towards the end of the gig, Chris Busby got up and smashed it to bits. We'd heard that The Move were smashing stuff up so we thought we'd give it a go. There was no health and safety back then, it could have taken somebody's eye out. On the same night, somebody pulled one of the leads and all of the amps came crashing to the floor.'

While The Casino was a regular haunt for Legay, The Nite Owl was where you would find both Pesky Gee! and Vfranie. 'We played on the Sunday afternoons,' said Paul. 'I remember going down to The Green Bowler one day and Wolloff said, 'Guess where we're playing next Sunday – the Owl!' All of us were really excited to be playing there.' Chris Busby: 'I was really nervous, it was a big gig for us, we supported Spring and Deuce Coupe. We were into the psychedelic look and sound at the time so it must have been a bit freaky for the audience as it was primarily a soul venue. I was wearing a blanket that had a hole in it to put my head through and had talcum powder in my hair, which I'd backcombed. I would shake my head and all of the talcum powder would fly out!'

While Vfranie played mainly in Leicester and Leicestershire, they also played gigs in London, Oundle, Wolverhampton, Peterborough and Nottingham. 'We supported Cream in 1968 at Nottingham University,' said Chris. 'It was on their Wheels of Fire tour, I think it was their final one. The strange thing about the gig was that we went on after Cream, which was a complete disaster because everyone had scooted off. I also remember Eric Clapton coming up to us afterwards and asking if we were a band of midgets!' Vfranie also supported The Fantastics at the St George's Ballroom in Hinckley and, on a few occasions, Jimmy James and the Vagabonds at Leicester University. 'We got really friendly with them,' said Chris. 'In fact, they used to occasionally borrow our kit. They went down so well with the audience, they were fabulous. I used to love playing the university, it felt like a proper venue with loads of people there.'

In the middle of 1968, Jimmy Rose left the band, followed by Paul Wolloff. 'Paul was a brilliant bass player,' said Paul. 'He would come up with a bass line and the rest of us would work off it. He went on to join Lynton Guest, who'd just left Love Affair. Martin Hayes joined us on bass and then Chris left so we limped on as a three-piece until Graham moved down to London with another band. I got married, sold my drums and that was it, we wrapped up in 1969. There's just me, Graham and Chris left now, Jimmy and Paul both died some years ago.' Chris Busby: 'I left in 1969, I went to work in Skegness on the donkeys for a couple of summers and the rest carried on. In the end it just fizzled out. I learned how to play the piano and keyboards and played by myself, never with anyone else. I haven't played in public since. It's a shame really, I often talk to Graeme about getting together, even if it's just an acoustic thing. I'd love to do something like that.'

Looking back, and while acknowledging that the sixties was a great time to be young, Paul also admits that he could have done with being about eighteen months older. 'I just missed a bit of it. The lads I was hanging around with were older than me and they saw The Beatles and the Stones, I was just a bit too young for that. By 1967/68 though, when I was seventeen or eighteen, everything was so intense. Day after day something new happened, the music scene kept changing. You'd hear Hendrix or The Doors for the first time, it was incredible. There were so many bands just in the UK that were good but then when the American bands came through, you never had enough money to buy all the albums you wanted or to see all of the gigs that were on. Even De Montfort Hall had good bands on, not like now, you really were spoilt for choice.' Chris Busby: 'It's probably not so much the bigger gigs that stick out for me, it was everything, I loved the whole thing. Except the Greenhill Youth Centre in Coalville, that's when the rockers threw beer mats at us, it was a right rough old place. I think to myself now though how on earth did I have the balls to do that, the thought of going up on stage is quite a scary one, especially when you look at some of the clothes we used to wear and the stage persona we took on. I was only fifteen when I joined, which was quite young really, and I was quite self-conscious but it gave me confidence. I loved it though, happy days!'

Klock Agency

'We turned our backs on the drug scene, it was so close to us. Nothing like what's available today though …' **John Aston**

Situated at 8 Market Street, Klock Agency managed, amongst others, five of Leicester's finest bands from the 1960s – Legay, Pesky Gee!, Family, Deuce Coupe and The Broodly Hoo. 'We actually started out at Great Glen,' said John Aston. 'An old lady, who was close on a hundred years old, let us have a room at the front of her house. I think we were there for about twelve months. There were four of us – myself, John Whitney, Maurice Ridgeway and Philip Wilson. John got us into it, he was in The Farinas at the time, we just latched onto him and did what he did but then we gradually started to take it up onto different levels. In those early days, John knew what he was doing while we didn't.'

During those early days of establishing Klock, John worked a night shift as a paper packer for WH Smith. He'd also run a disco at Leicester's Brucciani's café every Friday night. 'They went on until 10 p.m. or 11 p.m.,' remembers John. 'We'd got a lot of good American soul and Tamla Motown records, which was the core interest of what we were doing. Somebody nicked all of them though, never to be seen again. We expected to hear that some of them were being played in London or Manchester but it never happened.'

John Whitney and Philip Wilson eventually left, leaving John and Maurice Ridgeway to run the agency. 'Most of the bands were in their teens while we were in our early twenties,' said John. 'I managed Legay while Maurice looked after Pesky Gee!, who probably worked more than anybody, and Deuce Coup who were a Beach Boys type of outfit. They were the sort of band who you could go and have a drink and just listen to.'

Klock moved to its premises on Market Street in the mid-sixties, renting out two rooms on the first floor. 'You had to walk up a narrow staircase to get to them,' said John. 'The place had been on the market for a long time and we were ideal tenants for them. The overheads were massive though, the telephone in particular was unbelievable. We'd often close at five but then one of us would go back in case somebody hadn't turned up. Then you'd be on the phone trying to sort something out.'

The premises on Market Street would become the hub for Klock over the next few years. 'We had various meetings with people in there,' recalls John. 'A lot of them were guys who had committed themselves to buying a set of drums or a guitar and they weren't earning enough money to pay for them. There was nothing we could do about that though. I used to go down to Moore and Stanworth's about twice a year, I didn't know anybody there but they knew me. I couldn't tell the difference between a bass and a lead guitar, I wasn't interested in that side of things. Whether they thought that we were funding the HP arrangements for the boys I don't know but they would always acknowledge us being there.'

Whilst working for WH Smith, John would take the opportunity to read all of the regional newspapers to establish who was promoting gigs, barbeques or taking out regular adverts. 'I was trying to ensure that we had the lion's share. I'd flick through a paper and if there was something of interest, I'd either read it or buy it. We used to have loads of papers around the office, we'd spend a lot of time just tracking down promoters. A lot of them were students or someone who had offered to book bands or run dances for the local youth club. We needed them to come to us to book our bands. We spent hours and hours doing that, just to find work for them.'

For Klock, the promoters were more important than the bands because they were the ones with the money. They paid Klock's overheads including payment for the bands themselves. Finding the promoters, though, wasn't as easy as it sounds. 'We used to work hard, I used to drive miles, it was so boring it was untrue,' said John. 'Tracking down a vicar who ran a youth club in some far-off place but I'd seen his name two or three times in a newspaper that I'd scoured through. But he'd be so delighted that someone had phoned him, a month later he'd ring back and say he was organising a dance and could we send him a band. It sounds really small but those sorts of things gave me just as much of a glow as sending Legay to Sweden. Someone who organised four dances a year could spend £100 with us.'

Occasionally, due to the location of the offices, fans of the various acts on Klock's books would wander upstairs in the hope of a chance meeting with a band member. 'Invariably, we would give them a poster and they would go,' said John. 'You didn't want them hanging around but you didn't want to be rude either. We didn't hide the fact that we were there but we didn't advertise it either, there was no sign over the front door. It was a very open place, we had a couple of hairy moments.' A regular visitor to the offices was Ric Grech, bass guitarist with Family. 'Ric had a mini, I think it had rainbows painted on it,' said John. 'He would leave it parked on double yellow lines, right outside the door. He'd stagger up and stay for a fair bit of time. It could have been a tricky situation – you only needed the wrong guy up there at the same time and it could have gone horribly wrong.'

Klock made their money primarily by booking large and small acts onto the university and college circuit, in particular Loughborough and Leicester. 'We would book a mainline band into Leicester University, for example,' said John. 'There would be a certain amount of money to cover whatever the function was. We could, and did, give a London band that was earning between twenty-five and thirty quid a tenner more, they were well worth that amount. In return, we would get a gig at The Marquee for one of the Leicester bands. We'd got the operation to bring bands to the venues that we'd booked and that would be reciprocated with another agent, that's how it used to work.'

The reciprocal arrangements with other agents and promoters can be best illustrated via a 1966 local news item. It was reported that Jeff Kruger, owner of The Flamingo Club in London's Wardour Street, had offered The Broodly Hoo a three-month residency at the club. He also 'wants to handle their affairs as agent with Klock Agency continuing as managers'. The offer followed a particularly good set that the band had played at The Flamingo where they looked 'smarter than ever but nervous as kittens'. As a result of the residency, The Broodly Hoo played a lot more in London at venues such as The Speakeasy, Tiles and The Marquee. They also played an all-nighter for Rik Gunnell, who was a top agent at the time. When the other band failed to arrive, they covered their spot as well. This 'impressed Rik Gunnell so much he promised Klock Agency to fix the band up at the Ram Jam Club in the near future'.

Through Robert Stigwood, Klock booked The Bee Gees into Scraptoft Teacher Training College for £100, a week before they released their single, 'New York Mining Disaster 1941'. 'In fact, I think they got off of the plane and came straight to Leicester,' recalls John. 'As a result of that we got two London gigs, Legay would have certainly got one of those. Once you get a band into a location like that, you'd inform the *Melody Maker* and hope they'd turn up – there was nothing you could do if they didn't. A lot of bands got lucky and would pick up a line in the *NME* or the *Melody Maker* then people would start to ask about who they were and where they were from.'

At the weekend, Klock could have had over thirty bands out at the same time. This was the main reason why either John or Maurice would go back to the office in the evening, just in case anything went wrong. 'It could have been anything,' said John. 'The guy who ran the Nottingham Boat Club was a hard man but very straight, they used to have bands on a Sunday night. If he called because he'd been let down and you could get someone over to him at short notice, he'd give you three dates to send bands. The boat clubs had a great following, you could play there a couple of times and if the band had that spark, the four or five other venues in the area would then contact you to put them on. That kept bands like Pesky Gee! and Legay very busy.'

The variety of venues available for bands to play during this period was quite phenomenal. Youth clubs, village and school halls, pubs – the list was practically endless. 'Every now and then the phone would ring and it was the guy from De Montfort Hall asking for an act to fill half an hour,' said John. 'Deuce Coup would have been ideal for that. The bands would have worked all of the teacher training colleges within a thirty-mile radius of Leicester, we wouldn't get paid for those for at least a month afterwards. There would be a couple of schools that would have an end of term dance that would have been free admission to the kids, they would have found the money to pay for it from somewhere else. We would try and arrange for cash after the performance wherever possible but most of the educational venues would pay by cheque, that would come to us and then we would pay the band. There wouldn't have been a lot of money changing hands. Paying Moore & Stanworth though, or whoever, was the number one priority for the lads. Seventy to eighty per cent would have been paid to them and to offset the costs of the van. And paying us of course.'

While Family were the most popular band Klock had on their books, there was also a five-piece band from Rugby, a pop group who played soul, which went out for just £15. 'We kept booking them out,' said John. 'There was nothing different about them but they were reliable, did the job and were nice people. We would send them to every youth club within a forty-mile radius of Leicester. Once you'd made contact with a youth club that did four or five dances a year, the person making the booking would come back. All we needed to do was send them reliable acts. We probably had about ten or twenty of those but there was nothing different about them, they were there just to do a job.' Most of the organisers weren't bothered who the acts were as long as they turned up and did what they were told. 'If they were asked to turn the volume down, they did without any fuss,' said John. 'That was the difference between them and the likes of Legay who had just bought the Marshall stacks and wanted to up it. A few bands wouldn't get work because there was an individual within them who kept pushing it, usually over something silly like volume.' For John, all Klock were after was somebody to do a job and if they were a little bit different, then they would get behind them and do whatever they could to help. 'There was only so much we could do though. We would say if it's going to work, it'll work. That wasn't only with Legay, it was with one or two of the other bands as well.'

With bands such as Legay and Family on the books, acts with both talent and ambition, Klock would have had to have dealt with strong personalities and egos. 'Most of the bands had their characters,' said John. 'One of the guys in The Broodly Hoo, he was a lovely lad, would come in to see us and ask, "Why are we doing this gig?" And we'd say that the work came up, you wouldn't like anything else and it was there. He didn't want to do it because it was a youth club or somewhere that didn't excite him. But what the lads didn't realise was that their parents would be pestering us, asking if their kids would be earning enough money because he wants to buy this, he wants to buy that. When I think about it, we were nursemaids to them really, mainly because their eyes were bigger than their stomachs.'

Invariably, new bands would pay John a visit at the Market Street office with a view to getting onto Klock's books. 'It would normally be a band member and somebody who was looking after them, probably a parent,' said John. 'They would come into the office and say that these boys were just starting up and could you come and have a look at them, they're ideal for the club circuit, et cetera. We were there to tell them what needed doing and when and where they were playing. That was probably the limit of the conversations we would have with the representatives from the groups.'

With forever increasing overheads, Klock left its Market Street offices in 1969 and moved to nearby Saxby Street. 'It was cheaper and by this time, we were working a lot with the universities and colleges,' said John. 'It gave us a bit more freedom. Maurice lived there, we had a photography studio at the front and a garage over the road which made everything easier. Parking in the city centre was a pain even in those days. The students were around us, they could come in, have a coffee and book a band. They couldn't do that on Market Street.'

Although they were established within a fifty-mile radius of Leicester, the end of the mods, the psychedelic scene and a decline in the interest of soul music proved too much for Klock. 'We finished in the early seventies,' said John. 'People had grown tired of the music we had peddled for the best part of ten years. Music was going in all sorts of directions and it was very difficult. As a result, attendances at youth clubs and school halls, which were our bread and butter, dropped off. All of a sudden the London boys were dealing with Leicester University, they were looking for gigs for obscure bands which only a small percentage of the students were aware of.'

When Klock ceased trading, John went back to work for WH Smith. 'I've got no regrets, we learnt a lot from the experience. I'm not too sure I'd do it again but we had a good time, we were at the right age to enjoy it. We'd got a great lifestyle but we were always working, although it may not have looked like that. My wife and I wouldn't have gone to the pictures very often or anything like that, it would have been more we're going to this dance hall or that dance hall. I'd pick her up at 10.00 p.m. and then we'd drive to wherever to see one of the bands.'

Today, John spends most of his spare time playing golf. 'When I'm on the golf course, all of a sudden a memory will come back from the Klock days. I can remember paying £350 for Tom Jones to play the ballroom at Hinckley and playing darts with him. It was a hectic lifestyle though, we'd probably do about three or four different things on a Friday or Saturday night, we'd go and see a promoter or organiser, stop and have a cup of coffee and then move on to the next place. We were very lucky, at Christmas we used to have over fifty bands out all over the place, it was manic. But it was great, I loved it.'

John Butler

'Bands didn't rehearse they practised, very important to remember that. Rehearsals were for actors or presumably professional musicians, whoever they might be ...' **John Butler**

Born in Wigston, Leicester, in 1954, John Butler is a singer/songwriter and frontman of Diesel Park West. Comprised of Butler (vocals, guitar), Rick Willson (guitar, vocals), Geoff Beavan (bass) and Dave 'Moth' Smith (drums), the band released its debut single, 'When the Hoodoo Comes', in 1987. They released *Shakespeare Alabama*, their full-length album debut, in 1989. Since then, and with a couple of changes in the line-up, the band have released eleven albums and fifteen singles. John has also released three solo albums and one single.

A mainstay of the Leicester music scene for many years, John moved to St Saviours Road in Leicester after his parents split up in January 1963. 'Unlike today, divorce then was a very unusual happening,' said John. 'I moved from a Jelson new-build in Wigston Fields to a small terraced house next door to a factory where the machines kept going all day long. It was like going back in time, very rhythmic though. We didn't have a record player, not until much later on. To me, records were things that existed in the adult world, album sleeves seemed like ornaments to go with the polished gramophone players.' John's early music days were played out to a backdrop of two radio stations – in the evening Radio Luxembourg and by day, the BBC's Light Programme. On the TV, there was a choice of *Sunday Night at the London Palladium*, *Thank Your Lucky Stars* and *Juke Box Jury*. John went to Coleman Road Junior School in 1963 and Crown Hills Secondary from 1965–69. 'I loved Coleman Road and I think looking back, the Christian hymns were a big influence on me subconsciously. Great melodies and very dynamic too.'

The stark contrast between a relatively affluent Wigston Fields and an inner-city suburb didn't go unnoticed by John. 'The St Saviours Road area contained a lot of youngsters who were living quite austere lives, pretty much the same as those in the 1940s and 1950s. It was an old Victorian area and much of that recently departed epoch was still around vibe-wise, which, of course, I found fascinating. There was an old guitar teacher who lived on Jellicoe Road I remember in particular as being not too impressed with new developments in music. In the Humberstone Park area though, a bit further out, there seemed to be more kids who were into what was going on and, in contrast to those in the St Saviours area, had means to buy some equipment.'

One of John's first electric guitar experiences took place in the early sixties when he saw Bert Weedon, the first British guitarist to have a hit record in the UK singles chart, at Bentleys Garden Fete. 'He cracked a joke about high-class Braunstone so he must have been well primed,' recalls John. 'That was my first experience of class divide being mentioned. After all, we were all British and had just won the war together had we not? I can still remember the maroon-beige colour of his Fender amp, it would be an extremely valuable item if it were around today.'

Bentleys Garden Fete aside, for John the only places where you could go and experience live music were the various working men's clubs that were scattered around the city centre and its suburbs, most of which have now long since disappeared. 'Usually they had two or three solo singers on, all of which were backed by the resident organist and drummer. Later on, a beat group might have been on too. The first band I ever saw was The Rockets at the South Leicester WMC, which would have been in 1963, closely followed by the Stones in 1964 at The Odeon. Youth clubs were also a good source of gigs, in particular The Raven in Thurnby Lodge and Zodiac 67 in Netherhall. Locally though, Deuce Coupe and Legay were very good live and the Il Rondo was a great place for music and chicks. We saw King Crimson there, shortly after the Hyde Park gig with the Stones, they were on another planet musically, totally freaked the place out.'

John bought his first guitar, a red Vox Shadow with a coax input, in 1964 for eighteen guineas. 'Instruments seemed to come from ads in the paper or from catalogues that Vox or Selmer would produce,' said John. 'By now, though, the more established musical instrument shops such as Chaplin's on Charnwood Street or Chamberlin's on Waterloo Street started to display electric guitars in the window. Very modern and iconic. Moore & Stanworths on Melton Road became a very important and influential place, they stocked some quality gear. We used to go in there a lot, it was more like a social club.'

Switching to keys a few years later, John didn't pick up a guitar again until around 1974. 'That's why the left hand, upside-down thing evolved because I couldn't find a real left-handed guitar. The style has its built-in limitations but I figured it possible to develop a technique based on a sort of loose drone running throughout the chord changes. It was this that ended up providing the feel on songs such as "Like Princes

Do" and "When the Hoodoo Comes" later on for the Diesels. My job as a guitar player is to provide the backdrop to the song and augment the lead player.'

Influence-wise, John was more or less following the same bands as the other kids of his generation but with some exceptions. 'My brother had some really good rhythm and blues stuff which, even in my young head, I knew was sort of the real deal. "Bring It To Jerome", "Mama Keep Your Big Mouth Shut", that kind of stuff. The first single I ever actually bought though was "Nights In White Satin" when it came out the first time, I don't think it was much of a hit then. First album was *Buffalo Springfield Again,* their second album. I was a bit older then and had some dosh. Later on, after watching Legay and a few other local bands, I figured out that this could be a way not to work in a factory.'

In 1966, the twelve-year-old John managed to wangle himself into a club group, the exotically named Saketa 4 Plus One. 'I was a young kid when I joined but it was probably better than not doing it, I'm usually glad I did when I look back. The experience taught me that a band, any band, must gig to have any chance of finding out what's going on within itself. Kids needed to learn to play, so therefore "keep practising kid" was the ethos of the day. Usually it took place in pubs and certainly in church halls such as All Saints in Wigston. A lot of the kids at that time did nothing but practise though, which is okay, but I must have realised that onstage is where it all comes together. Or not.'

In 1967/68, John left the Saketas and joined up with 'a bunch of grammar school kids' who had a band called The Idle Rich. 'It was a good name,' recalls John. 'And they didn't play the clubs. We played a lot of West Coast and some good Stax stuff, "60 Minutes Of Your Love", that kind of thing. The kid who put me on to them was a bit of a hard nut from Thurnby Lodge by the name of Geoff Beavan. Geoff was related to one of the band members.' John first met Geoff outside a house on Uppingham Road, one late summer's evening in 1966. 'He was the kid who had taken my place in the Saketa 4 but he had become a bit pissed off by then,' said John. 'He told me there was this band called the Wretched Wretch who were looking for a couple of like-minded kids to complete the line-up. I thought "yeah that's a great name, I wanna be in that." But it turned out, in true Beavan style, he had got the name wrong and they were in fact called The Idle Rich. Nothing changes. He got blown out after a week or two but I stayed with them.'

In 1968, 'five minutes after being sacked from The Idle Rich for being too handsome', John joined Karavan, an outfit that he affectionately calls his first grown-up band. 'The bass player was my elder brother, Tony. I made my debut with them in Mansfield. I'd previously done out-of-town gigs with The Idle Rich, most notably Cannon Hill Park in Birmingham where we smashed up a load of old televisions like their local heroes, The Move. The implied adulation, and often humiliation, and the sense of achievement when something sounded good live was a particular driving force for me.' Contrary to The Idle Rich, Karavan had a pretty impressive tour schedule that took in most of the UK. 'The band's manager used to pin the names of gigs up on the practice room wall, there were a lot of exotic names on it like Sheffield,' said John. 'There were also a load of dates that were "Pending". I thought blimey, the band must be really big in Pending, wherever that is.'

Karavan mainly played covers, with the occasional original number. 'We had a great lead singer named Jeff Sanders who, before Karavan, was the singer with Hal C Blake,' said John. 'Jeff was fantastic, he always reminded me vocally of Jess Roden. We became actually very good live, very musically adept but with a defined edge and groove about us.' Eventually, Karavan morphed into a band called Ginger, going on to do numerous circuit gigs including, amongst others, The Marquee and The Roundhouse. 'We did the same circuit as Gypsy but without a record deal, which was possible then,' explains John. 'I don't know how an album would have sounded, whether it would have been a sort of rambling cod-prog rock or if it would have had something going for it. We certainly took it seriously enough with rehearsals and everything, it was very organised. By this time we also had a different singer, a guy named Jim Bowley who also played a weird sounding flute. He was a dead ringer for Steve Winwood.' In 1971, Karavan/Ginger broke up. 'There was a short-lived mark two but it was all over really,' said John. 'Anyway, I was an old man by then. Seventeen.'

Renowned today as the main songwriter for Diesel Park West, John didn't start writing his own material until much later in his career. 'I was thinking about it all the time during the sixties. Putting it down, though, is an entirely different discipline. There is not much else that comes close to the feeling of smug smart-arse satisfaction when you know you have just completed the three main ingredients and joined them together: lyric, tune and structure. It's like completing something you don't see but you know is there because you can hear it. And when it starts to gradually become visible, as it always does, it's the lyrics which make it happen. And how do you write lyrics? With a pen …'

One Leicester band that stood out for John during the late 1960s was Spring. 'They seemed different to everything else that was around, they started to really get it together. The stage act was loud and exciting, Pat Moran became an electrifying frontman with real charisma. When they got hold of a mellotron, their sound became something special. They were never as groovy as Gypsy but there was quite possibly a much broader width to the actual song writing from a lyric perspective. Spring's arrangements often got quite heady but they could mostly pull it off.'

With the demise of Ginger, John went to London for a year and then, in 1972/73, came back and formed a band called Pini with Geoff Beavan and Mick Pini. 'It was a prototype punk band but no one realised it at the time,' said John. 'We played driving rock 'n' roll and wore cut off duffle coats with drainpipe jeans in the era of flares. We played lots of gigs around the country including an unforgettable weekend at the original Liverpool Cavern, not the tourist attraction that's up there now. It was all booze, speed and blow. In those days, there was an especially vindictive drug squad copper who used to take pleasure in getting little hippie kids banged up with hardcore criminals doing proper jail time. Back then, they would put you away for a couple of years for one joint!'

Reverting back to the sixties music era, John then played in a Beatles cover band for a while before re-joining Mick Pini in a band called Baby. 'That was in 1974/75, we started to get regular dates at The Marquee where we had become quite popular. As a result, I started to get a lot of attention from within the business with regards to being a good singer, which I may have become but I knew I still had a lot to learn.'

Mott the Hoople offered John the opportunity to join them as a replacement for Ian Hunter but he didn't take up the offer. 'I did end up later with Mott's Luther Grosvenor (aka Ariel Bender) in his band Widowmaker when they lost Steve Ellis, their original singer. In the sixties he had been the vocalist for the Love Affair, he had a great voice.' Widowmaker released an album with John, *Too Late to Cry*, and then in 1977 toured the USA with Aerosmith, Foreigner, The Kinks and Ted Nugent as well as playing their own dates. 'We got to be a good band, especially toward the end. We were playing stadiums to 20,000 people per night as well as four nights at the Whiskey a Go Go in LA. They were fantastic gigs.' Due to a hefty dose of 'rock 'n' roll excess', the tour took its toll and Widowmaker fell apart. 'We were booked to do the Reading Festival right after the States, we were near to the top of the bill too,' recalls John. 'Instead, I ended up back in Leicester playing at the Full Moon on Coleman Road. I must have been mad.'

By 1978, John had formed Flicks with Legay and Gypsy's John Knapp and Dave 'Moth' Smith. 'We got signed, a very good deal with Ariola with lots of money sloshing about. We recorded an album at John Lennon's Ascot home which came out in 1979 called *Go For The Effect*. It's a flawed album and a bit daft in places, but it was a brave attempt right at the time when the new wave thing was sweeping the board clean. After that bombed it was the wilderness until 1987 when Diesel Park West got moving.'

From the humble beginnings of Saketa 4 Plus One, 1960s Leicester has played a pivotal role in the development of John Butler as a musician, as can be clearly seen by his CV post-Karavan/Ginger. The local connections with the likes of Mick Pini, Legay, Gypsy and Geoff Beavan are clearly there to see. The decade not only provided John with a true grounding in the music business (and life) in general, but also the ambition and drive to move forward outside of the city. 'In general, the sixties were sunny, smoky, sexy and stylish,' said John. 'Leicester, though, was going through an awkward transition between being an imperial light industrial powerhouse to the pink confused paper tiger it is today. There was a sort of resigned tension in the air. Culturally it alternated between the predictable and then, suddenly, the weird. And it still does that.'

Cert X with a young Moth on drums.

Vfranie.

Vfranie.

Klock Agency business card.

K L O C K

Agency

Telephone:
LEICESTER 20102
(3 lines)

Directors:
Maurice Ridgway & John Aston

8 Market Street

Leicester

Presented by M. Reynold

Black Widow at the Phoenix, poster by Circa Design.

Pesky Gee!

Kay Garrett and Baz Francis, Pesky Gee!

Pesky Gee!

Circa Design

'In the seventies you were defined by the music you listened to, but my tastes and preferences evolved in the thriving and dynamic atmosphere of the sixties. It was an exciting time to be a young designer and for me it was all about bands, festivals and psychedelic graphics ...' **Brian Plews**

Brian Plews was born in 1949, arriving in Leicester from the Leicestershire village of Church Langton in 1960 at the age of ten. 'Things could not have been more different,' said Brian. 'From rooted country bumpkin to Mowmacre Hill council estate rookie. I was naïve and apprehensive, especially at school where the other kids were so much more advanced than I was in the arts of fighting and playing truant. It wasn't a bad school but there wasn't the same emphasis on academic accomplishment as at my previous country school. Only two of us boys actually went on to grammar school.' The start of six intensive years at Gateway Boys' also marked the first, small steps for Brian on a journey with music at its heart. 'I had been captivated by the late-night offerings from Radio Luxembourg on a tiny, tinny tranny radio hidden under my pillow. Within a year, The Beatles were making waves with "Love Me Do" and "Please Please Me". Until then my barbwire hair was impossible to coax into the still fashionable quiff, no matter how much Brylcreem I applied. But the new national craze with the Fab Four suddenly enabled me to be right up-to-date with a distinctive sweeping mop. For the first time, I felt "with it". The first record I ever bought was "I Want To Hold Your Hand" and we didn't even have a record player.'

The other constant in Brian's life at this time was football. His dad, who was a long-distance lorry driver, was captain of the local British Road Services team and often took him along on a Saturday afternoon. 'I would kick a ball about to avoid hyperthermia while the teams vied to see who could collect the most amount of mud. It was the start of a lifelong passion. I remember the first time my dad took me to Filbert Street, we sat in the vertiginous "Double Decker" and watched Jimmy Greaves do his magic against a Leicester side which was lucky to come away with a 2–2 draw. From that point onwards, I hardly missed a home match for several years, rain or shine.'

For Brian, apart from football, Leicester had very little to offer the young teenager. So the arrival of Europe's largest ten-pin bowling alley in Lee Circle in 1963 was a welcome addition. 'The Top Rank Bowl was huge – thirty-six lanes on one floor, open all day, every day. Although my bowling prowess was inconsistent at best, I loved it and was a member of a team called the Spartans, resplendent with sew-on eponymous helmet. My 10-bob pocket money was quickly swallowed up though, it only just covered two games, a burger and a 7up.'

It was around this time that Brian started to become interested in fashion and eventually talked his mum into buying him the latest bell-bottom jeans from Irish Menswear. 'The jeans were my pride and joy and, owning only one pair, I insisted they were washed, dried and ironed in the shortest time possible.'

Now in the sixth form, Brian was working all day Saturday and then Sunday mornings at a car wash opposite the Tigers ground on Welford Road, earning a total of £2.10s for twelve hours' work. Brian was resolute though – he had a plan. And the time was right to put that plan into action. 'A classmate at school was selling an old Vespa 125 for the princely sum of £25. My parents were totally against the idea and did everything possible to dissuade me but I went ahead anyway and it changed my life.'

Brian grasped his new-found freedom with aplomb. He had his hair sheared at Ron's in Churchgate, bought a fishtail parka, blue jeans and desert boots and metamorphosed overnight into a mod. 'Despite being second-league compared to those of my friends, my scooter became my *raison d'être* and I proceeded to add every accoutrement known to mod, from a mass of mirrors and spotlights to a two-metre tank aerial. Who cared that they were cumbersome, or even dangerous, when it was the image that mattered.' A few weeks after his sixteenth birthday, Brian passed his motorcycle test at the first attempt. 'It opened up opportunities with the opposite sex as I could now zoom about with a girl on the back. There were a couple of prime meeting places, the Green Bowler on Churchgate and the Nocturne just off Wharf Street.' The Nocturne was ostensibly a coffee club and for Brian, it was exciting to be part of this new scene with pervasive parkas, soul and Tamla Motown blasting out of the jukebox and highly suspect dealings going on in the dimly-lit cellar. 'It wasn't long before it closed and quickly reopened as the Nautique, where it was pretty much business as usual. Emerging Leicester group Family used to practise in the back room of the Nautique during the day when the place was closed. Generally we met up at weekends and headed out en masse looking for house parties, some by invitation but usually not, or just rode out to the Leicester Forest East service station on the M1. Otherwise, we popped next door to The Three Cranes for a lager and lime and a game of table football.'

Riding home one night, Brian was distracted by a girl at a bus stop and drove into the back of a parked car. 'I found myself on the car's bonnet with my scooter bent in half. Nature was telling me it was time to move on.' Dancing became Brian's new calling, his parka giving way to a stripy blazer. 'The Palais on Humberstone Gate, the Il Rondo on Silver Street and The Casino on London Road were my favourite haunts. Not forgetting the infamous Nite Owl – a dark, sweaty cellar, famous for its all-nighters. I thought it was very seedy and only went a few times, one notable occasion to see Geno Washington. It had quite a reputation for pill poppers and didn't last long, it had closed down by 1968. That same year, I "worked" with Robin Hollick, aka DJ Owlin' Robin, at the Longship and he was full of stories of iniquitous goings-on there.'

Back at school, Brian's academic performance went from bad to worse as his interest waned and other distractions took over. 'As a sixth-former you were expected to provide your own discipline. Instead of studying, many of my free periods were spent improving my cue action in Osbourne's Snooker Club on Cank Street, or drinking coffee just up the road at the Art Centre. Somehow, I managed to take two out of the three A-levels I was studying, with the intention of returning for a third year as I was only seventeen and not old enough to go to university. Only a few days into the new school term, I realised I couldn't face another year. Fortunately, the college year commenced a month later and my supportive art teacher found an available design course at the local College of Art and Design.'

Over the summer, Bill Brown, the owner of the now defunct Nautique, together with a partner, started a new venture: The Longship. 'It was a sort of late-nightclub/ disco in an old factory space on Queen Street,' said Brian. 'It quickly became the preferred meeting place of the local West Indian community. It was here that I painted my first mural, naturally of a large Viking longship, and spent most evenings serving cola and burgers.'

College was fun but after the first year, Brian was ready for something more stimulating. 'I saw an advertisement in the local paper for a junior designer and I immediately applied. After calling every day for the next week, my attrition eventually paid off and I put my first step on the ladder for a princely £6 a week.' Brian's new job was in the studio of an associate marketing company at Gee Advertising on Regent Street, at the time the largest agency outside of London. 'It was all about ad men in sharp suits and mini-skirted secretaries, sixties sophistication personified. I loved being in a professional, creative environment and even took pleasure in the more mundane duties such as washing the paint palettes and acting as gofer for the senior designers. Being close to New Walk, it was a great location and when I heard that we were being transferred to a brand-new studio attached to vast merchandising production facilities on the Braunstone Industrial Estate my heart sank, especially as it meant catching two buses for an 8.30 start. Rising early was never my forte.'

By 1969, The Longship had closed and Bill Brown, ever the entrepreneur, told Brian about his next project. 'He had taken over premises on King Street and planned to open a shop/gallery called Circa selling work by local artists and his own range of leather garments. He offered me a room on the first floor. The rent was nominal and, albeit still very young and inexperienced, but with the Bill's encouragement, an opportunity beckoned. I set up my new studio as Circa Design on the tiniest of shoestrings and spent the next few months moonlighting between my day job in Braunstone and evenings in King Street, usually catching the last bus home.'

Circa caught the eye of the *Leicester Chronicle*. This article, written by Peter Barraclough in March 1970, neatly describes the concept of the organisation:

Leicester Artists Fight Mass Production With Brush, Potter's Wheel and Scissors!

Just over 12 months ago, a young man called Bill Brown, bored by his work in shoe manufacturing, hit on the idea of providing a platform for local artistic talent. His project was simple – to offer a service which would sponsor, encourage and sell work by amateur and semi-professional artists in the Leicester area, while at the same time catering for the ever increasing demand for the more individual goods.

The first floor houses a shop and behind this is a leather workroom in which Bill Brown turns out garment after garment from the stacks of various coloured hides which cram the shelves. Trading is often on a bring and buy basis. Artists bring in one of their efforts for sale, only to walk out with something which has caught their eye while on the premises.

The Circa organisation is completed by Bill Parks, a young freelance photographer, who has an impressive darkroom on the 3rd floor of the building, and Leicester sculptor David Seymour, who, although he doesn't work on the premises, is very much part of the Circa scheme.

If all this sounds very much like a self-contained community, this is exactly the sort of image which is sought. Many of their customers are personal friends and transactions are informal and friendly.

Bill Brown says the aim is to please people who would rather spend £8 or £9 on an original painting than the same amount on a print. It may not be anything special but at least it's something different, something unique which only they have. 'It's the same with pottery. We find that our customers like the homemade stuff and much of what we sell is made by a husband and wife who are teachers.'

Main plans for the future include concentration on clothes for toddlers and manufacture of homemade shoes, individually produced for the customer by a local designer called Phil Wilson.

At the time, there were no other design studios in Leicester working with local bands, providing Brian with a unique opportunity. 'Everything was in its infancy with few templates to follow, especially provincial design, and I pretty much made things up as I went along. I was very young and it was a bit of a roller-coaster ride. I had helped with free festivals on Welford Road Reccy and had already met several local bands who gave me a start with my first actual commissions. Also, my girlfriend was a scene designer at the Phoenix Theatre and introduced me to the manager, Robin Anderson (brother of Ian of Jethro Tull), and he gave me a job designing the publicity for their regular lunchtime events.'

Producing posters during the sixties was very different to the digital printing of today. The cost of printing large lithographic posters was prohibitive and almost everything was screen-printed by hand. 'In fact, everything was done by hand,' said Brian. 'Starting with a detailed pencil layout, separate stencils for each colour were cut with a scalpel on a translucent red film. Even the lettering required great dexterity. The number of colours was limited, often to one or two, but this could be increased by using a tinted paper.'

By now, Brian had developed a good friendship with a couple of other designers from work, Alan Taylor and Doug Powell. 'They took me to folk clubs and other genres of live music, including Leicester University, without which my music education would have been severely limited. My first experience of live big-name concerts, such as Free, Rory Gallagher and John Hiesman's Coliseum, took place standing in pools of Newcastle Brown and cigarette butts at Leicester Uni.'

The three friends organised their own version of The Beatles' Magical Mystery Tour, taking advantage of Leicester City Transport's favourable deals on coach hire. Everybody boarded on Humberstone Gate without a clue where they were being taken, the fact that it was a dark winter's evening adding to the intrigue. 'The final destination was actually the Bath Hotel in Shearsby which we had decorated the previous night,' said Brian. 'Later, after I had let them into my Circa Design secret, it emerged that they were also interested in doing something more exciting and we had dreams of going full-time together. But when it came to it, I was the only one to make the break. That being said, Alan's contribution to the success of Circa Design, and his guidance and assistance, were invaluable, and he continued to give up his evenings until the spring of 1970.'

Alan and Doug both drove vintage MGTs and in 1969, together with Circa photographer Bill Park, they set off for the Rolling Stones concert in Hyde Park. 'With what seemed like half the population of the northern hemisphere striving to get a view, and loaded with Bill's impressive photography gear, the two of us brazenly walked through the backstage stockade, climbed on top of one of the media trucks and had a perfect view as Mick and the boys made the dash from caravan to stage,' said Brian. 'Realising that access to the stage was out of the question, by the time we made our way back to find the other two, the Stones' set was well underway. The actual performance was under par and several contemporary commentators agreed that Family deserved all the plaudits.'

Brian first met Pesky Gee! in September 1969, just as they were breaking up in order to form Black Widow. They needed a poster for their first gig at The Casino. 'The Casino was one of Leicester's few proper venues and regularly hosted bands and discos, although by 1969 its main function was as a bingo hall. We had already produced the poster when the owner, local bingo hall impresario Drummond Macdonald, got cold feet and only relented when Alan and I tracked him down and somehow persuaded him to let the concert go ahead.' Drummond was suitably impressed by Circa's youthful enthusiasm and invited them to visit him at his home to discuss an idea they had been cogitating for an alternative use for The Casino: a multi-purpose arts and music centre. 'We showed him sketches of a proposed interior including a modular stage,' said Brian. 'The proposition went down well and we made plans to turn "The Village" into reality.'

Posters had been printed announcing its arrival and Brian had handed in his notice at work when Drummond pulled the rug on the project. 'It was very disappointing,' recalls Brian. 'But in retrospect, it was probably just as well as I wasn't really equipped at that age to undertake such a venture. Ironically, it was the catalyst for Drummond to rethink The Casino's use and he eventually decided to change it into Granny's Nightclub and I did all of its design work for many years.'

Now full-time at Circa, Brian decided to try his hand at being an impresario and organised a concert of his own. 'I had been working with a band called Aries, who were a little like Yes. They had just changed their name to Agony, not to be confused with Agony Bag, and needed a gig. I also knew Mick Pini from my schooldays and his fledgling band, Ned Ludd, was added to the bill. Finding a venue was more of a problem and Kirby Muxloe Community Centre wasn't exactly the most illustrious setting but, taking advantage of the City Transport coach service from the centre, we managed to attract enough people to cover the costs.'

Meanwhile Black Widow, who were working on their first album, *Sacrifice*, were beginning to cause a stir with their occult content and shocking performances. Circa had already created the band's 'flame' logo and demon symbol and had produced their first publicity leaflet. Following a successful pitch to the band's management company in London, Circa also produced the promotional material for the forthcoming album, comprising of stickers and posters as well as several giant 2.5-metre cut-out demons to display in record shops. This further extract from the *Leicester Chronicle* article describes the scene at Circa during this period of high profile creativity:

> The (Circa) centre includes a graphic department, a small paint spattered room which is providing a promising asset in these publicity conscious days when posters, slogans and eye catching advertisements are in demand. When I walked into the room, 20-year-old Brian Plews, a dark haired former art student, was struggling with an 8ft hardboard cut out of a giant demon, one of the half dozen ordered by CBS to promote the new LP by Leicester group, Black Widow. Association with Black Widow has proved to be a breakthrough. As well as producing the black and white demon posters, Brian and his part time assistant were given the contract to provide the inside cover design of the group's LP, which has now gone all over the world. Brian is particularly pleased with the effort which is a beautifully coloured illustration of hob goblins, demons, ghosties and the macabre, very

much in the style of 14th century painter, Hieronymus Bosch. The giant
demons, which Brian spent all night cutting out and spraying, are now
in London where they will adorn the shop windows of most of the
leading record shops.

'We were asked to create an illustration for the album cover,' explains Brian.
'Unfortunately, though, the powers-that-be decided it was too risqué for the outer
cover and it was banished to the inside.'

In 1969, Leicester Students' Union Rag Week had gained a new enthusiastic
and imaginative leader who had the ambition to give the 1970 event a stylish,
professional look. 'Circa created the Rag Imp,' said Brian. 'It was carried through on
a range of promotional material, including themed concert posters featuring both
big names and local support bands. It was a very bold approach for such a normally
amateur affair.'

The annual University Arts Ball, cheekily known as 'The Groupies Ball', was
held in the Top Rank Suite. It included an impressive line-up of acts including the
Bonzo Dog Band. 'We produced the poster which was inserted into the student
union magazine,' said Brian. 'The following evening, I had a party in a room above
the Chameleon coffee bar, which was a couple doors down from Circa, and a friend
from the Phoenix arrived with two members of the Bonzos. Unfortunately, they
both behaved themselves impeccably.'

One of Brian's contacts left university and went to work for music promoters the
Red Bus Company. 'He suggested I got in touch with them as they were putting on
a major event in May near Newcastle-Under-Lyme, called the Hollywood Music
Festival. Bill Brown and I signed an exclusive contract to sell posters, printed T-shirts
and handmade leather garments at the festival. It was the start of an unforgettable
year as we took our roadshow to every major music festival in the UK, culminating
at the legendary Isle of Wight.'

Now living in south-west France, Brian's affinity to music and art still forms the
basis of his work today. Working as a graphic designer at B Creatif (www.bcreatif.
com), Brian's commitment to eye-catching, contemporary design is still the same as it
was back in the early days of Circa. 'Looking back with the benefit of hindsight, I am
pleased to have made a small contribution to an important era in Leicester's musical
legacy. Admittedly, the city wasn't exactly the epicentre of contemporary music,
or contemporary design for that matter, but it certainly didn't feel like a cultural

backwater. To maximise your chances of fame and success though, particularly in the design industry, you had move to London, an attraction I always managed to resist. Perhaps I feared being out of my comfort zone, or just felt that the East Midlands was my home. Even when headhunted by London-based companies later in my career, when I would have felt confident at the highest level, I wasn't seduced by offers which meant giving up my quality of life. By luck or design, this led onto appreciable success further down the line and in many ways I have gone full circle, being involved in the same kind of work today that gave me enormous satisfaction over forty years ago. Neither would make me rich but, for me, that has never been what it's all about.'

Pesky Gee!

'I've lost the top end of my hearing due to standing in front of Marshall stacks, trousers flapping ...' **Chris Dredge**

Pesky Gee! started life in 1964 as Five-minus-One before changing their name to Inside Outfit. The band comprised of Kay Garrett (lead vocals), Chris Dredge (guitar), Bob Bond (bass guitar), Clive Box (drums) and Dave Vesey (guitar). When Vesey left, the band carried on as a four-piece until they were joined by Jess 'Zoot' Taylor (organ) and Clive Jones (saxophone, flute). The band then added Baz Francis (vocals) and Alan Hornsby (saxophone). In 1966, Inside Outfit became Pesky Gee!, Francis left and Kip Trevor (lead vocals) joined. In 1969, Pesky Gee! released *Exclamation Mark*, their only album, and the single 'Where Is My Mind', both on the Pye record label. After the album was released, both Hornsby and Dredge left and Jim Gannon (guitar, vocals) joined. Garrett left not long afterwards and the remaining band members continued under another name, Black Widow, releasing their debut album, *Sacrifice*, in 1970.

'We were called Inside Outfit but there was another band from Coventry called Inside Out and it caused a bit of confusion, mostly from a booking perspective,' said Chris Dredge. 'Promoters were booking us and expecting Inside Out and vice versa. Inside Out had a bit of a reputation and we were getting all of these hard guys with tattoos turning up at our gigs threatening to beat everyone up so Klock Agency advised us to change our name. We had a brainstorming session at Klock's office one Sunday morning, we pulled all of these names out of a hat but nothing came out that we wanted, so Maurice Ridgeway said, "I've had enough of all this, I've got a song here by Broodly Hoo called 'Pesky Gee', you can have that as a name and that's that."' Clive Jones: 'Klock chose that name for us, we weren't keen at the time but later grew to love it.'

For the first three years, Pesky Gee! were a soul band playing covers, never having any aspirations for writing their own material. The music they produced had a heavy bass and drum sound, backed up with an exciting brass section. 'When I joined, it was at the start of soul music's popularity so sax players were in demand,' said Clive. 'There weren't many of us around, we played what was at the time underground music as opposed to what was in the charts, the Wilson Pickett, Otis Redding, Sam and Dave type stuff.' Clive joined Pesky Gee! in 1965 from another Leicester band, Frank Lee Union. 'I was working at Morgan Squires when a guy who worked in the warehouse a few streets away found out I played sax and asked if I would like to come for an audition with Frank Lee Union, although there was never anyone called Frank Lee in the band. I was scared to death but because I had lessons I found it quite easy.'

Pesky Gee! were a mainstay of the Leicester circuit, in particular the Nite Owl on Newarke Street. 'George Parker, the guy who owned the Nite Owl, used to love us,' said Chris. 'We started off doing a couple of gigs and then he made us promise to do at least one a month.' The band played every other week, supporting big names including The Temptations, Jimmy Cliff and Mary Wells. 'After playing a gig elsewhere, we used to go on to the Nite Owl, usually arriving just after midnight,' said Chris. 'George would hand us a litre of scotch and a big bottle of coke and say to us, "There you go lads, get that down you and get on that stage."'

Like most other bands, Pesky Gee! were very conscious of their stage image. 'I used to be quite fussy about what I wore on stage,' said Chris. 'In fact, we used to get complimented quite a lot on our clothes. Some of my shirts were made by two girls who had a shop on Silver Street, they were superb, I had a couple off of them. I bought some fabulous clothes from them for next to nothing, mainly because they were samples.'

From a bookings perspective, Pesky Gee! were in a good negotiating position, mainly because organisers were guaranteed to make money due to the venues being packed solid. 'We were being booked seven nights a week and earning between £250–360 a gig, which was a lot of money in those days,' said Chris. 'We supported Marmalade once at Redcar, they'd just released "Ob-La-Di, Ob-La-Da", and they were on £75. We were the support band and we picked up over £200.'

While Pesky Gee! were regularly performing the main venues on the circuit, they also played at one of the city's less salubrious venues – Leicester Prison. 'I think we were the first band to play there,' said Clive. 'I fixed the gig up through my music teacher, Miss Mabbat. I had been having piano lessons but then became too busy to carry them on. Miss Mabbat asked us if we would like to perform there, she'd taken a few of her pupils to play for the prisoners and thought it might be a good idea. It was the most amazing time, I remember some of the band's girlfriends were there and when they walked in, the prisoners went crazy. Kay Garratt was our singer at the time, the prisoners just loved her, they had a collection the second time we were there and gave her some chocolates. I remember when the prisoners applauded it was so loud, they were really letting off steam.' Chris Dredge: 'A lot of the prisoners were in there because of drugs and they had heard of Pesky Gee! The guard said to us beforehand, "Don't expect too much, you won't get many there." Of course, it was heaving. There was one prisoner in particular who was quite small and he said to me, "I could fit into one of those speaker cabinets, get the back off." He seriously wanted us to smuggle him out in one of the speakers.' Afterwards, the prisoners helped carry the Hammond organ downstairs and made the band tea and cakes. 'The warden told us that after we had played, many of the prisoners used to get upset as it reminded them of what they were missing,' said Clive. 'Many of the cons, when released, would turn up at the Nite Owl and they would always look after us, promising that they would never steal our van – thanks guys!'

One gig that stands out in particular for both Chris and Clive was when they played with Chris Farlowe and the Thunderbirds at the Melton Mowbray TA Hall in 1966. 'They were number one at the time with the Rolling Stones' "Out of Time",' said Clive. 'Farlowe was doing a double up but on the way to the gig he lost half of his band so he asked us to back him. It went down a storm but of course he had to sing "Out of Time", a song we didn't know how to play.' Two musicians that were with Farlowe were guitarist Albert Lee and drummer Carl Palmer, later of Emerson Lake & Palmer. 'Albert Lee is my guitar hero,' said Chris. 'I can remember he sat there showing me how to play "Out of Time". We played, had a really good time and the crowd went berserk, even though it sounded awful. People forgot that we were actually Pesky Gee! and were asking for our autographs as if we were The Thunderbirds.'

Pesky Gee!'s first London gig was at The Roaring Twenties, an underground music bar. Located at 50 Carnaby Street, The Roaring Twenties, now a Ben Sherman shop, played host to a number of celebrities including the Rolling Stones, The Animals and The Who. On the way to the club, the van broke down and they were late. 'We didn't have a clue where we were going,' recalls Chris. 'We didn't know where Carnaby Street was to be honest, we got there at about midnight, unloaded the van and went inside.' Welcomed into the club, the atmosphere heavy with smoke, Kay was introduced as Lulu's little sister and the band played two sets. 'While we were on stage, something happened and the place went up,' said Chris. 'Apparently, some guy had been bottled or stabbed. The police turned up and started to drag out all of the under-agers and left. This guy was outside, blood gushing from the wound, it was all over the pavement. Next door was Ladbrokes' head office and the guard there ushered us out and we sat with him in his room until it had all died down. We didn't get back on stage that night but we got re-booked.'

Pesky Gee!, who by now had moved on to a more flower power/psychedelic sound, were playing a gig in Warrington when they got a phone call asking them to go to Pye Studios in London to record a single. 'When we got there, Ginger Baker pulled up in his Jenson Interceptor,' said Chris. 'He said, "Do you want a hand with the kit lads, I'm going in." We recorded the single quickly, leaving the studio with four hours' recording time to fill. They asked us to strip some tracks down for an LP and then go back later on to clean them up. We did about fifteen tracks, playing them how we would at a gig.' Clive Jones: 'We'd never done it before so we knew no better, we were all just desperate to make a record. There were many mistakes, all of which were promised to be taken out in the mix later but, forty-plus years on, they are all still there. And of course, I can still hear those mistakes, especially in "Dharma for One". The sax had a delay on the playback so I'm out of time all the way through. Well, that's my excuse.'

Exclamation Mark was released in 1969, the title coming about as a result of a classic record company mix up. 'Our manager rang to remind them to put the exclamation mark on the end of our name,' said Clive. 'But the girl on the phone got it wrong and called the album *Exclamation Mark*. I was able to correct this thirty years later on its re-release.' Both sides of the single are included on the album. 'We used to play "You Keep Me Hanging On", a Vanilla Fudge re-make of the original Supremes song,' said Clive. 'The follow-up was "Where Is My Mind" so we thought we would cover it. Our management liked it and despite having an original song that was going to be our release, "A Place of Heartbreak", they decided "Where Is My Mind" would be the A-side. It got a few plays and the intro was used for years afterwards on Stuart Henry's radio show.' Comparisons relating to the similarity of the riff on 'Where Is My Mind' and Legay's 'No-One' are dismissed by Chris. 'We had so little time to record it, I couldn't think of anything else to play, so if it sounds like "No-One" it's pure coincidence.' Shortly after recording the album, Chris Dredge and Alan Hornsby had a disagreement with the band's management and left. They received no credits for their role on the album or the single. 'Alan Hornsby was my fellow sax player and we always got on very well,' said Clive. 'He passed away in 2012 and many of us went to his funeral. We miss him very much and he will always be a member of the band. When we play the album, we are all together again.'

Kay Garrett left Pesky Gee! not long after Chris Dredge and Alan Hornsby. The remaining band members continued, changing their name to Black Widow, releasing their debut album, *Sacrifice,* in 1970. 'We never really finished,' said Clive. 'We just changed our name and became a darker, more progressive rock band. We were known as *the* black magic band. We made one, if not the first, black magic album which entered the charts. Our live shows included the sacrifice of a naked girl, which got us lots of publicity. We were a great live act but sadly, due to silly egos in the band, it was downhill after that.'

Nearly fifty years on since the conception of Five-minus-One, both Clive and Chris reflect on their time with Pesky Gee! 'It was the most fun time of our lives, I know everyone in the band agrees,' said Clive. 'We still get together and talk about the past and how much fun it was.' Chris Dredge: 'I have some great individual memories of the band, some stand out more than others but I can't say that they are any better than the whole. We enjoyed a really good social life together, which was quite rare for a band, but unfortunately it turned a bit nasty towards the end, which was the reason why I left. Up until then though, we all had a great time, every gig we played I thoroughly enjoyed. I certainly wouldn't change anything, it was the best ten years of my life.'

Mod Life

'Before I bought my scooter, I remember going to Skeggy in 1964 on the bus, I think it was with the Scout group. The scooters were parked all along the prom, it was unbelievable …' **Chris Busby**

Born in Leicester in 1950, Chris Busby lived on Evesham Road with his parents, Dorothy and Ed. Ed had his own painting and decorating business and Dorothy was a dinner lady. 'When I was twelve or thirteen, all you used to see was teddy boys, but we used to stay away from them,' said Chris. 'I used to listen to Bill Hailey and all that but that was only because my dad was into it.'

On a cold day in October 1962, Chris switched on his radio and, along with thousands of other young people across the country, heard a song that would change and shape his life forever. 'Me and my mate were playing on a slide at the top of a road somewhere, listening to a little transistor radio. All of a sudden, "Love Me Do" came on and that was it, that was when the transition took place. The music of yesteryear went, replaced by The Beatles, the Stones and my favourite band, The Who. I used to love Townshend's guitar playing, I still play it today, it's unbelievable. There's a clip of the High Numbers at the Railway Club on YouTube, it's brilliant. The mods are dancing like there's no tomorrow and are out of their heads on speed, exactly how it used to be.'

In 1964, aged fourteen, Chris decided to become a mod. The British youth subculture was sweeping the nation, its main emphasis focusing on music, fashion, Vespas, Lambrettas and all-night dancing, usually fuelled by a wide variety of amphetamines. 'Me and my mate said to each other, "What shall we become, mods or rockers?" The Brighton fights were taking place, we didn't like the greasy motorbike look, so we opted to become mods. The image and the scooters was a much cooler look than the rockers with their motorbikes and leathers. They also appeared to be a lot older than us.'

Chris left school when he was fifteen and started work at I&R Morleys, a warehouse situated on the corner of Oxford Street and Bonners Lane. The building is now part of De Montfort University. 'There were a few other mods there apart from me, mainly older lads though,' explains Chris. 'We would look up to them, especially the ones who were particularly cool, they were known in the mod hierarchy as "faces". I hadn't got my scooter then but there was a lad who worked there called Mark who had a blue Vespa. It looked great, he used to come to work on it. I thought to myself, I'd love to have my own.'

Shortly after Chris' sixteenth birthday, he bought his first scooter, a Lambretta Series 2. Launched in 1959 under the banner of 'Lambrettability', this particular model promised the opportunity to 'see exciting new places, enjoy exciting new experiences and make exciting new friends'. All very exciting, then. 'I bought it from a guy off Hallam Crescent for thirty quid, which was about five weeks' worth of wages at the time,' said Chris. 'It would be worth a fortune today. It had green and white striped side panels and fur on the seats. I preferred the look of a Lambretta to a Vespa, they were sleeker. It was scary, I didn't have a clue how to ride it. The first time I went out on it was really weird, you wouldn't have survived doing it today as there was much less traffic in those days. We went to Skegness shortly afterwards and I think to myself, how the hell did we get there and back in one piece? I had absolutely no sense of how to use the road.'

And it wasn't just about learning how to ride. It was about learning how to ride looking incredibly cool. 'To look good, we always used to ride right at the front of the seat and then lean back,' explains Chris. 'And of course, nobody wore helmets in those days. I had the mirrors and all that but I remember Otis, who played for Hal C Blake, he had a beautiful Vespa with chrome side panels and loads of mirrors. That's where you could spend your money if you had it.'

While it was all kicking off between the mods and the rockers on the south coast, Chris and his friends would instead make the shorter journey to the east coast and Leicester by the Sea. 'It would have took us 2–3 hours to get to Skeggy, I remember one day we went and got absolutely soaked, it was awful. There would have been about six of us, it wasn't like today when hundreds would set off. Once, we were in the parade ballroom and I could feel that something was going to kick off and all of a sudden these glasses came flying over, they came from the Nottingham lads. The smallest thing could have set it off, it didn't take much.'

The rivalry with the lads from Nottingham was not kept exclusively for Skegness beach. 'We used to go to Nottingham a lot because it was fairly local,' said Chris. 'You had to be careful where you went and what you said though because of the Leicester/Nottingham thing that was going on, as it still is today. I remember a load of Nottingham mods came over to Leicester one Sunday and there was a huge chase through the marketplace which led to a massive scrap. On bank holidays, we'd join up with the lads from Skegness, Boston and Lincoln and take them on.'

The Leicester mod scene was big and for a lot of people, the epicentre was Silver Street. 'It was probably Leicester's answer to Carnaby Street,' said Chris. 'You had Irish, The Gear Shop and other small clothes shops plus the Il Rondo, The Antelope and The

Churchill. Everybody used to go to The Churchill first to pick up some doobs before going over to the Rondo. They'd have bands on including Steam Packet, Julie Driscoll and a young piano player by the name of Reg Dwight, although we didn't know at the time he would become Elton John.'

Chris and his fellow mods would hang out at The Cadina coffee bar on Belvoir Street, where they used to park their scooters up on the opposite side, and the Kenco Coffee House on Granby Street which, up until recently, was also the site of the much-missed City Gallery. 'The Kenco used to stay open until late so we were there most of the time, it was full of mods,' said Chris. 'The Granby, which was a dance hall, was another great mod hangout, it was at the top of Burtons on the corner of Churchgate. The Green Bowler on Churchgate itself was originally a coffee shop but then they opened a room upstairs as a music venue. It would stay open until three in the morning so you used to get a lot of townies in there, they were a bit older and a bit more upper-class than us. The Palais was another big mod venue, it would nearly always end in a fight though.' No change there then …

As is the case today, Leicester during the 1960s was a culturally diverse city. When the local black kids began to mix into the mod scene, there was a general feeling of unity, mainly brought about by the shared passion of mod related music and fashion. 'A lot of them joined the mod scene,' said Chris. 'It caused a bit of friction with some people but mainly we were all singing from the same hymn sheet, we all respected each other. At the end of the day, it was all about the clothes and the music and they were all suited and booted like the rest of us. And they hated the rockers, which was a bonus.'

As with any youth culture, when it comes to fashion and grooming, there are places to go and be seen. The Leicester mods were no different. 'Everyone would try and outdo each other with the amount of buttons and vents you had on your suit,' said Chris. 'And it had to be made to measure. If you had it made at Jacksons on Gallowtree Gate then it was seen as better than having it made at Burtons, it was considered to be a bit classier. The queues outside both stores on a Saturday morning would be massive, guys either picking something up that had been ordered or waiting to be measured up for something. I wasn't a suit boy myself, I was more into Ben Sherman and Levi's, I wanted to feel comfortable. I'd get them from Irish and The Gear Shop, there was a real distinction between different styles.' Ron's on Churchgate was the main place to go to have your haircut. 'In fact, some would say it was the only place to go,' admits Chris. 'A lot of mods would come into town to get a haircut from Ron's because it was seen as cool to not only be there but to tell people you had been there. It's still there today.'

As seen on *Quadrophenia*, which Chris believes paints a pretty accurate picture of mod life during the sixties, there were a lot of house parties, some of which could last an entire weekend. 'Once it had got about that someone's parents had gone away for the weekend, it usually ended up in a party,' said Chris. 'Unlike *Quadrophenia*, though, I can't recall us ever trashing a house, we always used to respect where we were, although I suspect it used to happen. You'd usually find that there was something going on at a weekend via word of mouth, there were no mobiles or social media then.'

A lot of the house parties and all-night dances, in particular those at The Nite Owl, were fuelled by amphetamines. 'The whole drug thing was quite big within the mod scene, especially at weekends when you'd finished work for the week,' said Chris. 'Beer wasn't really seen as cool so we hardly ever touched it. I wasn't keen on acid, only took it the once, it intensified colours but that was about it. A friend of mine took it once and afterwards he said he couldn't get in the car because it was too small. As far as he was concerned, it had turned into a toy one and there was no way he could open the door and get in.'

Mods would take amphetamines for stimulation and alertness, as opposed to the intoxicating effect of alcohol. If the plan was to stay up all night, alcohol would have had the opposite effect and probably bring an evening, and the long-awaited weekend, to an early close. 'You'd try and get blues first with dexies as a second choice,' said Chris. 'We used to get eight blues or ten dexies for a quid, which would last you the night. The blues were great because it had phenobarbital in them, whereas dexies were an amphetamine. You took the blues first, the barbiturate would kick in and you'd feel really calm and then after twenty or so minutes, the amphetamine would kick in and you'd have such a smooth high. Dexies on the other hand would just give you a high with a horrible comedown.'

Spotting those that were 'blocked' wasn't hard, their eyes would give it away as would the fact that they would probably be constantly chewing. And while the Blue Beat Club on Conduit Street was the place to get your ten-bob cannabis deals, The Churchill was the place for amphetamines. 'There would always be someone in there flogging them,' said Chris. 'You knew who the faces were that were selling them. A mate of mine used to deal a bit and he'd got this massive bag of dex and he said to us, "Come on, let's go to Skeggy." We took them on the way there and we had a great night but it was terrible coming back, we were being sick all the time. You wouldn't drink with them as it would slow it down a bit and you'd have to eat chewing gum because your mouth would be going ten to the dozen. You'd end up chewing your tongue.'

Demand for the drugs led to some pretty drastic methods to ensure a supply. 'I remember that Timothy Whites was turned over once,' said Chris. 'They lowered a guy through the skylight on a rope and smashed into the cabinet, they got away with thousands of pills. A lot of chemists were being done during this time because the pills were worth such a lot of money on the street. The people who worked in the drug factories used to sell them on as well.'

Throughout the lifespan of mod culture, with its changing styles, fashions and music, there was to be one consistent: the ongoing rivalry with those pesky rockers. 'I remember being at The Casino one Sunday night and there were two rockers in there,' said Chris. 'I thought "bleddy hell, they're asking for it". Two mods went up to them and accused one of them of hitting their mate, which he denied all knowledge of. Then one of the mods smacked this rocker and he went flying. The guy picked himself off of the floor and the pair of them left. About half an hour later, everybody ran to the balcony – there were loads of rockers coming up London Road on their bikes, heading towards The Casino. The bouncers locked the door and the mods started chucking bottles and glasses at them from the balcony – we had high point advantage! I don't know how we got out of there in one piece, I think we left by the back door eventually.'

While the mods seemed to have taken over the city centre venues, the rockers would base themselves outside of the city in cafés on Frog Island, Braunstone Gate and Humberstone Road. 'We'd end up looking for each other,' said Chris. 'It was all a bit cat and dog to be honest. We were down the Green Bowler one night and there was a rumour that the rockers were coming down and it was all going to kick off. Loads of them turned up. We got locked in there as well.'

In 1966, Chris, along with Graham Morris, Jimmy Rose, Dave Smith and Paul Wolloff, formed Cert X (later to be called Vfranie), a mod band influenced by the Small Faces, Motown and Chris's heroes, The Who. 'I remember once we played at the Grand Ballroom in Coalville, it was a great place to play,' said Chris. 'We had to rush back afterwards so that we could see The Who, we'd still got our stage gear on by the time we got there. The guy at the door asked us if we were with the Joe Cocker Band so we said yes, and we got in for free. All of the mods were in there, it was a fantastic atmosphere, and this huge fight kicked off. On another occasion they played there, the stage was across the hall instead of facing down. The bar was behind us and John Entwistle, who was wearing a Union Jack jacket, and Pete Townshend came to the bar. Someone asked John if they could have his jacket and he told them to f**k off. They played the Granby Halls on a number of occasions, we went to see them every time.'

On another occasion, The Who played a short-lived gig at Leicester University. 'It was full of old rockers,' recalls Chris. 'Daltrey dedicated "Summertime Blues" to them and some guy threw a bottle and it hit Townshend on the head. He got his guitar and whacked the guy out. The gig finished there and then, Townshend was taken to hospital needing stitches.'

Alas, all good things must come to an end and the mods were no exception. 'Because the bands were changing, The Beatles, the Stones, et cetera, the fans moved with it,' said Chris. 'And that was the same for the mods, a lot of the acts went psychedelic.' A year on from the Summer of Love in '67, the psychedelic scene had gone. Like punk in 1976/77, once it had established itself and became mainstream, it morphed into something completely different. And Chris went with it. 'By 1967, I had the long hair and was wearing more flamboyant clothes but by 1969, after I moved to Skegness to work on the donkeys, I got into the skinhead scene, as did a lot of other casually dressed mods. The clothes were very similar, Ben Sherman and Sta-Prest trousers for example. The hair came off, either a number two or three, and I swapped my brothel creepers for Doc Martin boots.'

After three years in Skegness, Chris came back to Leicester in 1972 and got married a year later. 'I took up hairdressing in 1974, I took a course at the Government Training Centre on Humberstone Gate and have been doing it ever since. Paul Coles, the drummer with Vfranie, did the same course about six months later, he went on to work for Stag Hairdressers. I opened up my own place on Northampton Street and have been here ever since.'

It's interesting how with certain people, the essence of being a mod never goes away. And Chris Busby is definitely one of them. Paul Weller once said, 'I'm still a mod, I'll always be a mod, you can bury me a mod,' and I think that ethos would apply to Chris – he's still just as happy wearing his Levi's and Ben Shermans today as he was back in the sixties. 'The sixties was a great time, I loved my teenage years,' said Chris. 'When I walk past certain places I get a bit nostalgic, I think about all the good times we had there, especially if I hear some music from the time as well. Every song has a memory and it can set me off sometimes, all those ghosts from the past. For me, it all came to an end when I was twenty-three and got married. But I put so much into my life from fourteen onwards, experienced so many things, being a mod, being in a band, moving to Skegness, it didn't really matter. It still doesn't.'

The Farinas, The Roaring Sixties & Family

'We could have been The Beatles when we walked on that stage. I've never experienced anything like it, it sent a shiver down my spine, still does now …' **Harry Ovenall**

Formed in 1962, James King and the Farinas were Jim King (lead vocals, harp and later saxophone), Charlie Whitney (lead guitar, vocals), Tim Kirchin (bass) and Harry Ovenall (drums). Later that year, the band would shorten their name to The Farinas. Their story, like a lot of bands at the time, starts at Leicester Art College. 'I went to Stamford School, which was a public school,' said Harry Ovenall. 'I wanted to go to art college but I'd only got two O levels in art and general science. My art tutor wrote to Leicester Art College and told them that I was the best student that he'd ever had and they accepted me. By this time, though, I'd also started playing the drums so I'd got ideas in that direction as well. If I'd not gone there, I wouldn't have met Charlie or Jim so that was a big event in my life.'

At college, Harry met Charlie Whitney and Jim King. 'I was already in a couple of groups in Peterborough, The Teen Beats and The Monarchs. Another drummer would take my place if I couldn't make it.' Because the entire nation at the time appeared to be gripped by The Shadows, The Teen Beats fashioned their stage names around frontman Hank B. Marvin. 'I was Harry J. Vincent,' said Harry. 'We had Tiny B. Arthur on guitar, Rod Hurricane on vocals and Jess T. Claymore on bass. Our engineer was called Alias Black Jansen.'

Prior to The Farinas, Charlie and Harry formed a band with Tony Bart called Tony Bart and the Revels. 'I remember seeing Charlie at Great Glen,' said Harry. 'He was starting to play with other people, their drummer had an Eric Delaney plastic side drum on a stand. As soon as they knew that I had a proper kit, that was it, I was in. When Tony Bart joined, we became a Cliff Richard type of band. Tony then decided he wanted to do something else, he joined a band called The Strangers, so Jim King joined us. Jim was with us at art college, we thought he was a bit of a show-off, he was always going on about how much kit he had. He made out that he had all of these amps at home that we could only dream of. Of course, he hadn't – all he had was a little Vox amp.' With Birstall-born Tim Kirchin now on bass, the only thing left for the band to do was to find a new name. 'I went to the college library and picked out a book on design,' said Harry. 'I opened it at random and stuck my finger in what turned out to be a section about the Italian car designers, Pininfarina. That was it, we became James King and the Farinas.'

In 1962, the band recorded an EP at the Victor Buckland Sound Studios in Derby. 'John Brown of the Irish Manufacturing Company and his wife, Viv, got together with us,' explains Harry. 'We had this idea of making our own record. We recorded our own composition, "All You Gotta Do", and covers of "Twist and Shout" and "Bye Bye Johnny".' The band continued to develop their blues based R&B sound. 'We were English boys brought up on Cliff Richard who thought we could sing the blues,' said Harry. 'We used to go to the De Montfort Hall to see all of the bluesmen, we were absolutely blown over by the lot of them. We were heavily into Ray Charles. His album, *Ray Charles in Person*, was like our bible. We were totally into our music, a bit snobbish with it really, but it worked with what we did.'

Turning professional in 1963, The Farinas played gigs across the Midlands, London and also The Cavern in Liverpool. According to the website, Family Bandstand, in 1963 James King and the Farinas played The Marcam Hall, Cambridge, followed in 1964 by the Mayor's Charity Ball at Tamworth Castle, twice at The Assembly Rooms in Tamworth (supporting Roy Stuart and the Cyclones and The Trentside Four respectively) and again at The Marcam Hall in Cambridge. They also played the 100 Club in Soho supporting The Pretty Things and The Graham Bond Organisation. 'We used to pay for an insert in the club guide of the *Melody Maker* ourselves, that way people could see that we were very much a gigging band,' said Harry. 'I've still got a list of some of the gigs we did, we were working so hard. We'd do a gig somewhere and then come back and do an all-nighter somewhere else. We tried to make ourselves famous – there were no Simon Cowells in those days – although if a manager liked you, you'd almost become his pet and potentially he could have spent a fortune on you.'

A gig that Harry will never forget is one held at the Dorchester Hotel in London for the children of American servicemen who were based in the UK. 'We could have been The Beatles when we walked on that stage,' recalls Harry. 'I've never experienced anything like it, it sent a shiver down my spine, still does now. I actually thought, do they think we're somebody else? Every number brought the house down. The Americans really knew how to get the best out of anyone, they made you feel very welcome and when you hit a high note, they'd go mad.'

The 'look' of The Farinas at this time was similar to many bands of that era.

'There's an early picture of us wearing light blue, mohair jumpers, grey trousers and white shoes, that was taken towards the end of the Cliff Richard thing,' said Harry. 'John Brown from The Irish supplied us with all of that gear – he still goes in there today. We had handmade pinstriped trousers with cavalier front and braces, shirts and Anello & Davide boots. We found this place on Charing Cross Road where you could buy the boots off the shelf but we had to have ours handmade, unlike The Beatles. They had a book which had different samples of skins, everything from pony to patent. I had blue leather, Jim always had black patent. They were like a Chelsea boot but had a lovely Cuban heel and you could choose either a chisel toe or a flat end. After the pinstriped period, we got into normal, smart clothes that you'd expect blues men to wear on stage.'

In 1964, The Farinas were booked into the Fontana Studios in London to record their only single, 'You'd Better Stop'/'I Like It Like That'. With Jim King on lead vocals, the single was released in August 1964. 'Mim Scala, co-founder of the Scala Browne Agency, arranged for the recording to take place,' explains Harry. 'At the time, everything we did were covers except for "All You Gotta Do". I was in a record shop at the top of High Street in Leicester and I saw this 45 on the Jamie label. I'd never heard of it before, it was called "You'd Better Stop". I bought it and we covered it.'

In 1965, Tim Kirchin got married and left the band and nineteen-year-old Ric Grech was asked to join. A bass player, Grech was also known for his adeptness on the violin and cello. The following year, twenty-four-year-old Roger Chapman was asked to join the band as lead vocalist. Shortly after Chapman arrived, and now a five-piece, The Farinas changed their identity once more by turning into The Roaring Sixties. 'We were desperately looking for a new name,' said Harry. 'At one stage we became Farinas Soul and Roll but that didn't last very long. Because our look was very similar to the era of the roaring twenties, we thought we'd call ourselves The Roaring Sixties.' So far, so good. But then The Ivy League decide to release a single called 'We Love the Pirates' and rename themselves The Roaring Sixties just for that one song. 'We couldn't believe it,' admits Harry. 'It was back to the drawing board to find yet another new name.'

The overall image that The Roaring Sixties were portraying eventually led to them being renamed as The Family. 'It was all about the demob suits,' said Harry. 'At the time, we hired an American Packard car and driver and were driving around London looking like gangsters. We wore the suits all of the time. We were rehearsing in a studio in Gerrards Street and Kim Fowley, who was an American record producer, came by to see us. Because of our look, he said that it looked like a meeting of "The Family", which had Mafia connotations. We really liked it but we didn't change it straight away.'

The striped, demob style suits that The Roaring Sixties had adopted were created in Leicester. 'We found a shop on London's Oxford Street that had loads of stripy suit material that they couldn't sell,' said Harry. 'So we had the lot and took it to a guy on Evington Road and he made us the suits. If you look at the photo of us wearing them, Charlie and Ric are posing with scarves, whilst the rest of us have the smart, cool, American jazz men image, which was what I wanted us to look like. I didn't like the scarves, it was moving into the flower power thing, it just didn't work for me.'

Shortening their name to Family, the band began to tour across the UK. On one occasion, after finishing a gig at the Marquee, the band were summoned to a society party. 'This guy came in and said that Henrietta Guinness wanted to take us to a party,' said Harry. 'So we jumped into a taxi and off we went. It was awful, everyone was prancing around being nice to each other, it was all just so false. I used to hate all of that, it felt like we were her little group of boys.' The band were rubbing shoulders with the likes of Princess Margaret, Lord Snowden, famous models, actors and artists. 'Underneath the veranda was this American guy,' recalls Harry. 'It was pitch black, and he turned around to me and said "Hi". I couldn't see him very well but we started talking to each other – turned out it was James Coburn. He was at the height of his success but it was only afterwards I found out who he was, I didn't know.'

In the late sixties, Family were playing at Sybilla's, probably the most exclusive club in London. 'It was situated on Swallow Street and was the place to be seen, The Beatles used to hang out there,' said Harry. 'We had to get changed in the kitchen because there was no dressing room and I don't think we ever got paid. The waitresses would serve you the classic Scotch and coke in a tall glass with ice. It was a VAT 69 miniature and a bottle of coke on a tray and she would mix it in front of you. All of that would cost you a pound, that's about £18 in today's money. Excluding the white Sarenen furniture, the entire place was blue, including the stage.'

Family were now at the stage where they could think about putting their sound down on vinyl. After a further meeting with Mim Scala in Soho, the band began plans to record their first single. 'At the time, we were totally in love with Jimmy Miller,' said Harry. 'He was the guy who produced Traffic and also Wynder K. Frog's "Green Door" which had a beat that we were totally in to. I asked Mim if he would ask Jimmy Miller to produce the single, even though we didn't know what it was going to be. Mim went off and got John Gilbert, who was the son of Lewis Gilbert, to be our manager and Jimmy Miller as producer.' Later that year, Family signed to the Liberty record label and released their first single, 'Scene Through the Eyes of a Lens'/'Gypsy Woman'. Produced by Miller, the single also included Steve Winwood and other members of Traffic. However, Harry would leave the band before the single was released in September 1967. 'Because of the emergence of the flower power scene, I didn't like the way it was going. We'd played blues based music all the way through the sixties and done so well out of it and then suddenly it all changed. When we had the meeting at the House of Happiness, they said to me that my heart wasn't in it any more and it wasn't. We'd stopped playing the real music, the stuff that we'd enjoyed playing, and I was concerned about the direction we were going. So I lost it and walked out. Thank God I did because I don't think I would have survived.' Harry was replaced by Legay drummer, Rob Townsend. Family went on to record seven studio albums before calling it a day in 1973. They played their final concert at Leicester Polytechnic on 13 October of the same year.

The music that Harry was loath to depart from, the blues based R&B that was the trademark of The Farinas, was probably best encapsulated by the enigma that is Jim King. Jim left Family in 1969. He died in 2012. 'To this day, I can't believe how good a frontman he turned into,' said Harry. 'The sound we were getting at the time was incredible and it was all down to Jim on the harmonica. We had this thing where we could play both the maracas and the harmonica at the same time, a bit like Bo Diddley. He was a great singer and looked good – if you look at the early pictures of The Farinas, we would wear smart suits, he looked a bit posh. He was one of the last people in the world though that you would think would be a good blues harp player.'

Born in Kettering, Jim King lived at home with his parents on Argyle Street before departing for Leicester Art College. 'As with all of us, the music took over and we left a year early to turn professional,' said Harry. 'When we hit hard times, I became a driver for the TA and Jim worked at Lewis.' He took up playing the sax, he became obsessed with Sonny Boy Williamson. He had a natural talent for it, he had that special thing that the bluesmen have, a certain sharp tone when they suck out. The sax is such a difficult instrument to learn but within a year Jim had mastered it, it completely took him over.'

In the late 1970s/early 1980s, Harry used to run an antique stall near Wellingborough and had to drive through Kettering to get there. 'One day I had a phone call from Jim asking me to stop by his place, he'd had an idea about starting up a Jacques Loussier-style trio. He warned me though that he didn't want to talk about Family or the old days. He was living in his parents' house, they'd recently passed away, so I don't think he really needed much to get by. We went upstairs into a room and it was packed out with Yamaha saxophones, they all looked brand new. He put this music on and started to play. You'd never heard anything like it, I thought he was having me on. So I asked him to play it again and it was exactly the same, note for note. He was being serious. I was with the Brass Foundry at the time so I said I was committed to them and that it wasn't for me. That was the last time I saw him.'

The story of Jim King is surrounded by tales of eccentricity, his talent as a musician and his unquestionable place in the hierarchy of Leicester music legends. 'He started to get a little bit eccentric around about 1967,' said Harry. 'In the end, I think he had to leave Family because it was becoming a bit impractical. He was really into what he was doing and because Family didn't want him any more, he became totally immersed with himself. He got involved in a couple of projects, a bit of session work here and there, but he wasn't playing with anybody at all when I met him at his house in Kettering. But he had these great plans of forming this jazz trio. I spoke to him a couple of times afterwards but he'd gone, he was living in his own world.'

Today, Harry looks back with great affection on how it all began for him. 'It all started so simply for me. A guitarist at a youth club I went to in Peterborough back in about 1956 asked me if I fancied playing the washboard. They didn't actually have one so I ended up playing the draining board instead. Then somehow it progressed to me playing the saucepans and the whole drumming thing came from that – a set of saucepans. I eventually retired from playing the drums on New Year's Eve in 1986 although I still take part in the odd reunion whenever they come up. The thing about the sixties was that it was so "now", it was all about what we could do or create today in our band. They really were marvellous times.'

Clothes, Make-Up & Going Out

'People would drive past and honk their car horns at me, I don't think they could believe what I was wearing. In a way, I'd quietly enjoy the reaction, whether it was good or bad. The main thing was that I got a reaction and a response to what I was wearing, to what I had made.' **Mal Lawrence**

In the 1960s, if the girls wanted to wear something that was different to what was available on the high street, they would either take a trip down to London or make it themselves. Today's appetite to be a Primark lookalike wasn't the case back then – originality was generally both encouraged and applauded. It also helped if your mum worked in the hosiery trade and had a sewing machine …

Mal Lawrence was fifteen when she left school, taking up a job as a switchboard operator at the Co-op bakery. After leaving there, she went to work for a Leicester fabric manufacturer. By 1966, aged sixteen, the sister of Legay's John Knapp emerged onto Leicester's thriving mod scene. 'We all used to meet up in coffee bars, the Cadina in particular,' recalls Mal. 'At the time, John and Rod Read were big players on the mod scene, they used to jump on the train to London and get their clothes from Carnaby Street. Because of that, and the fact that they also used to go down to Brighton for the clashes between the mods and the rockers, they were held in such high esteem.'

At the time, Mal didn't have much of an awareness of fashion, instead she opted to watch and observe what everyone else was wearing, in particular John and Rod. 'I'd try to copy it but in a feminine way. One particular outfit I used to wear, which they had similar masculine versions of, was a navy top which was made in what we would probably refer to today as slightly thicker T-shirt material. It had big, bold stripes on it and was accompanied by wide, cream coloured trousers. They were huge at the bottom, they'd swing around with every step taken.'

Mal's people-watching at the Cadina led to a couple of rather odd observations. 'I remember that there were one or two couples who would dress the same, they'd wear exactly the same thing. In any generation that was a bizarre thing to do but there were a few people who would do that. There were also a few couples who stood out as being particularly precise with regards to what they were wearing, you knew they were together because their appearance was a variation of a theme. Their clothes were smartly cut, the girl's make-up would be perfect and there wasn't a hair out of place between them.'

Mal and her friends were the first generation to emerge from the war that had taken total control of their own lives. Although Leicester, like many other cities, had its limitations, most young people of that time were working in either the hosiery, boot and shoe or textile factories earning, and enjoying, good wages. For the first time, music, fashion, life itself belonged to them, it had nothing to do with their parents, grandparents or the war. They were the generation that actively fought against the moulds that their parents had made for them. 'Our expectations became a lot higher,' said Mal. 'Before, during and after the war you accepted "your lot" and you accepted the limitations that were out there. Once we got past the war and the rationing, our generation were almost like flower buds, we were awakening to the realisation that we could do anything we wanted. We didn't have to be told what to do, we didn't want to be told what to do or conform to any rules and regulations.' It was from this attitude that the fashion of the day developed – the younger generation were becoming increasingly bored with what was on offer. 'Out of the utilitarian choices that were available through the war and a few years after, we wanted colour, brightness and vibrancy and that came out in the fabrics and the designs. We weren't happy to live like our parents had lived and it exploded. Most eras develop slowly whereas this was one big explosion, it changed so fast. Unfortunately, a lot of people got lost along the way because it was too much, too soon.'

As with most young women of the time, Mal aligned herself to the designs created by Mary Quant. Quant was a key player within the UK mod and youth fashion scene and is famed for popularising the miniskirt. Her designs were a combination of simple shapes and strong, vibrant colours, the nemesis of post-war fashions. She encouraged young people to dress for fun and for any occasion. 'Mary Quant was quite revolutionary in her designs, as was Barbara Hulanicki for BIBA,' said Mal. 'Julia Read, Rod's girlfriend, was also into the Quant look, she was very prim and petite and always perfectly dressed.'

The influence of Quant, and a strongly growing attraction to Vogue designs, led Mal to start designing and making her own clothes. 'By now I was heavily into fashion so I had a lot of ideas floating around in my head. I would look out for materials that were different and which couldn't be found in shops. I used to get most of my fabrics from Leicester Market, it was a lot bigger then with a lot more choice. If I couldn't find it on the market, I'd go to Lewis's, they had a fabulous fabric department.'

Whenever possible, Mal would buy Vogue patterns. They would include a dress label that stated either 'Vogue Design' or 'A Vogue Design by …' which would include the name of the appropriate designer. These labels could be cut out and sewn into the outfit. Most of the time, however, Mal would design her own clothes, creating her own bespoke range of outfits, expressing herself via colour, fabric and style. 'I took great pleasure from sketching out ideas and coming to a final design. I'd put a bit of myself into the design so I knew I was in there. The longer I got into creating and wearing my own designs the more I didn't think about it so much, it brought out the person I was. I was never confident or outgoing but the reaction I would get to what I was wearing would boost my confidence. It was almost as though I'd become another person, a completely different character and persona. And I liked being that person.' Mal would hardly ever use a set pattern, opting to join together a few to make the design she wanted. 'If I wanted to make a coat, for example, I'd get a basic pattern for size and shape and then I'd cut it up. If I wanted to set in a stripe, I'd add on to the side to create this new shape. If I wanted the sleeves to come down into a tulip or a bell shape, I'd take the basic sleeve and cut it from the elbow down. My mum was a great help with this because she had always worked in the hosiery trade so she knew what to do.' Some of the outfits Mal wanted to design didn't have a pattern so her mum would help if it became too complicated. 'She would say that she had to have something to go by and then we would look at the Vogue patterns, find something I liked and then we would adapt it. But for some designs, we would work it out together. With Mum's help, a coat for example would take about a week, because I'd have to line everything with a satin lining, it needed to hang properly and look right.'

Whatever Mal wore couldn't be bought in the shops, it was completely bespoke based on an idea that she'd had. 'People would drive past and honk their car horns at me, I don't think they could believe what I was wearing. They probably thought I looked stupid but I didn't care because it was my design and that's how I wanted to look. In a way, I'd quietly enjoy the reaction, whether it was good or bad. The main thing was that I got a reaction and a response to what I was wearing, to what I had made. I guess it was quite a brave thing to do at the time but it didn't particularly bother me because I knew I was a bit different when it came to fashion.'

Occasionally, Mal would have an idea, make it up and then later on would see an element of her design incorporated into somebody else's. 'I certainly wasn't influencing anyone, I just felt that because I was designing and making clothes for myself, maybe I was picking up on ideas before they were being mass produced. That was a huge boost for my confidence.'

In general, when it came to clothes, there were the girls who would buy from the shops and those who would make their own. 'If you wanted to buy clothes off the shelf, you'd go to somewhere like C&A because the larger department stores would be too expensive,' said Mal. 'The girls who bought their clothes would sometimes stare at you because you were looking completely different, they didn't understand what you were wearing. It was accepted though because, ultimately, they didn't want to look like you, they were happy with what they were wearing. They accepted the fact that you looked different.'

Apart from a few fashion faux pas, Mal always tried to look as though she was wearing quality clothing, a basic rule that went back to the days of being a mod. Even if she made it herself, the outfit had to make a statement. And on one Saturday night, she certainly achieved just that. 'I was going meet this guy so in the morning, I went into town and bought some green velvet material and a pair of green tights and a green see-through top. Out of the velvet material, I made a miniskirt which was about 12–18 inches in length. I made it, lined it and wore it in the evening. I must have looked awful but it was what I wanted to wear on that particular day. I don't think I wore it again after that though!'

While Mal Lawrence was making her own clothes with the help of her mum, Helen Garner, from Fleckney, took another direction. 'Because I could never get what I wanted I used to have my clothes made for me by a lady called Mrs Flowers, she was a professional dressmaker,' recalls Helen. 'Everything had to match – shoes, boots, everything. I'd buy a pattern and Mrs Flowers would adapt it for me. She made me a powder blue corduroy skirt – my dad used to call it a belt – and a fitted jacket. I couldn't find any boots to match it so I dyed a pair I already had along with some ribbons for my hair. On another occasion, I remember going to London and getting a pair of white, lace-up boots, they were completely different to what was available in Leicester. I came back, bought some white leather material and asked Mrs Flowers to make me a fitted jacket and skirt to go with them. She used to charge me 10/- a dress, I think the most she ever charged was 11/6.'

On one occasion, when Helen went to see Legay, she wanted something different, something in red, and she knew she wasn't going to be able to buy it in the shops. 'I couldn't go and see them wearing the same outfit as last time so I went into Leicester on the Midland Red bus, bought the material and some dye, and took them up to

Mrs Flowers. I asked her to make me a plain red, short fitted dress with zips at the side. In those days, having a zip at the side was unusual and I can remember the poor woman looking at me gone out. I took the material to her at 3.00 p.m. and by 7.00 p.m., I was wearing it. In between, I'd dyed my boots and left them outside to dry with strict instructions that no one could move them!'

Getting ready to go out could take anything between one and two hours. If you were out with your girlfriends, then the chances were that between you, you'd probably decide beforehand what you were all going to wear, mostly depending on where you were going. After the outfit for the night had been decided, there was the make-up to apply, an art in itself that required a very steady hand. 'The eye make-up was almost painted on with a heavy black eyeliner on the top and bottom, it really was quite thick,' explains Mal. 'Then you painted white onto the top of your eyes and then either a dark blue or grey line around the eye socket. After that, you'd apply a thick line of eyeliner, mascara or false eyelashes and then thick mascara on your bottom lashes. You'd finish it all off with heavy foundation. It used to take hours but it's what we had to do before we went to a gig or for a night out.' Mal had picked up her eye make-up style from John Knapp's girlfriend, Linda. 'She'd been doing it like that for such a long time. Later on, I learned how to adapt it to my style. I don't think I wore the false eyelashes though, I wore eyeliner instead.'

Unlike today, there weren't any celebrity perfumes available during the 1960s, choices were mainly restricted to the likes of Tweed, L'amour, 4711 and An Evening in Paris, the latter being another legacy from the Second World War. The Chanel perfumes were available but were out of the price range of most young people. The majority of perfumes could be bought from department stores such as Morgan & Squires, Lewis's, Marshall & Snelgrove and Simpkin & James, places where ladies used to lunch, still wearing their leather gloves and handbags, a remarkable remnant of post-war Britain. 'Traditionally, you would have your perfume bought for you at Christmas and when it had gone, it had gone,' said Mal. 'But now, because we were working, we had a bit of extra cash available so we could go out and buy some more. The more that people went out to work and earned, the more disposable income they had to spend on nice things.' The availability of perfume was, like most commodities at the time, be it fashion, furniture or food, beginning to develop and evolve. 'We expected more choice so we were given more choice,' said Mal. 'There was a youth market evolving, the first generation after the war that was coming of age. We'd entered an extremely revolutionary period where everything had changed or was changing.' One perfume in particular, Estée Lauder's Youth Dew, had become extremely popular, probably because it had become more affordable to the younger generation. 'Nearly everyone was wearing it,' said Mal. 'I used to buy that and all of Estée Lauder's associated cosmetics, including shampoo and bubble bath. I could afford it because I was working and still living at home. Our wages provided us with our first taste of freedom and sophistication and Estée Lauder certainly provided you with the latter.' Youth Dew might also have benefitted from coming with a health warning. 'It wasn't everybody's favourite,' remembers Helen. 'It was a very heavy fragrance, if you put too much on you could get a terrible headache.'

Depending on the day of the week, most girls would head into Leicester and to the various venues that were scattered around the city centre, including the Il Rondo, Nite Owl and Casino. 'Leicester was a really vibrant, exciting place to be,' said Mal. 'It didn't have the London buzz but then again, nowhere else had either. Not many people had cars back then so once you were ready, we'd get the bus into town, picking friends up on the way. Afterwards, we'd all walk back to St Margaret's Bus Station together and get the last bus back to Birstall, the Midland Red L85. I'd get the bus with Ray Read and if I had to get off on the Loughborough Road, he would always walk me home. It was well out of his way but there was no way he would let me walk back on my own. You knew that if you were with Ray, you were safe, he would always look after you. He wasn't afraid to take anybody on.'

While drugs were readily available in Leicester, it's surprising how few girls used to take them. 'I never used to touch drugs,' said Helen. 'Actually, I never used to drink much either, if I did it used to be a gin and orange and that would last me all night. There was a lot of speed and purple hearts available but it never interested me, I never needed it, I was always happy and on a high anyway. There were lots of people who didn't touch drugs, especially the girls, I think it's been made to look like a big thing when in fact it wasn't.' Mal Lawrence: 'Drugs were there for everybody to try but it really didn't interest me nor my friends. In fact, most of the time I wasn't aware of what was going on, I was a bit naïve in that respect. I didn't mix heavily with the people that were into that particular scene although I do recall that drugs were very easy to come by.'

The 1960s were pivotal in the development of both Helen Garner and Mal Lawrence's personality and characters, the mod-related qualities of the time shaped the way they would look, think and be. Inspired by the likes of Mary Quant and BIBA, both women demonstrated a creative flair to the fashion of the time, in particular with regards to creating their own bespoke designs, either with the help of their mum or the unflappable Mrs Flowers. For Mal, the sixties represent a time of change, togetherness and a unique feeling that you were at the centre of something rather special. 'I've always said that whoever lived through this period was very lucky, the sixties was an awakening of a generation and it formed the basis of what my life is today. I still try to wear nice clothes, it's something that I've carried over from the sixties, John's the same. By talking about it today, I hadn't realised just how much of the mod way of thinking, in particular with regards to fashion, was still relevant in my life. It's quite revealing, it hadn't occurred to me at all.' The wartime generation, the parents and grandparents of the sixties generation, always believed that the camaraderie, the closeness of the community during the conflict, was the best ever. 'But that's how close everyone was in the sixties, we were always looking out for each other,' explains Mal. 'Every day was exciting, there was always something new happening, you felt you could do anything. Everything seemed to have a special aura about it, mainly because we were all doing it together, we were all discovering new things together. I'm convinced that we were all very aware that we were playing a part in something special, it was completely alien to what our parents had done so we knew it was all new. It was a remarkable time – I wouldn't have missed it for the world.'

Kenny Wilson

'It's been said that if you can remember the sixties you weren't there. I've got the opposite problem. I can remember so much I can't see how I managed to fit it all in. I have lots of separate memories of things but I have a job working out the chronology.'
Kenny Wilson

Kenny Wilson, guitarist, singer/songwriter and film-maker, was born in 1951 in Knighton, Leicester. His mother loved listening to music, in particular the Bakelite wireless with its extension speaker in the other room. 'She liked to play it loud as she did the housework so my early years consisted of listening to light orchestral music played at a deafening level. I loved it though, it became the soundtrack of my life.' Kenny's next-door neighbours, members of the Salvation Army who played in a brass band, were very supportive of him when he first got into playing music. 'Most of the people I knew didn't play anything. I think they saw it as a luxury they couldn't afford. If it didn't bring money in then it wasn't worth doing.'

By the time Kenny left Avenue Road Junior School, pop music was making an impact on his life, even though he didn't have a record player nor could afford to buy records. 'It was at this time I learnt a skill I thought everyone had but now realise they don't,' said Kenny. 'I could memorise a whole record and play it back in my head. At times, I even managed to "improve" on it and preferred my virtual version to the original.' Having failed his eleven-plus exam, in 1962, Kenny went to Lancaster Boys School. 'I didn't feel like a failure, in fact I was glad to be going there. It was a new school in nice grounds and there was a girl's school next door that proved significant in later years.' Lancaster Boys was given the remit to get its pupils to pass exams and had one of the highest pass rates in the city by the mid-1960s, including the grammar schools. 'The official school leaving age at that time was fifteen and passing the eleven-plus didn't guarantee success,' said Kenny. 'Lancaster Boys was seen as a good school and I enjoyed being there.' In the first few weeks of the new term, pupils were given the opportunity to play a musical instrument. 'We could try all sorts of instruments: trombones, cornets, clarinets, euphonium. It was great fun,' said Kenny. 'I decided on clarinet because at that time there was a big hit by Acker Bilk called "Stranger on the Shore". I was obviously still heavily influenced by light orchestral music!' Lancaster had a school wind band run by a visiting band

Chris Busby, learning to play the guitar.

Chris Busby, on the road again.

The Roaring Sixties.

Kenny Wilson, late sixties.

Hank, a student friend of Kenny Wilson 'who didn't seem to attend many lectures.'

The Beatniks.

Rob Townsend, The Beatniks. 'After every gig he used to be completely knackered. I don't know why, he's only a drummer.'

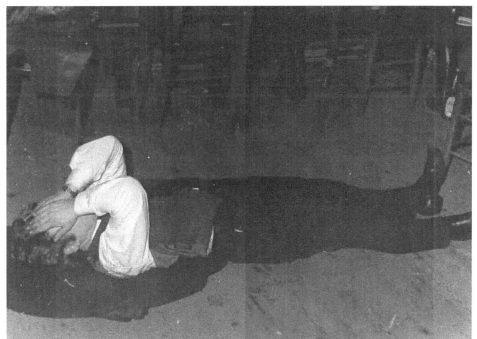

Hal C. Blake.

Hal C. Blake.

The Nite Owl - Jimmy James and the Vagabonds.

The Nite Owl - Zoot Money.

master, Mr J. Ord Hume, a relative of a famous military band composer. 'We didn't have actual lessons but he showed us the basics and then we just learnt on the job,' recalls Kenny. 'He showed us the music and we learnt the notes and he shouted at us if we got it wrong. He did his own arrangements with some really easy parts so anyone could be part of the band right from the start. Then there were more difficult parts as you got better. It actually sounded very good and set me on my path as a musician.'

In 1963, the intense fan frenzy that was Beatlemania struck and life was never the same again. 'This was the watershed, it opened up the floodgates of new possibilities,' explains Kenny. 'This was when youth was liberated from the conformity of the past and I lost interest in light orchestral music. With the emergence of the Rolling Stones shortly afterwards, I became a total convert and spent most of my time singing or playing records over and over in my mind until they actually became a part of me. I wasn't a passive consumer, I was living it.' Kenny had a problem though. Although he understood perfectly what was happening, he didn't know how it was done. 'I had no access to the instruments used in pop music and my music theory was poor. When I discovered how chords worked it was an epiphany: "So that's how you do it – you play chords and sing along to them!" Once I worked that out there was no looking back. It took quite a while to reach that point though.'

Nineteen sixty-five was a significant year for Kenny. Now a teenager, he was also part of a wider subculture; the mods and the rockers. 'I was on the periphery of both although I tended towards the mods. The rocker connection was that I attended the Avenue Road Youth Club, which was a rocker stronghold. They were quite impressive with their powerful bikes and reckless ways. I can remember them doing speed trials around Avenue Road and Bulwer Road where occasionally one them would crash into a wall. They were a bit moronic but I liked their macho swagger, leather jackets and studded belts.' The mod connection at this time was more by association. Although Kenny and his friends were aware of what was happening, they were too young to go to the clubs and coffee bars frequented by the mods. Instead, their time was spent hanging around in parks, the town and getting up to mischief, including casual shoplifting, illegally travelling on trains and performing dangerous dares, mainly on building sites and railway lines. They were on the outside looking in, absorbing mod culture in every detail. 'The mother of my best friend at the time had a hair salon on Queens Road,' said Kenny. 'She had an apprentice who was a fully-fledged mod with a real scooter and he became a source of information about what was happening and where the best places were, even in London. These stories were passed on with a sense of awe and wonder that was virtually religious.'

For Kenny, 1965 was one of the best years for music with the release of albums such as *Rubber Soul* and *Highway 61 Revisited* and the singles, 'House of the Rising Sun', 'Mr Tambourine Man', 'My Generation' and 'Like a Rolling Stone'. 'There was also a remarkable string of Beatles hits. I internalised many of the songs at this time to such an extent they have effectively become a part of what I am and I still perform them now.' At this time, singles were the most important format as they were affordable to nearly everyone. In Leicester, the main stores were Brees on Churchgate and Cowlings on Belvoir Street. 'We also listened to the Top 40 on the radio and jukeboxes that could be found in the many caf cafés. We also went roller skating at the Granby Halls on Saturday afternoons where the latest hits were played on a loud PA system.'

In 1966, Kenny became bored with being a delinquent and decided to become an intellectual. 'I wasn't exactly sure what this entailed but I realised that knowledge is power and that if I continued following the path I was on I would end up either in borstal or a boring job.' Kenny started going to the recently opened Phoenix Theatre, which was staging a range of avant-garde plays at the time. 'I was particularly impressed by *Little Malcolm and his Fight Against the Eunuchs*, which I saw several times. I related to Malcolm's rage against normality and mediocrity. I also went to the De Montfort Hall to the classical and jazz concerts, you could get a cheap ticket if you stood at the side. I saw some remarkable events there such as The Modern Jazz Quartet, the Duke Ellington Orchestra and Dave Brubeck, who I watched sitting on the stage just behind where he was playing.' Kenny bought several records cheaply from a Leicester market stall. 'I particularly liked Bix Beiderbecke and still play the records now. I also developed a lifelong love of Louis Armstrong, who I think is the greatest jazz player of all time. I saw Jacques Loussier at De Montfort Hall and found his jazz treatments of Bach pieces quite compelling. All in all, it was a time of growth and awareness for me. I was breaking away from the conformity of the working/lower-middle-class attitudes around me that I found so stifling.'

Kenny had also gained a new set of friends and was old enough to start going out at night. 'The mod thing was still happening and we bought made-to-measure suits from John Collier and fancy shirts and shoes. At this time I was doing three paper rounds so I had a bit of money to spend.' The main venues they went to were The Green Bowler on Churchgate and the Casino Ballroom on London Road. 'This is where I first encountered the local live music scene,' said Kenny. 'When the bands weren't playing, there was a disco. Contrary to what many think is mod music, the majority of records played were soul and bluebeat.'

By 1967, Kenny was working towards taking his O levels. It was also the year of the 'Summer of Love', the hippie social phenomena epitomised by Scott McKenzie's anthem, 'San Francisco (Be Sure to Wear Flowers in Your Hair)'. 'I welcomed it with open arms,' said Kenny. 'It beat the pants off the kind of casual violence that epitomised the mods and rockers. It also felt incredibly liberated. Later that summer, Leicester had its very own "love-in" on Victoria Park. Local poet Terry Wilford read his poems, people strummed guitars and we all felt very clever as the police looked on.'

For many, the hippie explosion was seen purely as a commercial opportunity and many club owners cashed in on it. Alex Barrow closed the Bluebeat Club and opened up the House of Happiness on Campbell Street. The Chicane Club was advertising 'flower power' and a new club opened called the Fifth Dimension. 'There were plenty of people who became known as "weekend hippies",' recalls Kenny. 'They had straight jobs during the week but freaked out at the weekend. But all this misses the point that something actually was happening, attitudes were changing. There was a new autonomy amongst the young and their older sympathisers.' Home-grown businesses started emerging selling alternative clothes and other paraphernalia. The area around Silver Street became a hive of enterprise and alternative culture. An underground press emerged on a national level, most notably with the newspaper, *International Times*, which was distributed clandestinely. 'At this time, the established record companies briefly lost control of their product,' said Kenny. 'The fans and the musicians were calling the tunes and were in control of their own culture. It was a liberating time where, for once, what was best was also the most popular.'

Nineteen sixty-eight was the year that Kenny started playing his own gigs, with blues guitarist Mick Pini being a particular inspiration. 'He had an electric guitar and was the first person I knew who had a Marshall stack. I went back to Mick's house and he demonstrated it to me. As he played, the house started shaking and I thought the window frames were going to fall out, it was monumental.' Kenny was also becoming influenced by avant-garde jazz. In Leicester, records could be borrowed from Goldsmiths Music Library for a small fee. It mainly stocked classical music but they also had a folk and jazz section. 'I was impressed by recordings of Ornette Coleman and Albert Ayler,' said Kenny. 'I decided to dust my clarinet off and start playing free jazz. I found that I could make it sound a bit like an electric lead guitar and I also used it to create weird screaming noises. I got really experimental – I once played the clarinet underwater in the Town Hall Square fountain on one occasion!' Kenny started to write apocalyptic poems influenced by William Blake and the language of the King James Bible, performing them alongside free jazz improvisations. 'My reputation as a performance artist increased and I began to be invited to perform at gigs and jam sessions. I think I was seen as a bit of a novelty act but at least I was out there doing it.'

Kenny got his first paid gig at Raynor's, a slightly seedy fifties-style nightclub tucked behind the Grand Hotel. 'It was rumoured that the owner was associated with the Krays,' said Kenny. 'This could be true because Charlie Kray lived in Leicester for a while in the early seventies, I met him in The Town Arms once.' The club held a hippie night every Monday evening called The Crocodile Club, featuring live bands, DJ Stuart Greasley (who called himself Gensian Sprunt) and 'the best light show outside of a Pink Floyd concert'. The light show was created by dripping different coloured inks onto a slide projector, bubbling up and moving as it heated up. 'Stuart wore a crash helmet covered in wire wool and as a finale, he covered it in lighter fuel and set it on fire,' said Kenny. 'He was a bit of a prat but very entertaining. He got the idea from The Crazy World of Arthur Brown and he would play their record, "Fire". No health and safety then. When I finished my gig, it went down so well they invited me back the following week. However, the doorman hated me so much he refused to let me in until the organisers intervened.'

Kenny's first real success as a musician was to be invited by the poet Boyd K. Lichfield to form a band with him. 'I had already performed with him on several occasions creating a musical backdrop to his poems. We were later joined by a musician who played a dulcimer-like instrument called a Chinese Banjo. This created a kind of shifting drone which gave a rhythmical base to the performance. All the music was improvised and spontaneous, it never sounded the same twice. We ended up playing all over the country, including the Roundhouse in London, on the same stage as the likes of The Doors, Jefferson Airplane and Pink Floyd. Heady stuff indeed!'

Leicester had a vibrant poetry scene, mainly due to the efforts of Lichfield. Born in Romford, Lichfield came to Leicester in the spring of 1968 and was the epitome of the 'romantic poet'. He was prolific, looked the part and was a brilliant organiser of events. The main venues for poetry readings in Leicester were The Town Arms on

Pocklingtons Walk and the Chameleon Coffee Bar on King Street. There were also a lot of events taking place at Leicester University, presided over by G. S. Fraser who was a published author and professor. The chairman of the Leicester Poetry Society, Alan Bates, was a frequent visitor to The Town Arms and would hold gatherings at his house on West Avenue for poets, artists and intellectuals. 'Another interesting character at the time was Charles Hickson, who was a brilliant poet, an incredible raconteur and looked like a caricature of George Bernard Shaw,' said Kenny. 'He still holds the record as the only person I've ever known to have read all of the novels by Proust.'

The Town Arms was also the centre for acoustic and folk music in Leicester as well as traditional jazz, which still had a big following with an older crowd. 'Russ Merryfield, a stalwart of the folk scene, started a jazz band there and continued to do a regular Friday slot for at least twenty-five years after that, maybe more. He gets my award for the longest-running residency of all time! Local promoter, Tony Savage, also ran a club there which featured some of the best folk singers in the country such as Alex Campbell and Bert Jansch. They were paid well and you could make a good living in the folk clubs. They earned more in a night than most people earned in a week.' Bluegrass musicians George and Thadeus Kaye were also regulars at The Town Arms. 'They sometimes had impromptu jams in the bar downstairs. They were incredibly good technically and I picked up lots of tips from them, especially George who sang, played guitar and became an expert fiddler.'

Kenny was also spending more time hanging out with Mick Pini, usually around New Walk, the Chameleon and the Art Centre Café on Cank Street. 'They were very nice and let us sit there for hours over one cup of tea which they even sometimes gave us for nothing,' said Kenny. 'It was like a social club for hippies and misfits and they played some really good records. Eventually they started putting folk concerts on there at night with candlelight.' Leicester University and Leicester College of Art, now De Montfort University, were also hosting gigs by some of the biggest names in music at the time, including The Who and Pink Floyd. 'Mick and I, especially Mick, got quite friendly with Fleetwood Mac who played in Leicester quite regularly. Mick actually stayed with Peter Green in London and it has been said that he carried Peter's style forward into the seventies and eighties. He was certainly a big influence and a superb guitarist.'

At The Chameleon, you could drink real coffee and listen to cool jazz. It was here that Kenny got into the music of Miles Davis and Thelonius Monk. 'Legendary local singer/guitarist Maurice Coleman used to play there regularly. At the time, his gentle jazz ballads seemed incongruous compared to the psychedelic scene I was part of but he was a truly great performer who I grew to love.'

It was at this time that Kenny met Hank, a student at Leicester University who didn't seem to attend many lectures. 'Hank was amazing, I think eventually he was expelled. He played the guitar and harmonica and sang in a gloriously mournful, out of tune voice. He sounded a bit like Tom Waits but many people thought he couldn't sing. I thought he was brilliant, well before his time.' Hank sold Kenny his first guitar for a pound, an old jazz model with F holes. He also taught him his first chords. 'Hank had a brilliant repertoire of songs, many of which I still play now. It was from him that I also learnt the basics of blues harmonica and how to bend notes and this became a new string to my bow, or rather a new blow to my harp!'

Highfields had become the bohemian area of Leicester and people often opened up their flats and bedsits for gatherings, events and parties. 'The "King of the Hippies" in Leicester was Dave Brookes,' said Kenny. 'He was a painter of weird, exotic fantasies that he would bake in an oven so they looked really old. He had a book by Laurence Lipton called *The Holy Barbarians*, it was like a manual of how to live the hippie life based on the community at Venice Beach, Los Angeles. This became a kind of blueprint of how to furnish your room with Indian tapestries, rugs and low-key lighting with different coloured bulbs. Very atmospheric. His girlfriend caused quite a stir when she posed nude in the shop window of a newly opened boutique on Silver Street.'

At one party, Kenny discovered the album, *The Velvet Underground & Nico,* and was immediately struck by the dissonant qualities of the music and one song in particular. 'It was a track called "Heroin" and it fitted in well with the kind of music I had been making using drones, feedback and extreme lyrics. After a short while the party host rushed up to me and told me to change the record. He hated it even though he had bought it. I told him I thought it was great and he gave it to me on condition that he would never have to listen to it again. It became my favourite record of 1968, I played it so much I virtually wore it out.'

Nineteen sixty-eight was also a time of great political upheaval. In May of that year, Paris erupted into riots when French workers joined student protesters for the first time with a one-day general strike. About 800,000 students, teachers and workers took over the French capital, demanding the fall of Charles de Gaulle's government and protesting at police brutality during the riots of the past few days. In October, a big anti-Vietnam war demonstration took place in London. An estimated 25,000 took part in the march with trouble erupting outside the US embassy in Grosvenor Square. 'Leicester had its own anti-war demonstration which passed quite peacefully,' said Kenny. 'Although there were scuffles on the junction of London Road and Charles Street if I recall. I ended up being pushed into a cordon of police, which was quite scary.'

By 1969, the dream was over for Kenny. 'A friend of mine committed suicide shortly after having a bad acid trip. His death still reminds me of a quote from Allen Ginsberg's poem, *Howl*, that the "best minds of my generation were destroyed by madness". People seemed to be either getting religion or joining extreme left-wing political parties. Personally, I had no desire for spiritual salvation or replacing a bad system with something even worse. The year of the Woodstock festival seemed to be the end of an era for me. The good times didn't seem so good any more.' Kenny spent the summer in Folkestone staying with a friend and in September, went to Middleton St George College of Education, County Durham, to train as a teacher. 'Nineteen sixty-eight remains to this day the period I remember as my "golden age", a time and a feeling I have constantly tried to get back to and I think, in recent times, I have begun to achieve that.'

Hal C. Blake

'There was nowhere to play, the police were starting to close all of the clubs down and the remaining venues were completely different to what we were used to ...' **Rod Brown**

Formed in 1966, Hal C. Blake were Tony (Otis) Weston (vocals/lead guitar), Nick Gay (bass guitar), Dave Edwards (keyboard), Rod Bates (drums), Ray Percival (saxophone) and Rod Brown (trumpet). 'We based ourselves on the likes of Geno Washington, Otis Redding and all of the other American soul acts,' said Ray Percival. 'Originally we were quite mod-looking but that changed as we progressed. Our first gig was upstairs at The Pelican on Gallowtree Gate. We'd play two forty-five-minute sets, all covers, with each song blending into the next one. It was hard work for a brass player as we were also doing all of the moves that went with it.'

Ray joined the band after reading an advert in Moore & Stanworths asking for a rhythm guitarist. 'At the time, there was only Tony and Nick in the band so I went over to meet them. I said I was responding to the advert for a guitarist and they said that they were really after a saxophonist and asked if I could play one. I said no but I'd give it a go. Within three months of rehearsing we were up and playing.' Rod Brown joined the band straight from secondary modern school. 'My brother's friend was the drummer in a band called Martin and the Munixs, Ray had also played with them. He asked if I wanted to join a band and I said yes, why not. I was pretty skint at the time, I was playing a £15 Selmer trumpet that I'd bought from Moore & Stanworths. The trumpet player from Fearns Brass Foundry wasn't getting on with his Besson International, a very expensive instrument, so he traded it in for another one. I asked my mum if she would stand guarantor for it, it was about £100, which was a lot of money back then. I've still got it now, it's in immaculate condition.'

The eagle-eyed amongst you will notice that there was in fact, no one in the band called Hal C. Blake. 'It was the title of a single,' said Ray. 'We were stuck for a name, Tony was looking through his record collection, pulled a single out and said "we'll call ourselves this". As far as the punters were concerned, though, Tony actually became Hal C. Blake. He was also known as "Otis" because of his dance moves, they were a bit like James Brown. Tony had seen him on TV once performing a routine where he pretended to faint so he decided to copy it. We played The Casino one Sunday afternoon with Vfranie and he fell on the floor, he was doing this James Brown thing. He couldn't get back up though so we all had to help him back on his feet. He was a real showman, the last I heard of him he was in the oil business in America.'

As the brass section of the band, Ray and Rod used to rehearse in Ray's parents' house on Tudor Road. 'Imagine a sax and a trumpet playing together in a small front room of a terrace house,' said Ray. 'The noise must have been tremendous! As a band, though, we would rehearse at The Windmill in Humberstone and the Nite Owl in Leicester. We used to rehearse at the Owl on a Sunday afternoon, we'd leave the kit there from the night before and start rehearsing at 1.00 p.m. before it opened at 4.00 p.m. for the afternoon session, which was usually put aside for local bands. Tony used to have records imported from America so if there was something out in the States that nobody had heard of here, we would get it first and rehearse it. We were all about covers, Tony wrote some songs of his own but I don't think we performed any of them.' Rod adds: 'Because of these imported records, as far as the audience were concerned we were constantly playing new stuff which they probably thought we'd wrote ourselves because they hadn't heard it. We certainly didn't want to disillusion them.'

With their home bases comprising of The Casino and the Nite Owl, Hal C. Blake gigs were renowned for their party-like atmosphere which was fuelled by the band's two West Indian dancers, Sam and Denzel, who would stand at the side of the stage and get the crowd moving with their energetic dance routines. 'We started with nothing and within six months we'd got a following, it happened so quickly,' said Ray. 'In the early days, we'd play the Nite Owl one week and then two weeks later, Pesky Gee! would play. We'd rotate every fortnight, which went on for a good six months. Sometimes we'd support Legay and on other occasions we'd be on the same bill as the Peskies, it would be a full-on soul gig. There wasn't a lot between us to be honest, we were very similar, the main difference was the fact that we had Tony, people came to see him. His interest in soul music was incredible and that came through on stage.'

With their following growing by each gig, the band relished playing The Casino. 'We loved playing there, every time was like a homecoming gig,' said Rod. 'We'd try and book in there every few months as it was few and far between when we played Leicester, we were that busy. It was the same faces at each gig but we would have changed since the last time they saw us, we'd progress and move on so quickly over that short period of time.'

The emerging talent of the band's brass section hadn't gone unnoticed. 'We were playing a gig somewhere and The Equals were in the audience,' explains Ray. 'They were looking for a brass section and asked me and Rod to join them. The pair of us sat in the Café Rialto in the marketplace the next day discussing whether we should join them or not and in the end we decided that we were alright as we were. Next thing, they release "Baby Come Back" which eventually got to number one.'

By 1967, the band were supporting some big names from the national music scene. 'We played a lot of outdoor gigs at the time, Whittlesey was a big one,' said Ray. 'We were expecting a couple of thousand, it turned out to be around 18,000, we couldn't believe it. There were some big names on that bill – Peter Green's Fleetwood Mac, The Move, Amen Corner, Donovan to name just a few. We were bottom of the bill but we were still there, it was a great experience.' Rod adds: 'We got The Move kicked off at Nottingham University once. We were at the top of this building, we were on first and somebody from the estate over the road complained about the noise. By the time the police arrived, The Move were on and they closed the show down.'

Hal C. Blake were now playing gigs across the UK, which inevitably meant that a lot of time was spent on the road travelling into the early hours of the morning. 'We had a great roadie but every now and then by the time it came to leaving a gig, he would fall asleep and I'd end up driving the van back home,' said Rod. 'It was very frustrating for me and Ray because we used to be the last ones home, it would be about four or five in the morning when we'd get in. Inevitably there would be a bobby on the beat somewhere on his bike and he'd make us empty the van so he could look for drugs. On occasions, we'd even have to unscrew the amps and take the drum skins off. The irony was that as a band we were clean, we didn't really take anything.' Being on the road also meant that on occasions there was little chance to eat anything so a raid on the kitchen cupboard and the frying pan was almost a necessity, even in the early hours of the morning. 'I set fire to our house once,' admits Rod. 'We'd played a gig somewhere and I got back about four in the morning. I put the chip pan on and fell asleep on the settee in the next room. I was woken up by my brother, the house was full of black smoke, the polystyrene tiles on the kitchen ceiling were on fire. As you can imagine, I wasn't very popular after that for a bit.'

The arrival of the flower power era sparked a visual change in direction for the band. 'We were supporting Jimmy James and the Vagabonds at London University and we wanted to make an impression,' said Ray. 'We parked up on Carnaby Street and went into this shop looking for kaftans, bells, beads, incense sticks – anything that we could link into the flower power thing.' Rod adds: 'The next night we came back to Leicester to play a gig at The Casino. Ray and I dyed our boots lime green and went on stage wearing the kaftans and everything else that we'd bought the day before. You could see that everybody was thinking, "what on earth are they wearing?" They'd never seen that sort of stuff before, it was certainly something that you couldn't buy in Leicester.'

In late 1968, Tony and Nick left the band, taking the name with them. 'They wanted to be a bit more progressive in their sound while we carried on with the soul,' said Ray. 'Tony kept the name but it didn't really work out as people were turning up expecting to see a soul band. We got an American singer in called Ted Dyson and we formed Donnell Jackson and the Broadway Crowd. Just as Tony was seen as Hal C. Blake, Ted became Donnell Jackson.'

Donnell Jackson were Ted Dyson (vocals), Jim Gannon (lead guitar), John Savage (bass guitar), Barry Stevens (drums), Ray Percival (saxophone) and Rod Brown (trumpet). The name was created by Klock Agency who wanted them to sound like an American soul band. 'In the beginning with Hal C. Blake, jointly we were good, individually we weren't that talented,' said Rod. 'We stepped up a gear when we made the transition to Donnell Jackson, the chemistry in the band was really good. We had a phenomenal guitarist in Jim Gannon, who'd previously played in The Broodly Hoo, he turned us around a lot just in terms of sheer quality. John Savage fitted in great on bass, he worked well with Ted, and Barry Stevens was excellent on drums. They all added to the band having a better-quality sound.'

Donnell Jackson were gigging all over the country playing four or five times a week, sometimes twice on a Saturday night. 'As with Hal C. Blake, we were backing some really big acts even if we were at the bottom of the bill,' said Ray. 'The RAF camps were good, there were about four or five of those. We'd also play the All Stars Football Eleven shows, they were good fun to work on, we'd be on stage with the likes of Kenny Everett and Dave Lee Travis. We'd very often do one gig on the Saturday night outside of Leicester and then finish off at the Nite Owl later on for an all-nighter. Then we'd probably play the Casino on the Sunday afternoon so we'd have played three gigs within twenty-four hours.' It was also during this period that the band supported Joe Cocker at The Tin Hat in Kettering. 'He'd just recorded "A Little Help From My Friends" and it hadn't done anything,' explains Ray. 'We played our set and then we stepped back to watch him, he was only young. All of a sudden, the hall doors open and this guy walks through the audience wearing a dressing gown and slippers. He climbs onto the stage and walks up to the plug sockets on the wall and switches everything off. Everybody just stood there and watched him. Then he turned around, stepped down from the stage and walked off. He was obviously a very disgruntled neighbour complaining about the noise in his own way.'

The popularity of the band, with its new line-up and sound, also enabled them to turn professional. 'We did that for about six months,' said Rod. 'We couldn't really go to work and play in the band as well as we were gigging too much. We were sometimes earning up to £100 a gig, which was a lot of money, a fee you would only get by playing the bigger venues. The Casino on the other hand would pay you about £15 a gig, so there was a big difference.' The band even found time to record a one-hour show for BBC Radio Nottingham. 'I was the only one who had a recording of it,' said Rod. 'It was on a three-inch spool of tape and when I moved house twenty years ago I sold my reel-to-reel deck and a load of tapes and I forgot it was in there. I'll never forgive myself.'

Ted Dyson, the band's lead singer, is yet another contender for a Leicester Music Legend Award. If only anyone could find him to give him one. 'We used to play a few airbases and on this particular occasion we played the American one at Alconbury,' explains Rod. 'Ted was in the audience and he asked us if he could get on stage and do a number with us. Jeff Sanders was our singer at the time. Ted was incredible – he'd jump into the crowd and really got them going. He joined us not long after that. I was a bit naïve at the time, it was only later on that all of the pieces fell together – Ted was in the armed forces, Vietnam was on and he was singing with us. Basically, he'd gone AWOL. To us, although he was based at Alconbury, we assumed he'd sorted everything out with them to join us in the civilian world. We never thought anything of it until he was arrested.' As far as the band were concerned, they'd got an amazing singer and showman. It was only a matter of time though before somebody would put two and two together and want to know why this young American guy in his early twenties was in a band and not at war. It was a routine stop near the Six Hills Hotel on the A46 that lead to Ted's arrest. 'The copper was asking us all our names,' said Ray. 'The problem with Ted was that he was named after six American presidents so when it came to his turn, he started to reel off all of these names. The copper thought he was taking the mick and arrested him there and then. We all had to go to the police station where they grilled us all night. We never saw him after that and to this day we don't know exactly what happened to him. He was a great guy, very funny, he used to say that he'd just got back from Vietnam but he didn't like it there because they shoot you with real bullets and you break out in little holes. He told me that he used to play the guitar in the bars of Philadelphia when he was a teenager, he taught Jim a couple of bits, more in style though than in technique. I've tried to find him but there's no trace of him anywhere.'

Not long after Ted's departure, Donnell Jackson called it a day. 'If it hadn't been the fact that we were coming to the end of an era with the seventies approaching, we would have certainly shifted up a gear,' admits Rod. 'If we'd got another year out of that band we probably would have moved on to greater things. For me though, in the end it was a combination of reasons why we finished; I'd got a lung problem – I started to cough up blood after a gig, way too much rehearsing and playing probably – Ted got arrested and the sixties was coming to an end. There was nowhere to play, the police were starting to close all of the clubs down and the remaining venues were completely different to what we were used to.'

The music scene was changing and the venues that characterised that scene were either disappearing or turning into something else. As with musicians of any era, once the performing has stopped, the reality check was that you had to get a job. 'I was one of seven kids and I was the only one who "didn't work" as far as everyone was concerned,' said Rod. 'But there was never any problem getting a job in those days, if you said you wanted to be a train driver you could be one and that never really changed until the late seventies. I'd left the band and just got married so I needed to earn some regular money. I tried playing afterwards, I was in a band called Equity, but I couldn't get used to the fact that people weren't really listening any more. When we at our best, they were queueing at the door to see us. I found myself constantly looking at the clock – that's when you know it's time to quit.' Ray adds: 'After Donnell Jackson, I got a job and joined a band called The Film and then another outfit called Talk of the Town. In 1987 I was playing in a band called Lets Go Round Again and we'd just learnt John Miles' "Music", it was a big orchestral thing and we got it note perfect. We played it at Spinney Hill Club and someone shouted out, "Can you do the birdy song?" That was it for me – we'd put in about three rehearsals for just this one track and they wanted the bloody birdy song. I called it a day not long after that.'

For these two best friends, who between them comprised the brass section of both Hal C. Blake and Donnell Jackson, looking back on their time in both bands brings obvious feelings of pride and great affection. 'We were young kids, we'd get on stage and we were stars,' said Ray. 'Rod would come down to my place on Tudor Road and we'd rehearse for a bit and from there we'd go down to the Il Rondo, it was a meeting place for bands. In the afternoon, if we didn't go bowling, we'd go to the pictures and then we'd meet the rest of the band at the clock tower and go off to a gig, that was our day. Happy times.' Rod adds: 'I remember everything with absolute bliss. I joined the band literally straight from school and by the time we'd finished in the late sixties, all of my friends were going down the clubs every night, playing snooker and darts and so forth. I hadn't seen any of that world at all and by the time I was twenty it suddenly struck me that that's what people were doing at night. So when I left the band, I went through a period of catching up with all of that. Later on in life, I got a job as a manager at Premier Drum and I bumped into some old school friends there. They were looking back, telling me stories of when they left school and I thought to myself you know what, I had a bloody good time. You really do forget how well off we were in non-monetary terms. I honestly believe that we were in the greatest era and position of our lives and we enjoyed it the best way that we possibly could. We missed out on a lot but we missed out on nothing really.'

The Beatniks

'We knew that if we were playing The Pit, the queue would be all the way down East Bond Street. That was always a great gig …' **Gus Turner**

Formed in 1961, The Beatniks were Brian Lee (lead guitar), Pete Illiffe (bass), Rob Townsend (drums) and Gus Turner (vocals and piano). 'Mick Miller, our original lead guitarist and the founder of the band, decided to leave,' explains Gus Turner. 'So I thought about it and asked him if he minded me forming a new line-up and to carry on as The Beatniks and he was cool with that. I knew Guy Sheppard, a local art student and drummer, and Brian Lee, a guitarist, so I asked them to join me. Guy knew Johnny Davis, who was a bassist. Sometime later Guy and Johnny left so I asked Rob Townsend to join. Rob knew Pete Illiffe and that's how we stayed until the end.' The Beatniks would go on to support Manfred Mann, Billy J. Kramer, John Lee Hooker, The Who and The Fourmost to name but a few. 'We worked alongside John Lee Hooker a couple of times,' said Gus. 'We all felt highly complemented when he told us he enjoyed working with us. He said that if his backing band weren't available at any time, we could step in for them, which was a huge compliment.'

The Beatniks would rehearse once a fortnight at The Royal Mail on Campbell Street and The Wig & Pen on Wellington Street. In general, the band members went along with whatever Gus suggested as the choice of material. 'Little Richard and Ray Charles's vocals were what turned me on but it was Jerry Lee Lewis's piano playing, not his singing, that really inspired my playing. My first real influence, though, was an instrumental called "Bad Penny Blues" by Humphrey Lyttelton. It got into the Top 20 in 1956 and I learned how to play it by ear from a 78rpm record. I performed it at my first public solo performance when I was thirteen, it went down a bomb at a parents evening at Lancaster Boys School.'

Right from the inception of the band, the dynamics of the four musicians worked exceptionally well with minimum upsets. 'Basically it worked okay,' said Gus. 'We all got on great together. Pete was a brilliant bassist but very quiet, he and Rob used to hang out together. He used to have to copy my left-hand bass riffs which was sometimes difficult. Pete once suggested changing a rock and roll song, I think it was "Mean Woman Blues", he wanted to play it in the style of Bo Diddley. It went down a bomb. Brian was an exceedingly good guitar player, not only playing lead but because the piano was more prominent than most bands, he had to combine lead and rhythm. I got on with Rob probably the best though, we used to laugh a lot and I always used to look out for him. He had, and still has, a most acceptable personality. Fame has not changed him, unlike some I could mention. He's a very good, solid drummer, rock steady, never ever made a mistake. I remember telling him to hit the snare harder, so he always carried a spare snare drum with him just in case he bust the skins, which he used to do now and then. If we had a gig in the week, I used to wait for him outside Winterton's, where he worked, and bomb straight off when he knocked off. He was always hungry and after every gig he used to be completely knackered. I don't know why, he's only a drummer. I have a photo of Rob after a gig looking as knackered as I was, we both seemed to be the only two in the band who threw all we had into it.'

The Beatniks would play a storming set, comprised mainly of rock and roll numbers with a hint of blues including songs from Jerry Lee Lewis, Little Richard, Ray Charles and Chuck Berry. 'I had a decent tape of a gig, but it's long gone,' recalls Gus. 'The blues numbers, "Stormy Monday" for example, weren't very well received. We covered "Twist & Shout" by the Isley Brothers a long time before The Beatles, that track always went down well. I remember Pete saying that the Fab Four must have come to one of our gigs to get it!'

As an early publicity stunt and photo shoot, the band once broke one of the sacred rules of Leicester City Council – they climbed all over the fountain in Town Hall Square. 'A city council jobsworth shouted at us, telling us to pack it in before we caused any damage or he would call the police,' said Gus. 'I shouted a load of abuse back at him and threatened to sort him out. He asked us what band we were and I said, "Tony Bart and the Strangers and don't you ever forget it, you tosser." Then he rang the police. We all ran off and to this day, I don't know if Tony was ever questioned about it.'

The Beatniks were now a regular fixture at some of Leicester's most popular venues including The Pit, The Corn Exchange, The Trocadero, Leicester University, Loughborough University, The Granby, The Casino and Syston Assembly Rooms. 'We had two cars to take us to the gigs, Brian and Pete in one and me and Rob in the other,' said Gus. 'We knew that if we were playing The Pit, the queue would be all the way down East Bond Street. That was always a great gig. It had a piano but it was only a five octave and it was so bad I never used it. The Spinney Hill WMC on Frisby Road was a venue which not many bands knew about. It was a fantastic, regular monthly midweek gig, it was always packed every time we worked it. The Co-op Rooms on Uppingham Road was another one. My favourite venue however had to be The Corn Exchange, the women there were always very friendly. I used to do the gig and in-between spots I would be on the door, sorting the naughty lads out. It provided me with a little bit more wonga on the night.'

As with a lot of bands, playing more than one gig in a twenty-four-hour period was not unheard of, as Gus explains. 'I recall we once played a Saturday afternoon at the Corn Exchange, struck the kit and went on to The Casino on London Road. We played there until late, struck the kit again and set up in the Percy Gee Building – three gigs in one night. There would also be some weeks where we would play three or four gigs. If we worked a working men's club over the weekend, it would be Saturday night, Sunday night and a Sunday lunchtime as well. I hated those lunchtimes, my voice was still sleeping. We also had some Saturday morning gigs in cinemas, The Coliseum in Leicester and the Odeon in Rugby in particular. At times, we couldn't hear ourselves for the screaming, which was something I noticed starting once The Beatles had made it. One song in particular which used to attract screaming was "Fortune Teller". It was also around this time that I noticed something strange was happening. At the majority of gigs, the lads in the audience would gather around the piano and when we had finished, they'd come up to me, shake my hand, pat me on the back and say how much they liked the show. Meanwhile, the others would be swamped by the girls who, on occasions, would throw sweets, cigarettes and even "teddys" onto the stage. Never any knickers though …'

The Beatniks were also influencing a future generation of Leicester bands. 'It was probably around 1962–63 that I first started to take a serious interest in playing in a band,' said Pesky Gee! guitarist, Chris Dredge. 'The Beatniks were one of those bands that really inspired me. We would, as fluffy faced sixteen-year-olds, go to the Corn Exchange in Leicester Market Place for a Saturday night out. The resident band there, or so it would seem to us, were The Beatniks – none of them could've been much older than me. The Corn Exchange was big and held probably between 200–300 people and they were all held by the band. Rock and roll was their stock in trade and very good they were at it. My recollection after fifty-plus years were that they were professional, exciting and very entertaining and I suppose that, given different circumstances, they could have been "big". They seemed very loud and somewhat decadent, but by today's standards they were probably little angels.' Legay keyboard player, John Knapp adds: 'The Beatniks were the first band I ever saw live, it was down The Pit, and I can remember it like it was yesterday. They were so exciting, the crowd loved them, there was so much energy coming from the stage it was unbelievable. These were definitely not wimpy musicians. I was only sixteen at the time but their mixture of rock and roll and a couple of blues tracks really left an impression on me. I remember thinking Gus was a bit scary but I liked that about him, I had the same sort of feeling the first time I saw Pete Townshend play. Watching them live, as well as listening to music at home, really convinced me that this was what I wanted to do.'

One memorable gig for Gus took place at the Peterborough Corn Exchange in 1964. 'We used to play Peterborough quite a lot and on this occasion we were sharing the night with my long-term pal, Freddie Fingers Lee, and The Fourmost. The management informed us the place was being demolished the following week and that we were the last band to ever work there and we could wreck the place if we wanted. I pushed the baby grand piano off the stage with Fred standing on top of it, the punters went wild. There was no way anybody was going to play that piano again. I swung from the curtains, threw water on the drummer as he played a solo and had a staged fight with Fred. He would throw his glass eye at me, I'd catch it and drop it into a glass of beer and then he'd drink it. That was a good night.' On another occasion, Gus remembers how Brian's electrical handiwork would, on occasions, literally bring the gig to a grinding halt. 'One of Brian's jobs was to set up the power/plug boards. Because many halls still had the old 5 or 15 amp sockets, he never changed the plugs to suit, he just rammed the bare wires in and used matchsticks to keep them in place, which was really quite naughty. Sometimes, though, the wires would fall out and we would lose power. One night, after the third time of being unplugged, I got upset and I turned to Rob and said "that Brian's a f*****g idiot". Unfortunately, I said it just as the power came back on, the mics picked it up and the whole sentence boomed out through the PA. He just looked at me and smiled, he had a smile that made you forgive him of anything. The gig was at a university and when the audience heard my rather crude working-class gob they all gave out a massive cheer and started singing "Why Was He Born So Beautiful". Wha'ra laugh!'

In 1964, Gus closed the band down, mainly due to the organisational and logistic demands of the job. 'I decided I would try and join a load of different bands as a guest artist,' explains Gus. 'I went on to play with a couple of local and regional bands including The Danny Klyne Five, The More than Five, Revival, The Freddy Finger Lee Band and Albatross. The idea was that I'd come on and do a set or two, make some good music, do the business and go home. No more working out the pay or waiting for the band to load their gear into the van and driving them all back, which meant I was always the last to get home. For me, it now meant that there would be no PA to load because whoever the band was would have their own. All I had to do was pull the mics out of the piano, grab my amp and I'm away – simples!'

For Gus, the 1960s was an incredible time to be a musician, providing a unique opportunity to develop individual styles. 'The music scene in the sixties was unbelievable – freedom of expression, you could do whatever you wanted to do and there was plenty of work about. It wasn't unusual back then to have a five or six band gig and on some occasions, two bands would work together. I used to really enjoy working with The Farinas, for me Jimmy King had a phenomenal voice, and Harry Ovenall's drumming was the dog's cojones. I truly loved it, it really was sex, booze and rock and roll. At seventy-five years of age, though, I look back with a little sadness because there were quite a few casualties along the way. For me though, the good times well outnumber the bad and many of my compadres are still around and we still tell stories and bullshit about the old days. Sadly, Pete passed away a long time ago. I've seen Brian a couple of times and Rob and I still keep in touch and meet up now and again. There are some regrets but not enough to say anything about, we just got on with it right to the end without exemption. It would appear haphazard but I was very careful with planning along the way. As a man at a gig once said, "you are your own man" and more important to me, I did it my way. I never had a care in the world, it was all there for the taking – 100mph living, full on hedonistic fun and I filled my basket to the rim.'

The Nite Owl & The White Cat Café

'I knew at the time that I was involved in something special and I wasn't wrong, I've never seen or experienced anything like it since ...' **Kathy Chamberlin**

The Nite Owl, the self-proclaimed home to the 'Midlands' best rave all-nighter scene', was situated at 31 Newarke Street. Opening in 1966 and based in a former shoe factory, the Owl boasted two floors that were open to the public – the bands played in the basement while the ground floor was a coffee bar. The building burnt down in 1968 in what many still describe as quintessential 'mysterious circumstances'. The Owl was best known for its dark corners, soul music, dancing and its now legendary all-nighters. It also had a reputation as a venue where drugs, in particular speed, were widely used. 'The Nite Owl was my Great Uncle George's club,' said Natalie Kent. 'My aunty Kathy worked there, it was the first of its kind in Leicester and not very popular with parents whose kids were out all night. It was a fresh and exciting place where you could listen to good music and meet friends. Every club has its problems but the soul of the place was built on good intentions by a very talented man who made his own luck.'

The Nite Owl was owned by George Parker, who was not only one of the more colourful characters on the Leicester music scene but also one of the most innovative. George was born in Coleorton, Leicestershire, in November 1929. His father was a coal miner and his mother a housewife who looked after both George and his sister, Irene. As a result of working down the pits, George's father had to have part of his lung removed after contracting Coal Workers' Pneumoconiosis (Black Lung Disease), a condition caused by long exposure to coal dust. 'I really liked his mother, she was very strict but because I was always polite, there was never any problem between us,' said Kathy Chamberlin, George's niece. 'She was a cleaner and was obsessed with keeping the place spotless, it was immaculate. She was a solid lady but didn't know how to show love – George always said that he wasn't allowed to play, he was supposed to be seen and not heard. She wanted George to be a coal miner like his father but he didn't want to. Ironically, when he was a teenager, he was conscripted to work in the pit as a Bevin Boy. He hated it though and swore that he would never go down the mines again, he'd seen how it had affected his dad and all of the other men around him.'

Years later, George set up a business called Parwilco, named after the three partners, Parker, Wilson and Cooper. Parwilco had a licence to mend fruit machines, pinball machines and jukeboxes. 'Everywhere had one of George's jukeboxes,' said Kathy. 'They had a young lad who went around changing all of the records. The venue had no choice regarding what went on the jukebox though, it was whatever was new to the charts. The venue would take half of the profit and George would take the other and that would pay for the records.'

In 1966, George opened the Nite Owl. He would eventually own the Crossroads Café, which was situated next door to the Nite Owl, the White Cat Café on Duns Lane and cafés on Havelock Street and Millstone Lane. During this time, George had also become the proud owner of a brand-new, all American, Ambassador car. 'The Ambassador was beautiful, it was an automatic,' said Kathy. 'He let me drive it. I was too young for a provisional licence but he still let me have a go. He used to say no wonder these Americans had got a better way of life without having to use a clutch! George was a bit flash but not a show-off. If he had any money he'd love to spend it, especially on the kids, buying presents and ice cream. He bought me and my sister, Anna, tickets to go and see the Rolling Stones at the Trocadero because we were so upset at missing out on seeing The Beatles.'

Kathy Chamberlin was fifteen years old when she began working for her uncle at the Nite Owl in the spring of 1967. 'George wasn't happy with the staff he'd got, they weren't taking any money,' said Kathy. 'He went to my mum and asked if I could work for him. Although I was nearly sixteen, I'd already got a job in the offices of Wolsey. I wanted a job that was above board which would pay my tax and my stamp. I didn't know how I was going to fit the Nite Owl in, I was working Monday–Friday, was at night school and played volleyball one night a week at Westcotes School. It was a bit hectic but you were expected to work in those days. George wanted me to finish my job at Wolsey but I wouldn't, I was learning how to touch type and general office procedures, there was no way I was going to pack that in.'

Shortly after Kathy started, George brought in Barry Benson, aka 'Handbags Barry', as manager of the Nite Owl. 'George wanted reliable staff who wouldn't let him down,' explains Kathy. 'The previous manager wasn't very nice and there was a horrible atmosphere. He didn't like that I was related to George, he was always shouting at me, telling me what to do. Barry got on really well with Ricky, who used to work the door, they looked after me while I was serving behind the bar. Ricky was lovely, he was a small, solid guy. He really enjoyed working there, he loved the music and was always singing. He'd mop the floors, he'd do anything.'

According to Kathy, on a busy night the Nite Owl could probably hold between 900–1000 people on both floors. 'It's often referred to as Leicester's cavern but it was bigger than that, you couldn't touch the ceilings. The ground floor had lots of chairs and tables, a massive jukebox, toilets and a big area for dancing. You'd climb down one set of steps to get to the basement, that's where the bands would play. The bar area was the full length of the factory, it was massive, Barry would often come down and sit with me there. I'd got an electric bell that I had to ring if ever I was in trouble but I never did as all of the staff would be around to check if I was okay. There was a grill behind the bar that I cooked the burgers on and soft drinks were served from soda fountain taps. I worked out that if I strapped a ruler across the taps with elastic bands, I could pour three drinks at once to cope with the demand. I'd have two pots of fresh, good quality filtered coffee on the go at all times, one really strong and the other normal strength. It smelt gorgeous and it kept me going. There wasn't a lot of filtered coffee around in those days but I would make loads of it. By four in the morning, the kids would be wanting the strong stuff. The girls would be literally falling asleep on their boyfriend's shoulders, totally shattered. I never stopped, I used to take a break when the kids started to get tired and their parents came and picked them up.'

The upstairs floor was used as a dressing room for the bands even though, officially, it wasn't part of the Nite Owl lease. 'The stairs had been blocked off,' said Kathy. 'The only way up was via the lift which was locked off, only George and Barry had the key. Everyone who went up there was escorted.' The dressing room boasted settees, tables and bottles of alcohol in the far corner. If needed, the area could be split into two if more than one band was performing. 'You had to come downstairs for coffee, George didn't want me to leave the bar. The bands, their managers and the rest of their entourage were the only ones who had access to the alcohol. It was a free bar, we couldn't charge for it, the police wouldn't give George a licence to sell alcohol because he couldn't guarantee that the kids were old enough to drink it. George would go up there and have a drink with the bands but his staff weren't allowed.'

Even though the bands had their own space upstairs to get changed, George was frustrated because they had to make their stage entrance via the lift, the stone stairs and into the basement through the audience. Not only did it not look right, it took a long time for the bands to get to the stage. A grand entrance aside, it also wasn't exactly the safest route in for the artists, with much groping and hair-pulling to be had and enjoyed by the fans. George wanted the bands to enter the stage from behind so there was only one obvious thing for it – he had to build a tunnel between the Nite Owl and the café next door. As you do. 'I don't know how George got permission to build the tunnel but he did,' said Kathy. 'The building next door was empty when George took over the factory and then a café opened, it was called The Crossroads. It was a big place but no one was ever in it. It was a pretty miserable place to be honest, I think the owner tried to pick up trade from the Nite Owl but it didn't succeed. So George brought in a builder, he was a structural engineer. Everyone helped out building the tunnel, even the bands, Ricky was as black as the ace of spades by the time he'd finished.' One of the band members who helped construct the tunnel was Legay's Robin Pizer. 'I remember digging from one cellar to another. We used buckets and wheelbarrows to take out dirt and bricks and we loaded them onto a lorry. It was dark but we had lights, it was a bit like being in a mine. We did it after normal work hours so the lorry could park outside. I remember someone using a jackhammer on parts where there was thick concrete. I can't remember how long it took but I don't think it was more than a week or two as quite a few people were helping. After it was finished, we whitewashed the walls. When it was completed, it worked well.' As soon as the tunnel was finished, the dressing room moved next door and the bands had easier access to the stage. 'Before the tunnel was built, the kids could see the bands coming and going and using the lift, it just wasn't right,' said Kathy. 'When the dressing room moved, the bands had their own entrance and exit and would enter the stage from behind. It looked and worked much better.'

One of Kathy's favourite memories of the Nite Owl was when it embraced the psychedelic scene and was kitted out in fluorescent lights and paint, a style which George had seen in a club in Spain. 'He brought some art students in from Leicester Poly and they painted murals all over the black walls with fluorescent paint in return for a free night out. It looked fantastic, it really changed the place. The lads used to love wearing white shirts and the lighting made their shirts glow in the dark. If anyone had caps on their teeth they would show up as well, I remember one girl always used to dance with her hand in front of her mouth. George also got into the swing of things, I remember him once dressing up in top hat and tails with flowers coming out of his hat for one event. He also arranged for coaches to take all of the 'Nite Owlers' to Spalding for the music festival, they all wore Nite Owl T-shirts.

Hendrix was on the bill, he was also given one to wear. I remember him wiping the sweat from his face on it and chucking it into the crowd.'

Every week, new posters would go up confirming acts that had been booked in. It was relatively cheap to get in to the Nite Owl with a small increase for the all-nighters. 'George never wanted to rob the kids,' said Kathy. 'Even when we had the bands on he didn't charge much more. He used an agency that would bring all of these American acts over. I can remember him having a conversation with Barry, he'd just booked The Temptations which probably cost a lot of money, and he made it absolutely clear that he wasn't going to charge more for it.' Along with The Temptations, the Nite Owl featured some of the best groups of the time including Amen Corner, Edwin Starr and local soul band Pesky Gee!, who were regarded by many as the house band. 'I'd never experienced an "all-nighter" until the Nite Owl,' recalls Pesky Gee! guitarist, Chris Dredge. 'At 6.00 a.m. on a Sunday morning we would all spill out into Newarke Street, adrenalin still high. By today's standard, the Nite Owl may not seem particularly outrageous but at the time there was nothing to compare. It was a bit of a dodgy place actually – 90% of what I could tell you about it is unprintable, it was a den of iniquity. One minute it was there, the next it had gone. We were George's favourite band and he tried to book us in eight days a week. We would generally arrive about 1.00 a.m. to be greeted by either Little Ricky or Handbags Barry, the two doormen – George never called them bouncers. Little Ricky was about 5ft 7inches tall and 8ft wide, Barry had a market stall selling handbags. They used to keep bottles of coke behind the door – if there was any trouble, Barry would pull a bottle out and open the lid using his teeth. It was enough to put a few people off. George would always appear in the changing room with a litre of scotch and two large bottles of coke for, as he put it, "night-time refreshment". There was no bar, so it was always welcome. You could always recognise the drug squad looking to nobble a pusher – they were dressed as really naff hippies in big, black shiny boots and they usually fell asleep at about 3.00 a.m. Owlin' Robin, the resident DJ, would be belting out all the American soul imports, a lot of which had yet to reach England. He let us borrow them so we could learn them, that way we were always that one step ahead. The names we played with there could fill a book – The Temptations, Junior Walker and The All Stars, Wynder K. Frog, Amen Corner, Alan Bown Set, Roy C – the list is endless. If any memories endure of the sixties good times it will always be the gigs at the Nite Owl.'

The attraction of the Nite Owl, with the wide variety of gigs and music on offer, is critiqued here by one of its regulars, Nick Hairs. 'I was introduced to the Nite Owl by a girlfriend who used to go to The Burlesque and other places. As I loved my music, it was mainly the bands that interested me. My first visit was on 28 January 1967 to see Herbie Goins & The Night Timers. I loved this type of music along with Tamla and Stax. I used to go to college further up on Newarke Street so I knew the area well, we used to hang out in the Crossroads Café during the week to find out who was playing at the weekend. The Nite Owl was always packed and the feeling that you had on Sunday morning was great in so much you knew that you'd had a good night out. There was a guy from college who went there a lot, a real pill head, and we used to laugh a lot on Monday mornings when he recounted his weekend escapades. Wynder K. Frog was a favourite gig of mine there, I used to love the Hammond sound from Mick Weaver. And of course, Geno Washington – the Nite Owl must have broken every health and safety law when he played. Alan Bown was another great act I saw there, I'd seen him before at the Il Rondo. Pesky Gee! were always good, I loved seeing them – Kay had a great voice. The Chris Farlowe gig was funny because they were so late getting there, I think the support played again to appease the crowd. Turns out that they went to Newarke from another gig as opposed to Newarke Street!'

Leicester musician Kenny Wilson also recalls some of his favourite gigs at the Owl. 'I saw Georgie Fame and the Blue Flames and Geno Washington and his Ram Jam Band there. Another brilliant group who played there was the Graham Bond Organisation who had Jack Bruce as their bass player. Legay were also a regular feature who I saw quite often on Sunday afternoons and were fantastic as usual. They also featured many American soul stars there. It was a very good place until it burnt down and I'm not speaking metaphorically!' Vfranie drummer, Paul Coles adds: 'The Nite Owl was like our Cavern, it was really hot and the atmosphere was electric. There wasn't much going on during the week, it was mainly the weekends, Sunday afternoons were the best. It wasn't a big place – a stage, a tiny dressing room, a room upstairs where you could get a coffee and an area where Owlin' Robin did his DJ thing.'

Robin Hollick, aka DJ Owlin' Robin, started out at The Burlesque on Humberstone Road before moving on to the Nite Owl. 'The Burlesque was the venue that changed things in Leicester,' explains Robin. 'It was like a large shop with wide steps going upstairs. You'd walk up, turn right and the toilets were directly in front of you. A bit further on was the band's dressing room. Then there was a big room with a stage in the corner, it had a sort of curved front.' The Burlesque, along with The Nite Owl, were famous for their all-nighters, most of which went on until 8.00 a.m. 'I cut my teeth as a DJ on the 4.00 a.m.–8.00 a.m. slot,' said Robin. 'Obviously, not everybody stayed all night but a lot did. I remember slowing things down for the last fifteen minutes, as I was to do later at The Nite Owl. I used to finish with Lorraine Ellison's "Stay with Me Baby".'

As with The Burlesque, alcohol wasn't on sale at The Nite Owl. 'People used to smoke and drink coffee or pop,' said Robin. 'I don't recall alcohol being a major issue in those days and drugs weren't as rife as we are now led to believe. The Nite Owl wasn't a boozy environment, it was more about the music and the dancing. People knew the score and didn't bring it on the premises, it just wasn't a problem.'

As with Jim Gregan, DJ at the Il Rondo and The Palais, Robin would keep up to date with the latest music via one of the local record shops. 'There was a guy who worked in Advance Records, he looked like Thunderclap Newman's piano player, who was really good to me. He let me go in and listen to records and keep up with the new stuff.'

Stand-out acts at The Nite Owl for Robin include Amen Corner, Wynder K. Frog, Gas, Geno Washington, Zoot Money, Jimmy James and the Vagabonds and Alan Bown. 'A dodgy London agent sent us The Four Tops and they definitely weren't. We also used to have good local support acts such as Pesky Gee! and Legay. Pesky were more appropriate for the evening shows while I seem to recall Legay doing a lot of the Sunday afternoon shows. They were very much the band that the girls wanted to see.' Some of the gigs held at the Owl, however, were not so popular. 'I was with Roger Chapman in the Chameleon on King Street and he said, "Let's ring a few people and see who we can get together for a gig at the Nite Owl",' said Chris Dredge. 'We did it that evening. There was me, Roger, Rob Townsend, a bass player and Zoot on keyboards. We did about an hour and a half of blues, a complete one-off. I don't actually think anybody was there, well at least no one who would admit it.'

As with most young people of his generation, the burning desire to do things differently than his peers was paramount for Robin Hollick. 'We were starting to do things our parents hadn't done. Yet some of our friends, who were only five years older than us, were still spending time at the Palais talent shows and formal dance halls. They were still attached to a townie culture when it was the time of the mods and rockers. There were no proper nightclubs in Leicester apart from Ambassadors on Charles Street and that was for the older crowd. They used to have acts on such as Matt Monro and The Bachelors. The Nite Owl was for the kids. They didn't have the expectations of today's teenagers because they didn't really have anything in the first place. No pristine conditions but it was ours.' At some point during the mid-sixties, the local authority brought in fire regulations and any new club would need a licence to open. 'The Penny Farthing was the first one if I recall,' said Robin. 'It was quite luxurious compared to The Burlesque and The Nite Owl, which weren't really nightclubs as such but entertainment and music centres.'

For Robin, the sixties were all about music, clothes and fashions. 'I distinctly remember walking around in a fur coat my aunt had given me. We were the first generation not to go to the Palais, we wanted to be completely different to our parents. Most of us worked hard all week and then played hard at the weekend. From when I first entered the Peep Hole on Wharf Street in 1965 and heard Gobbi playing soul and blue beat music, I knew then my life was going to change. It was a wonderful and innovative time.'

The Nite Owl was one of the few venues for all-nighters, people would travel from all over the country to enjoy its soul-inspired atmosphere. 'It wasn't just Leicester people in there,' confirmed Kathy. 'It never ceased to amaze me just how far some of them had travelled – London, the North, the West Midlands, literally everywhere. They all looked amazing as well, the clothes that they used to wear were out of this world. The mod boys were always clean, well-groomed and immaculate and the girls looked stunning. They'd never wear the same outfit two weeks on the trot and a lot of them would save up their money just to buy new clothes for the all-nighters.'

Inevitably though, the availability of drugs did cause problems for the management and it was the success of the all-nighters that gained the Nite Owl its reputation as a pill-popping venue and a so-called 'den of iniquity'. 'From what I saw, it was never a den of iniquity, I never saw anybody collapse through drugs,' said Kathy. 'I think it had that reputation because in those days, if you were young and out after 3 a.m. in the morning, it was assumed that you were up to no good. Staff knew that the police would be in there and George didn't want any trouble so there was an active policy to get the pushers out. If there were any known pushers in there, or if you were found to have drugs on you, you'd be kicked out. We knew there were pushers outside and it was our job to keep them out so everyone was searched on the door. Even inside the club, people were being watched if we thought they looked suspicious. The outer toilet doors were always open, they were never allowed to close, and we had a guy who would sit opposite, watching who was going in there. If we thought anyone was pushing, he'd be on to them straight away.' According to

Kathy, the drugs squad never raided the Nite Owl but they seemed desperate to find any form of illegal substance on the premises. 'It was never raided but to be honest, I was so young I don't think I was able to spot a policeman even if he was standing in front of me. I used to see older men though, who we assumed were the police, talking to younger couples. After a while, the younger ones would look uncomfortable, move seats, and come up to the bar and ask for a coffee. It was as though the police were wanting to find problems.' Georgie Wright, George's niece adds: 'Everyone was searched, including the plain-clothed police officers who were always around checking. Drugs were rife at the time though and some managed to get stuff past the lads on the door, but they'd always get kicked out if they were caught.'

Chris Lewitt, who interviewed Robin Hollick, observed that it seemed incredible that the all-nighters happened during a time of quite stifling social conditions. 'It was still only twenty-two years since the war had ended. There was no all-day drinking then, pubs closed at 10.30 p.m. each night and opened for two hours on a Sunday lunchtime. Most people's work patterns were the same and pub hours revolved around this. Drinking was all about going to the pub with the old man or down to the working men's club and sit in the concert room with all of the family. Teenagers in the mid-sixties seemed to know their place in an uncomplicated, accepted way. Because of this, the all-night club sessions at The Nite Owl must have gone down badly with the locals. At the time, there were only two other all- nighters in the provinces, The Twisted Wheel in Manchester and Black Cat/Mojo Club in Sheffield.'

On Sunday mornings, after an all-nighter, the prospect of a cooked breakfast at the White Cat café on nearby Duns Lane would act as a magnet for many of the Nite Owl's clientele. The café acted as a Sunday morning recovery zone before the journey back home and was very much part of the Nite Owl scene. 'My mam ran the White Cat and we lived above it,' said Georgie Wright. 'We would have the psychedelic crowd and the mods, with their parkas and scooters, in on the Sunday straight after the Owl had finished and then the rockers during the week. They'd dance to all of the records on the jukebox. My mam, Norah, was called the "Green Dragon" because she wouldn't stand for any funny business and barred anyone if they didn't behave, but all the kids were pretty mild-mannered and respectful. If my uncle thought that any of them had taken anything, he made them get a breakfast and straighten out before going home. He really was the coolest uncle ever.' For Georgie, the records played on the White Cat's legendary jukebox, whether it be mod, psychedelic or anything else, provided her with a unique education in great music. 'I can remember being asked by my music studies teacher at school what we listened to at home. I didn't know where to start – the teacher was a bit flummoxed by my repertoire. I was living over the café and the jukebox would blare out all day and night, it was immense.'

George decided to open the White Cat on Sunday mornings because he was concerned that the Nite Owl clientele, some cold and wet, had nowhere to go after the all-nighters had finished. 'He felt really sorry for them,' said Kathy. 'The kids would huddle up on the doorstep and ask him to stay open until later but he couldn't as he had to get the place ready for the Sunday afternoon session. He'd ask why they hadn't gone home and he would get a variety of reasons – it was Sunday morning, they hadn't got cars, they couldn't park their scooters on Newarke Street, their parents wouldn't pick them up, they couldn't afford taxis, the buses didn't start until 10 a.m. – the list was endless.' After working an all-nighter, Kathy would head back to the White Cat, where she lived with her mum and little sister Georgie, and start serving the hungry throng. 'They'd have coffee and a breakfast – I don't think I've ever cooked as many bacon and sausage sandwiches as I did there. The kids were warm and after they'd had something to eat and drink, they were back up dancing to the jukebox. Then as soon as it turned 10 a.m., they'd all slowly disappear and get their buses home, it was always empty by 11 a.m. I was really happy doing it but eventually my mum took over the Sunday morning shifts. After working eight hours at the Nite Owl, I was totally knackered and I had to go to work the following morning. To this day though, I still think that the main reason why George opened it up was because of kindness, he really was concerned about the kids.'

With flashing lights around its windows, the White Cat was viewed by many to be one of the few proper food cafés in Leicester. With freshly baked deliveries every day, the café was completely different to the various greasy spoons that were scattered around the city. 'We had all of the mod-cons,' said Kathy. 'And it was clean and scrubbed every day. We had booths that were fixed to the ground, a jukebox and pinball machine that never stopped and two one-armed bandits. Sometimes, the customers could get through twenty-quid's worth of tanners on a Saturday afternoon. When we first took over, it was open between 7 a.m. –6 p.m. but then it changed to 10 p.m., much to my mother's annoyance. The kids would come in at night-time and hang around until the end, they didn't want to go drinking so they'd sit on bottles of coke. The bikers started to come in later on, they were the softest bunch you'd ever seen, nothing like the American lot you see on the telly. They were a nice little group though, half of them hadn't even got motorbikes but they'd still meet up with their mates. The mods would use the place at the weekend and we didn't have any trouble from them at all.' A couple of doors down from the White Cat was Brian's Scooter Shop. 'He sold new scooters as well as second-hand ones,' recalls Kathy. 'He used to service them as well. The mods used to park their scooters down a little side street. He used to have more room on the front than us so they'd park their scooters there as well and come in to the café for a coffee. The bikers would be there as well but nothing ever kicked off, my mum knew how to control them all. She wouldn't stand for any trouble or hanky-panky.'

The music at the White Cat would be on all of the time, even when the builders and car mechanics who worked over the road came in for their breakfasts first thing in the morning. 'They'd put records on the jukebox while they were waiting,' said Kathy. 'It was endless. We used to put the music on as soon as we started, even when nobody was there. The keys to the jukebox were in the till so we'd put some money in, choose a record, and then take the money back out again. Mum let us do that because half of the profit was ours anyway. They used to change the records every week, that way we could guarantee we'd got the latest hits and the new number one. I was given all of the records that came off of the jukebox, I've still got some now.'

Running the café, especially at night, wasn't without its problems as Kathy describes one particular incident. 'I was mopping the floor down when these four lads walked in, it was about ten minutes before we were going to close. Although I didn't know it at the time, they were some of the hardest men in Leicester. There were still a couple of customers in the café who were about ready to leave. One of the four lads walked straight to the back of the café so I told him that we were closed and everything was switched off. I was furious, he was walking all over my mopped floor with his muddy boots so I very politely told him to leave. After they'd gone, one of the customers asked if I knew who I'd just kicked out. He was terrified, shaking, but I wasn't because I didn't know who they were. I said I haven't kicked anybody out, I asked them to leave and they did. I wasn't having anybody walk over my mopped floor with muddy boots and I definitely wasn't going to wash it again.'

A law came in during the 1960s that stated if you were a venue that had fruit machines, you would not only need a licence but would have to become a club. Consequently, the White Cat Café turned into the White Cat Coffee Club. 'After that, we had to sign people in,' explains Kathy. 'I'd have to go up to whoever was playing the machines and ask them if they were a member and if they weren't, they'd have to join. The money George earned from the fruit machines and jukeboxes though enabled him to open up the Nite Owl so it was worth it.'

While Saturday nights, with its gigs and all-nighters, were for the serious music buffs, Sunday afternoons at the Nite Owl were for teenagers who were simply thrilled at being allowed to do something grown-up in the adult world. 'George opened up on a Sunday afternoon because of pressure from parents and from letters that he'd received from the younger kids pleading with him to let them in because they were so desperate to go there,' said Kathy. 'They were too young to go to the all-nighters and their parents were worried that they would try to get in. There wasn't really anything to do on a Sunday in Leicester apart from bowling, which a lot of them didn't want to do, so George opened up the Nite Owl. I used to get there early and the queues to get in shook me solid. I can remember the first Sunday opening, it was only advertised in the *Leicester Mercury*, everything else was via word of mouth. I walked past the White Cat Café and St Mary de Castro Church and came on to Oxford Street and I could see the queue from there. The girls who I worked with at Wolsey were all there asking if I could get them in but there was only one doorway and it was packed. Ricky had to literally grab me and pull me in. The doors would open at 2 p.m. and they would close between 5–6 p.m. We couldn't close no later than that because a lot of the buses stopped at 6 p.m. and some of the kids would have had trouble getting home. There were loads of cars on Newarke Street though because their parents didn't mind picking them up on a Sunday afternoon.' Georgie Wright adds: 'A lot of parents were kicking off about their kids being out all night. It was a big hit, again just soft drinks on sale, and they came out in their droves. I think these sessions became popular because they were seen as very cool for the younger age bracket. Opening the club to kids for a daytime disco provided a way for them to express themselves through dance and it promoted an interest in music.'

At first, the Sunday sessions were disco orientated until George decided to mix things up by adding in some of the local bands. 'Legay were the band that pulled the teenagers in on the Sunday afternoons,' said Kathy. 'They were the most outrageous band I'd ever seen, mainly because of their black make-up. You could also tell that they were a bit special as well, they were proper musicians producing a completely different sound to what everyone else was making. No one would have dared to have played rock music in the Nite Owl but Legay got away with it. All of the music that was played, though, was out of this world and Owlin' Robin was a brilliant DJ.

The kids wanted to dance and they did, upstairs and downstairs. We even let the parents in – I can remember one mum sitting with me while her two daughters were downstairs, she couldn't believe that we'd let her in.'

The Nite Owl closed its doors for the last time in 1968. One of Leicester's most unique and exciting venues was no more. Stories abound regarding the reasons why it closed but the reality of the situation was that the club was refused its application to renew its music licence. 'George had got his licence and then in the third year, it was refused by both the police and the City Council,' said Kathy. 'He appealed it and lost, I actually wrote the appeal letter for him. He was heartbroken, it nearly broke him because he hadn't done anything illegal or wrong. The police were determined to close it down though, there was one policeman in particular who was always in George's face, and in the end they succeeded. You couldn't run a club without a music licence so he closed it down.' After the Nite Owl closed, George moved to London where he concentrated on a nightclub that he co-owned with three others. His wife was left to run the café businesses.

The final nail in the Nite Owl's coffin came one night in May 1968, as described here by the *Leicester Chronicle*:

> A passing motorist reported that the Nite Owl discotheque, on Newarke Street, was on fire. Within minutes, pumps attended. The unoccupied four-storey building was well alight and further pumps were requested, including eight units from Wigston, Syston and Kibworth. Jets were concentrated on the front and rear of the building to stop the fire spreading but the roof and gable end collapsed on to the neighbouring building. The brigade had the fire under control within an hour, using nine hand jets and two turntable ladders.

As described in the report, and contrary to urban myth, the Nite Owl had been closed for a few months by the time fire took hold of the building. 'My sister said that it was closed for a long time afterwards,' said Georgie Wright. 'It was just an empty, old, rundown building although there were rumours about someone else reopening it as a club.'

Kathy Chamberlin started working at the Nite Owl when she was just fifteen. She was seventeen when she left. 'George wanted everyone to be happy, he loved watching the kids dancing and enjoying themselves, it was probably because he was denied it himself when he was a child. He was a people pleaser and if he made some money along the way, all the better. As for the White Cat, like most of Duns Lane it was pulled down years ago. There's a garage there now where, ironically, I take my car for its MOT. The address of the garage is 3–5 Duns Lane and the White Cat was number 3. Sometimes, when I'm waiting for the work to be done on my car, I stand there and remember how it all used to be. I knew at the time that I was involved in something special and I wasn't wrong. I've never seen or experienced anything like it since.'

Nearly fifty years on since its closure and now in his late eighties, George Parker reflects on the Nite Owl. 'I remember bands and singers used to audition on Monday afternoons to play the following weekend, Rod Stewart was one of them. I told him he couldn't sing and not to bother – look at him now. My mother used to call me "the night owl" because I never slept and was always out, that's how the club got its name. It just seemed like a good idea to open it, we'd been all around the country looking at clubs and there was nothing like it in Leicester. I loved music and it seemed as though there was nothing for the kids to do. Looking back though, I don't think Leicester was quite ready for it. The kids were but the police and the authorities weren't, they thought it was a bit of a nuisance. They couldn't contend with the amount of people that were there, even though there was never any trouble. I've got no regrets about the Nite Owl though, just a feeling of sadness that we weren't allowed to carry it on.'

ND - #0275 - 270225 - C0 - 234/156/14 - PB - 9781780915500 - Gloss Lamination